A STUDY IN SHERLOCK

13 Years of Sherlock Holmes
Artwork 2000-2013
By Bret M. Herholz

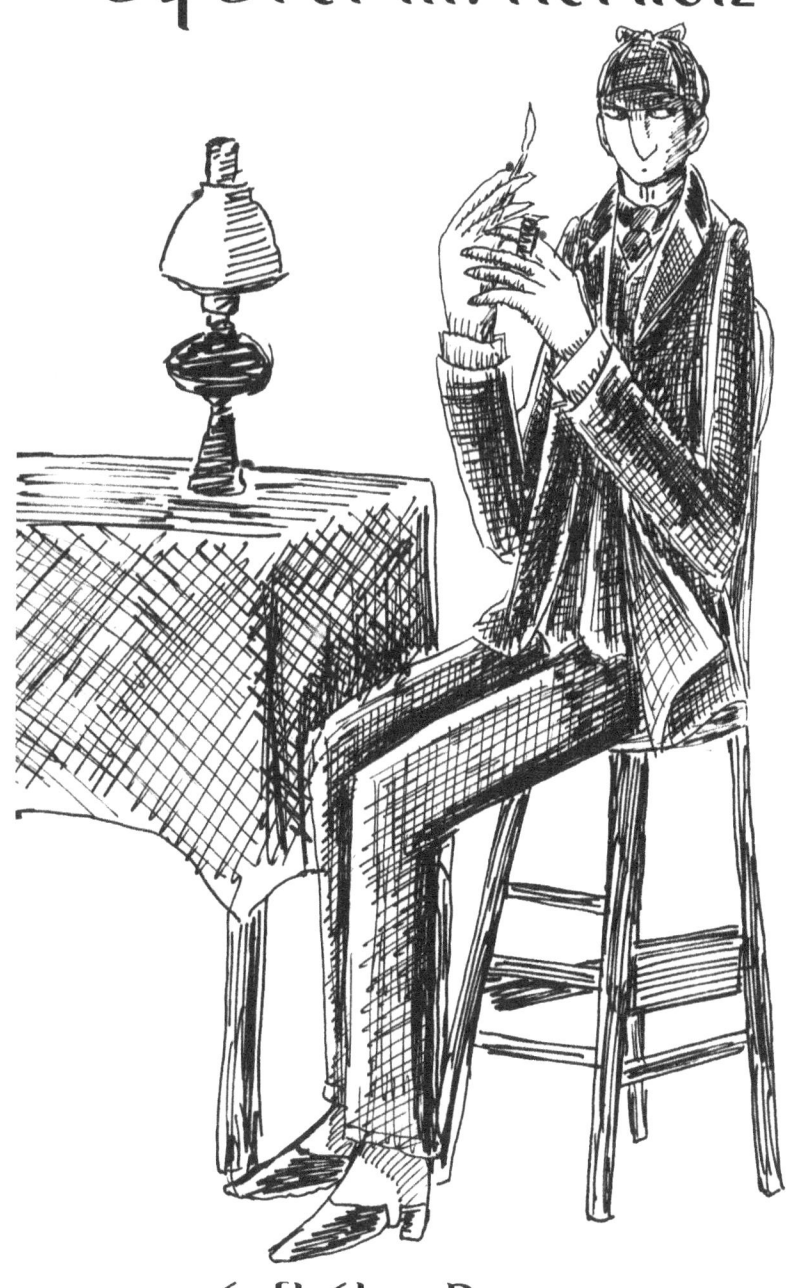

Soft Shoe Press
Northampton . Worcester Mass

The story represented in this publication is a work of fiction. Any similarities to events and persons living or otherwise is purely coincidental.

A Study in Sherlock:
13 years of Sherlock
Holmes Artwork
2000-2013
2013 Firt Print Run

c. 2013 Bret M. Herholz
herbertzohl.blogspot.com

Based on the characters created by Sir Arthur Conan Doyle

Published by Soft Shoe Press

This book contains most, if not all, of the Sherlock Holmes illustrations I have completed between 2001 to 2013.

Probably the most difficult part when compiling 13 plus years of work is trying to create some sort of chronological order to what piece goes before which piece. I can remember the first piece I did. I can even remember the ink I used.

It was Pelikan. Nowadays I use Deleter Black Drawing Ink.

It's all the pieces in between I have difficulty remembering. So I did my best to put exact years to those ones. But even that was a bit difficult. There were ones I was certain I did in 2004 and was surprised to find out I actually completed it in 2002.

Not all the work showcased are gems. But what they do is represent a different stage of my life and my development as an artist. We all have to start out somewhere. And we're always developing.

Most of the work featured in this book are unpublished until now. Although, I have included several pieces that are either previously published or works in progress. Along with many of my early illustrations, I have also included my comic art, photographs as well as set design and sketches.

When I did that very first drawing the thought of a production of Sherlock Holmes set in a contemporary setting was unthinkable and I wanted nothing to do with the Gillette stage play.

Funny how things change.

One thing hasn't changed for me as far as the character is concerned. Sherlock Holmes will always reside in those upstairs rooms at 221B Baker Street.

Whether it be 1891 or 2013

Bret M. Herholz
May 2013

First and foremost I wish to thank Peter Simeti and Erin Kohut of Alterna Inc. for taking a calculated risk and publishing my graphic novel SHERLOCK HOLMES: THE PAINFUL PREDICAMENT OF ALICE FAULKNER. I am forever appreciative in the faith they had in my work.

A special thanks to authors Lyndsay Faye, R. Lee Shackleford and Bert Coules for the kindest of permission to use the artwork I created inspired by their respective Sherlock Holmes tales. All of which are authors who have a great understanding and take the utmost care in their interpretation of the character. I highly recommend you check out their stories.

And thank you to Ken Hailey of the Kentucky Repertory Theatre for bringing my work to life on stage and for allowing me to use some of the photo's taken from the play itself to be reproduced in this book.

This book is dedicated to William, Basil, Peter, Christopher, Robert, Jeremy, Benedict and the many faces that have brought Sherlock Holmes to life on stage and screen over the years.

ILLUSTRATIONS

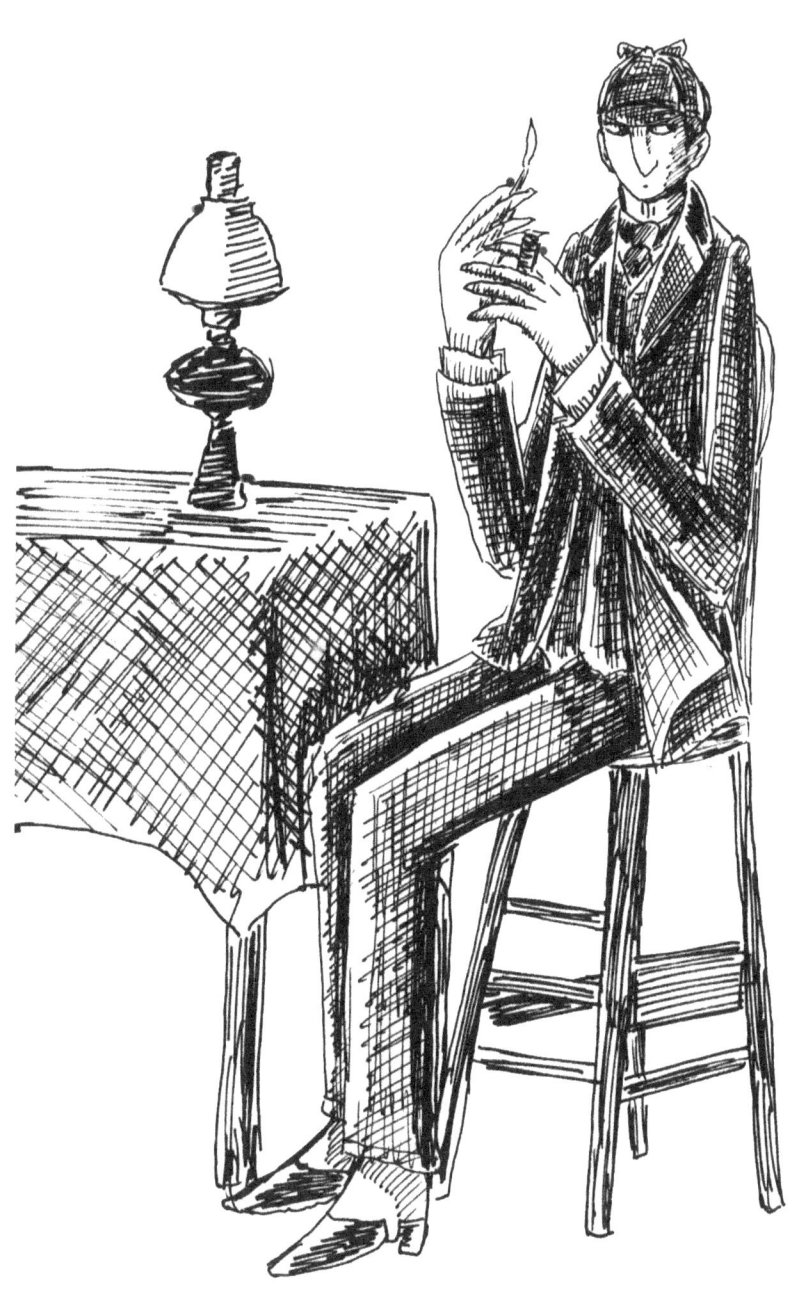

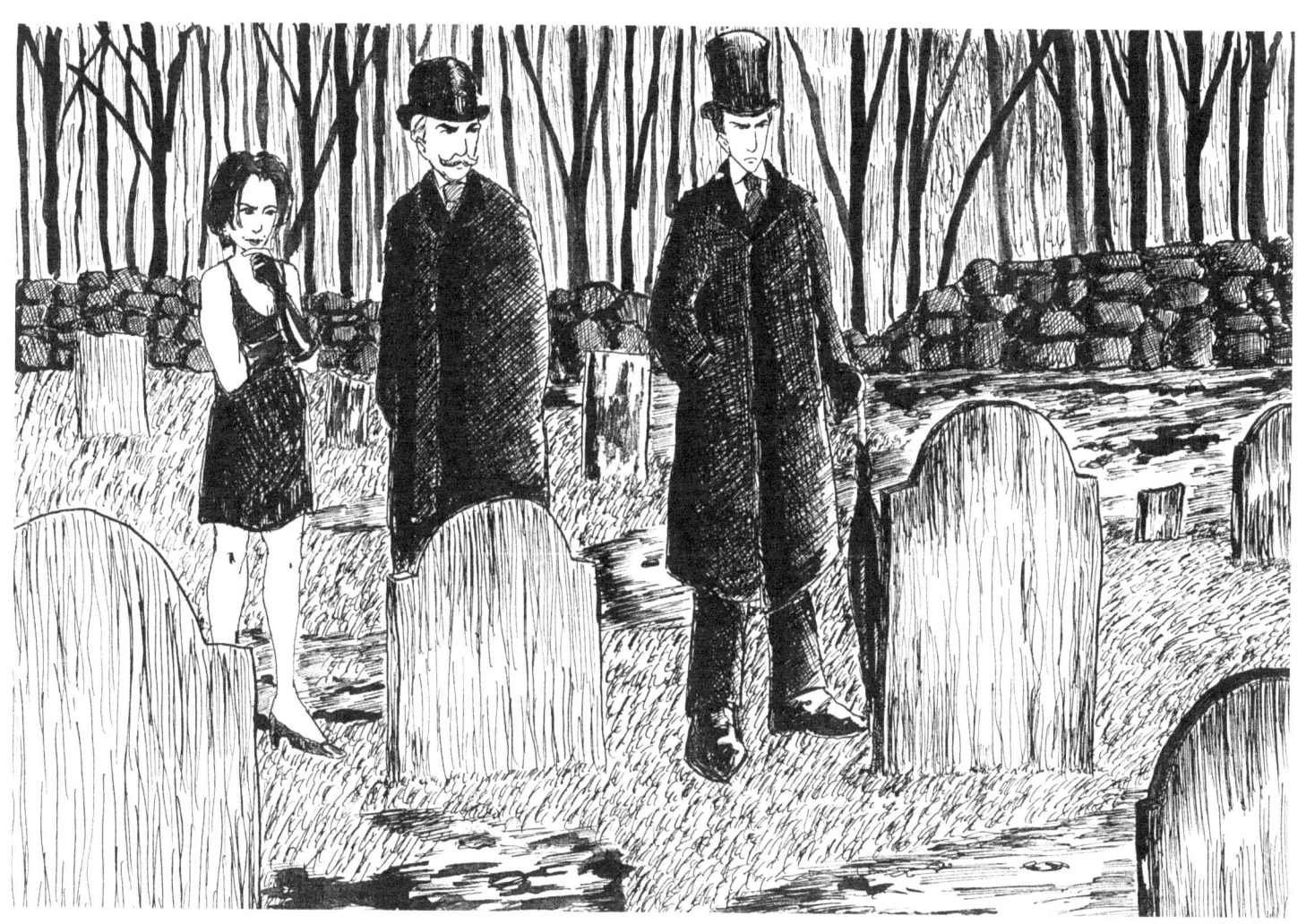

Untitled 2000
This is the very first Sherlock Holmes illustration I did. This one and the next eight are part of an untitled series.

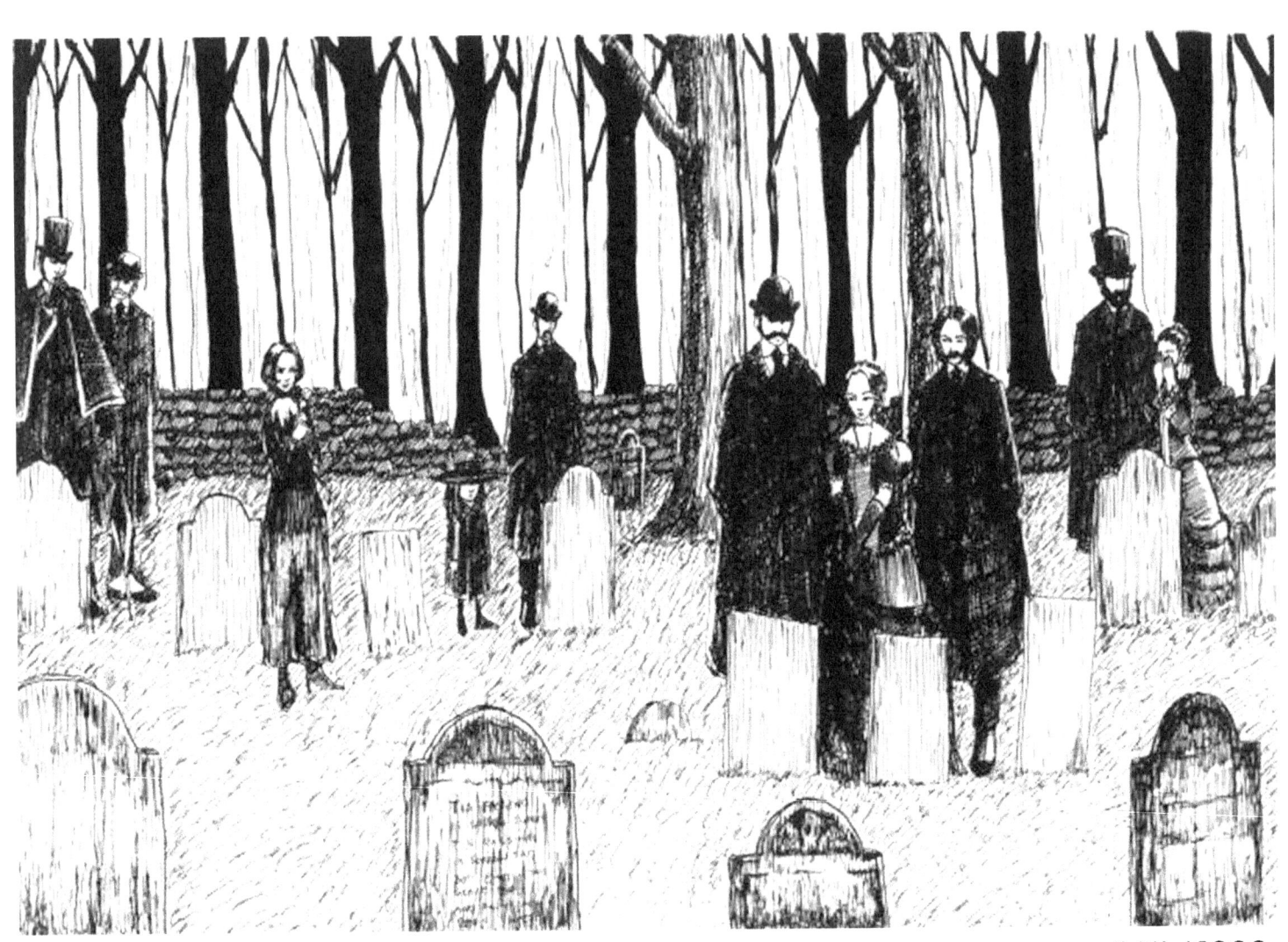

Untitled 2000

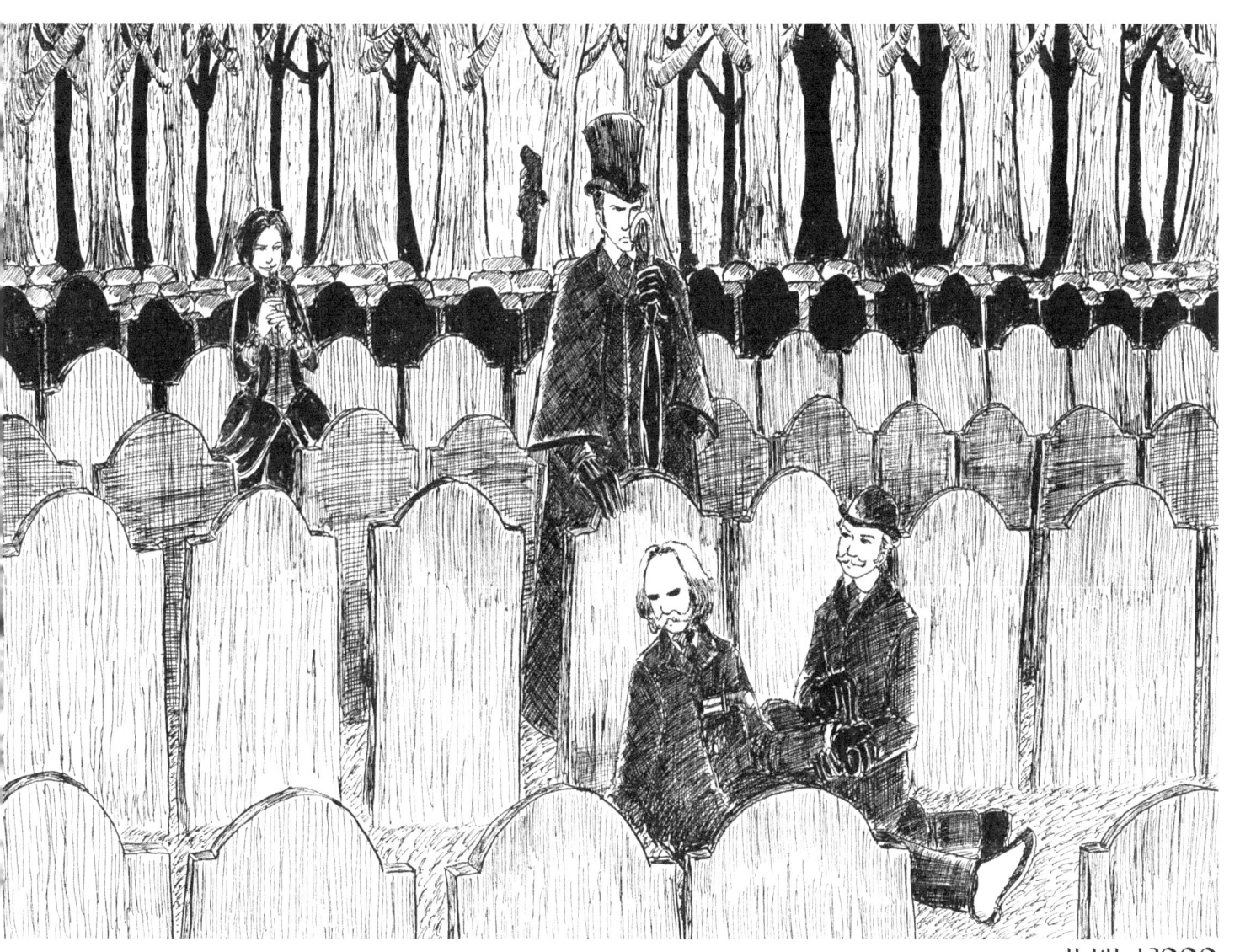

Untitled 2000

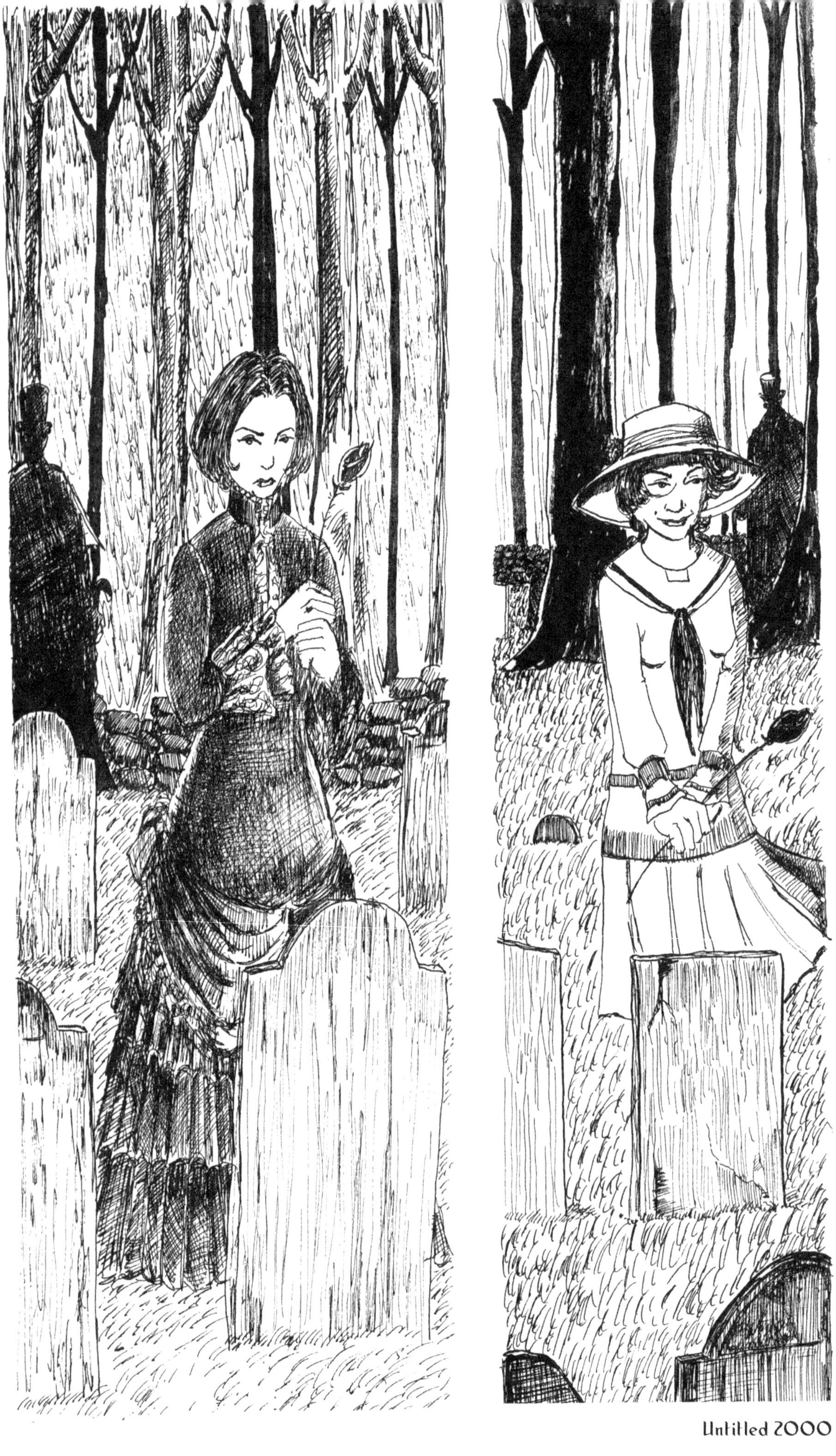

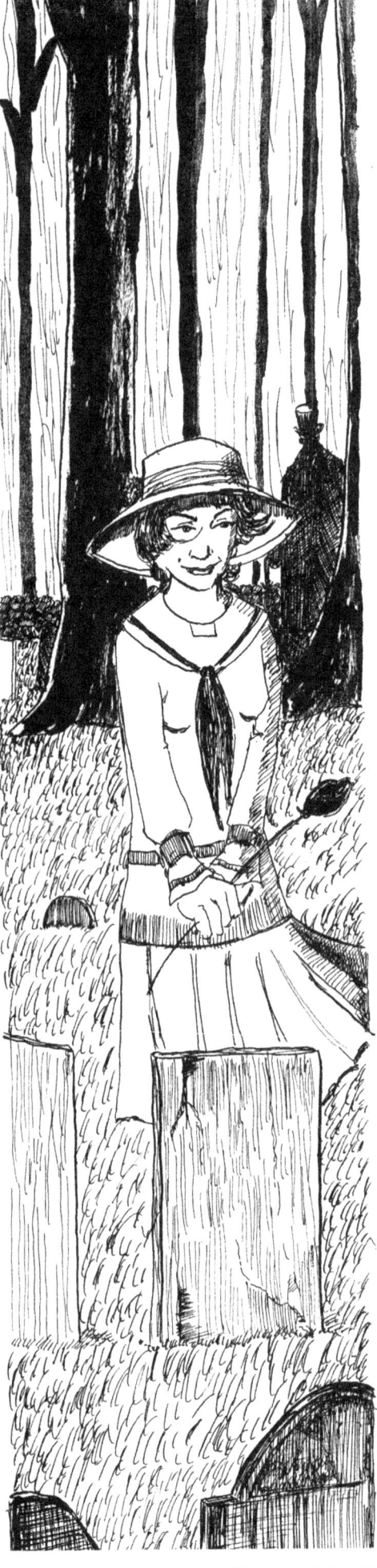

Untitled 2000

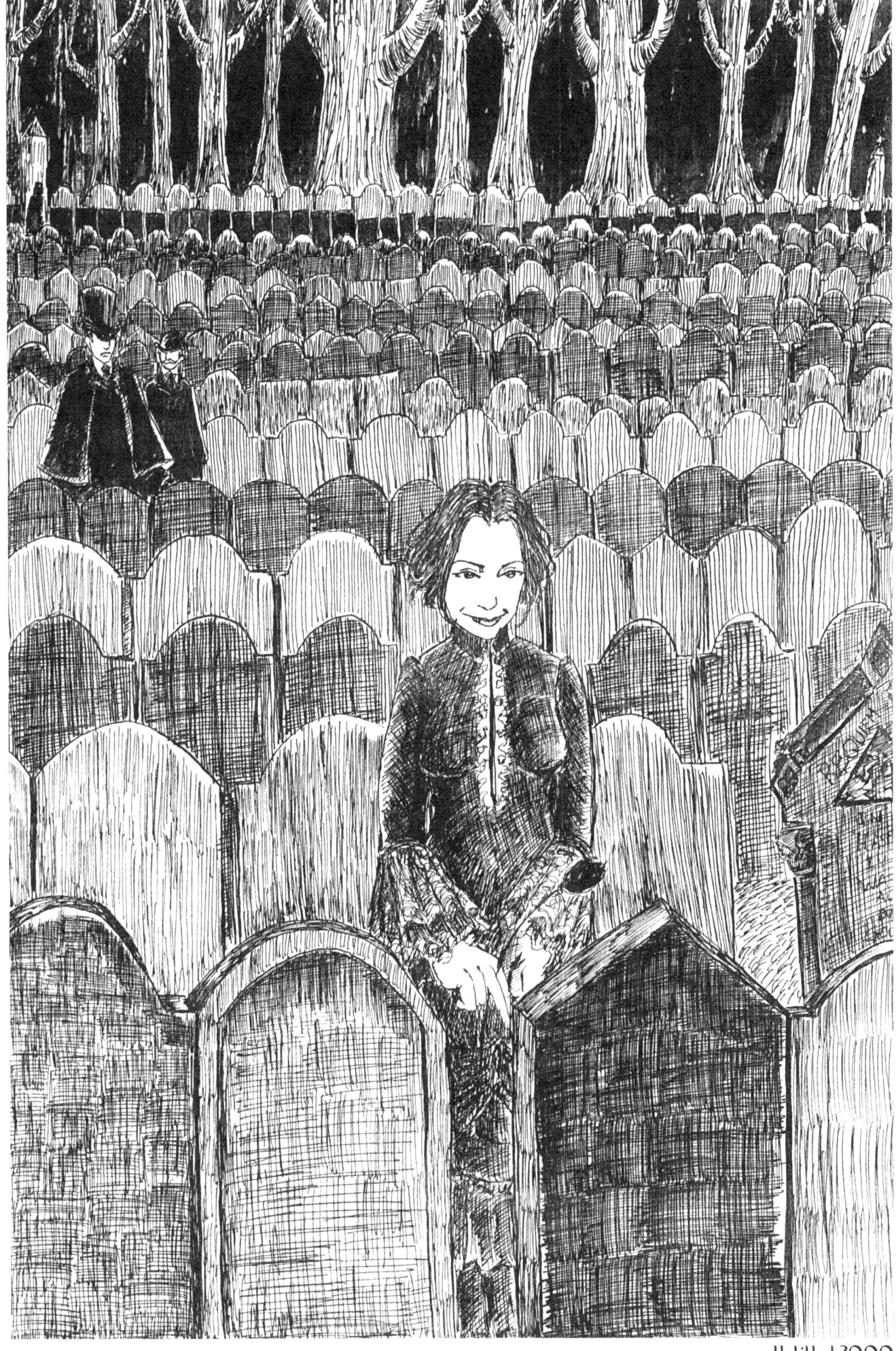

Untitled 2000

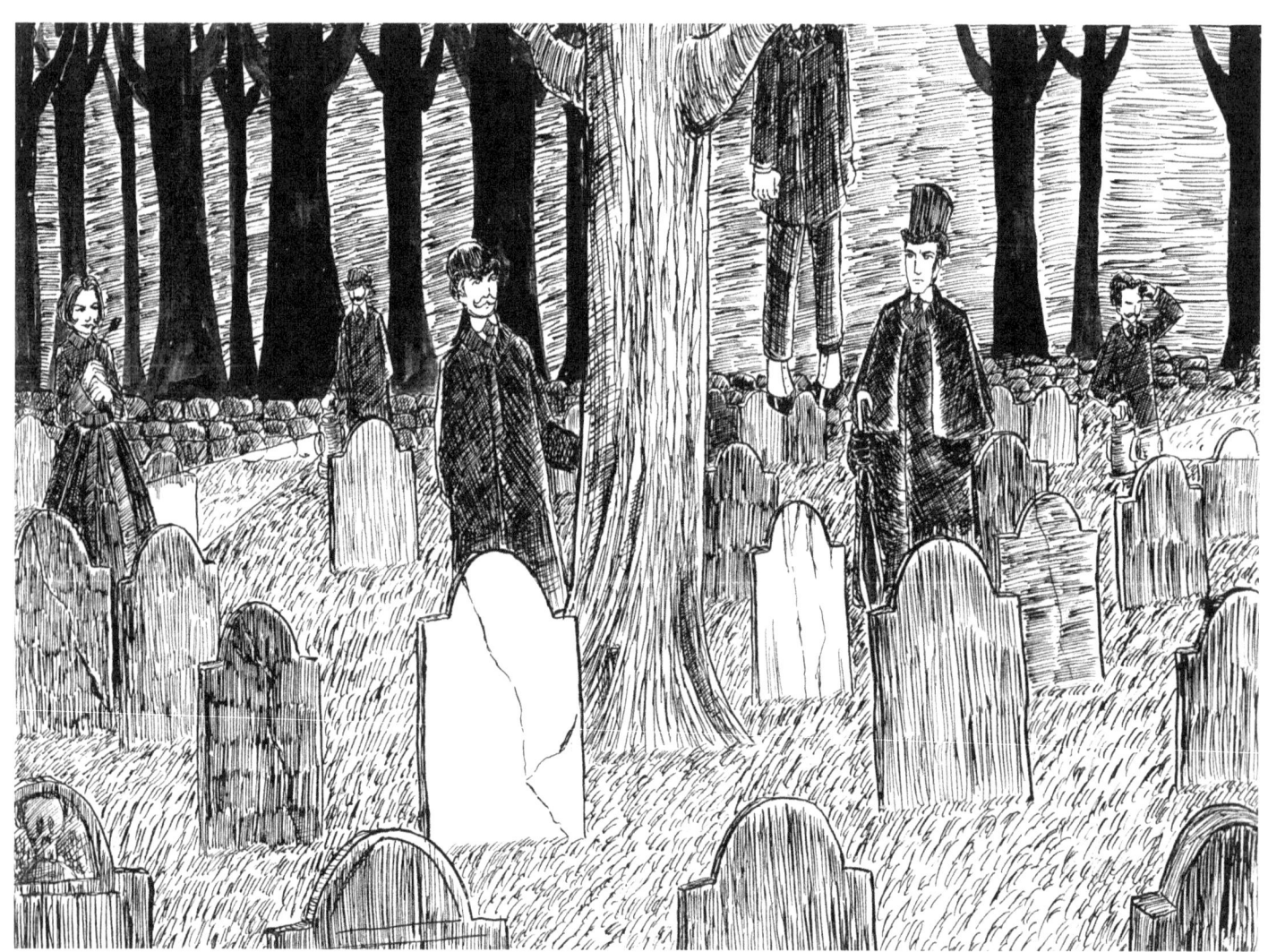

Untitled 2000

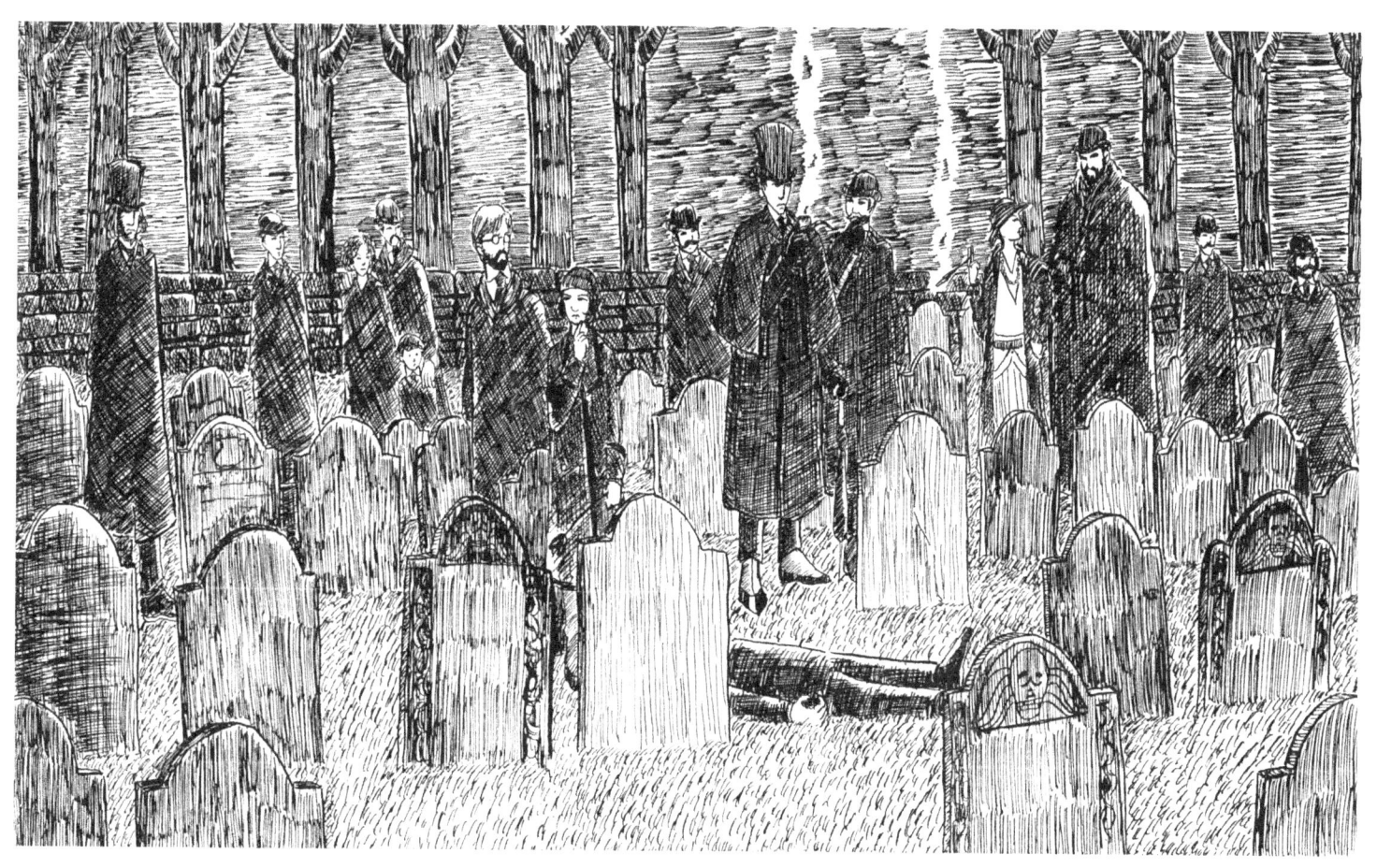

Untitled 2000

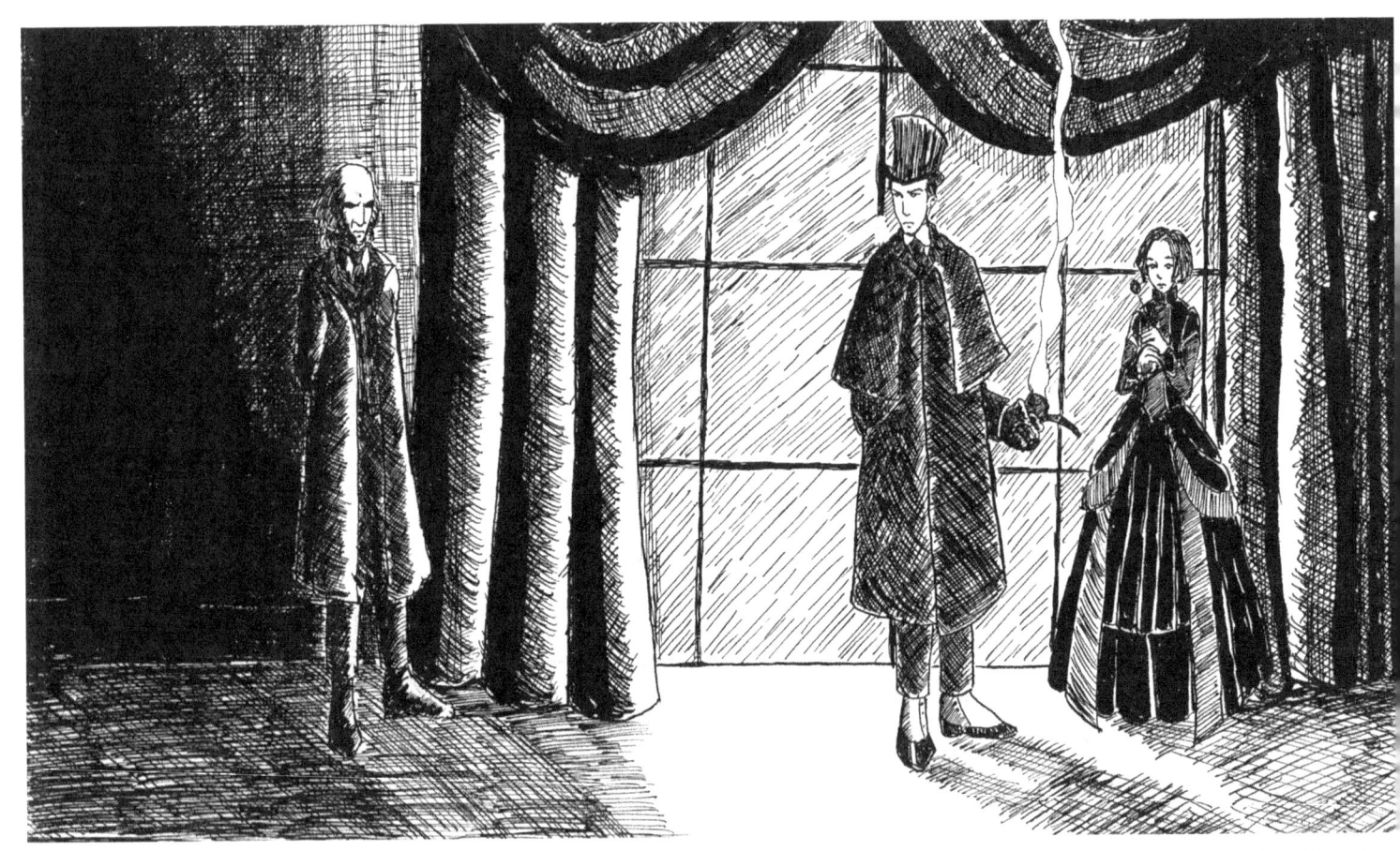

Untitled 2000

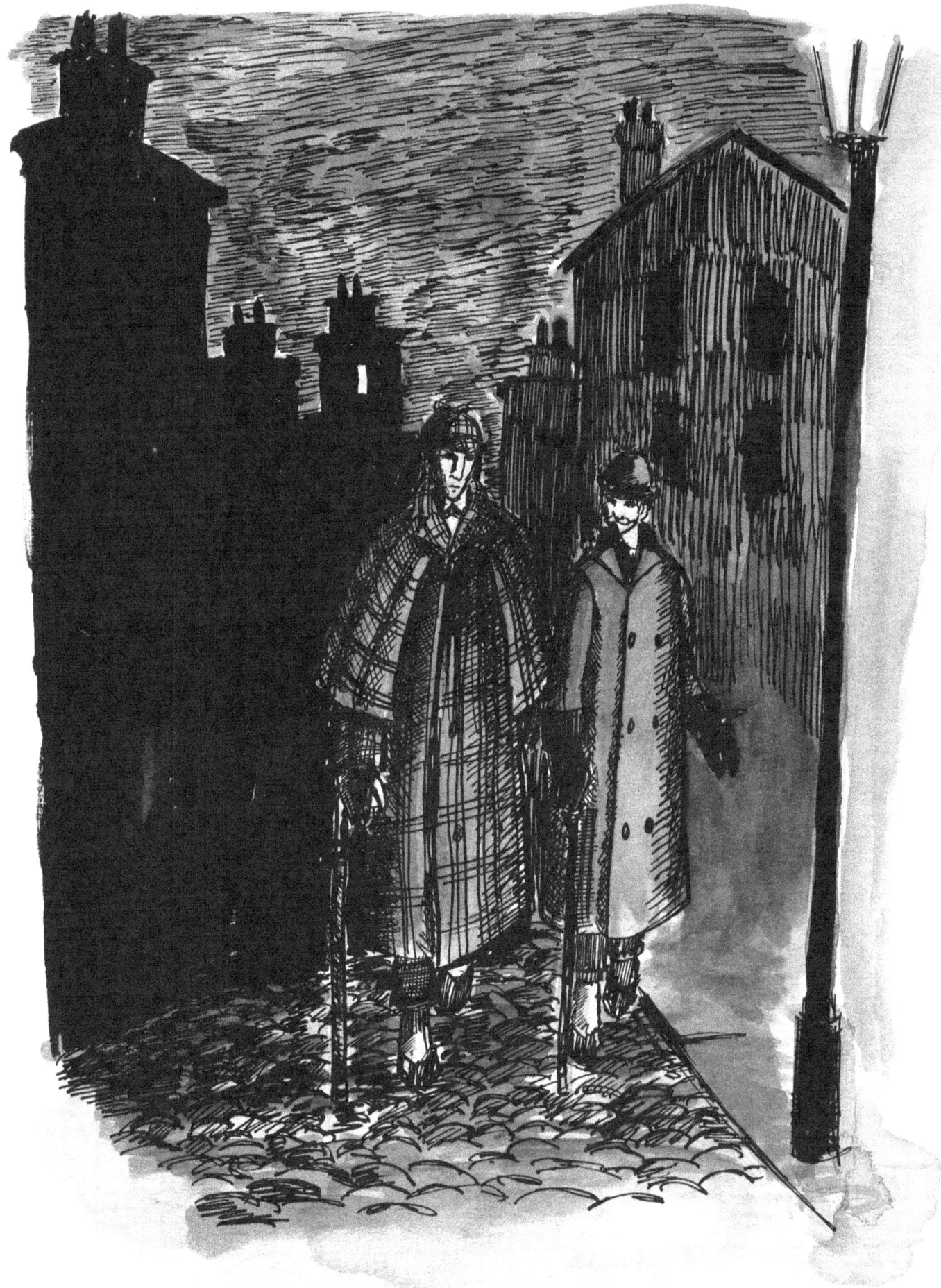

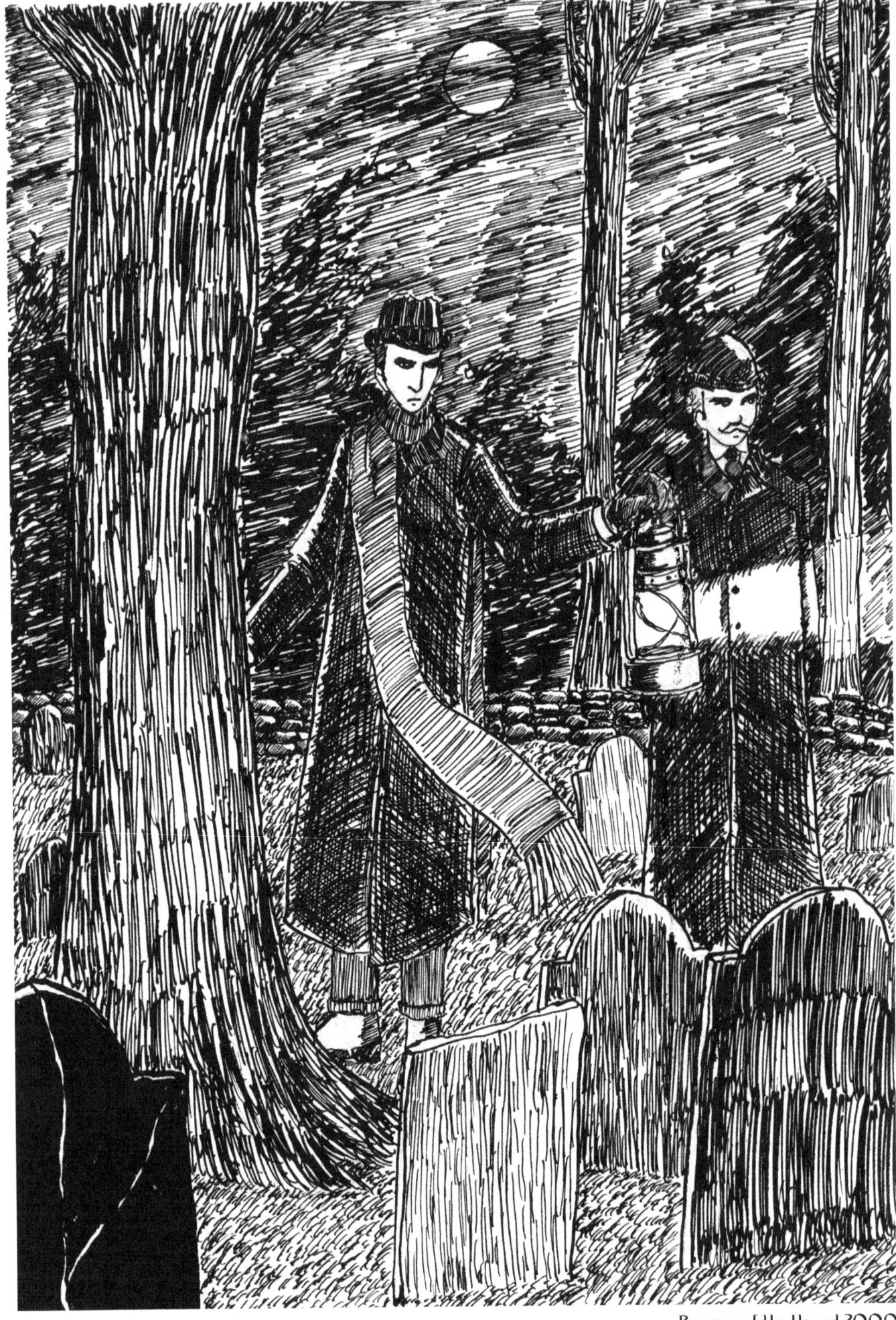

Beware of the Hound 2000

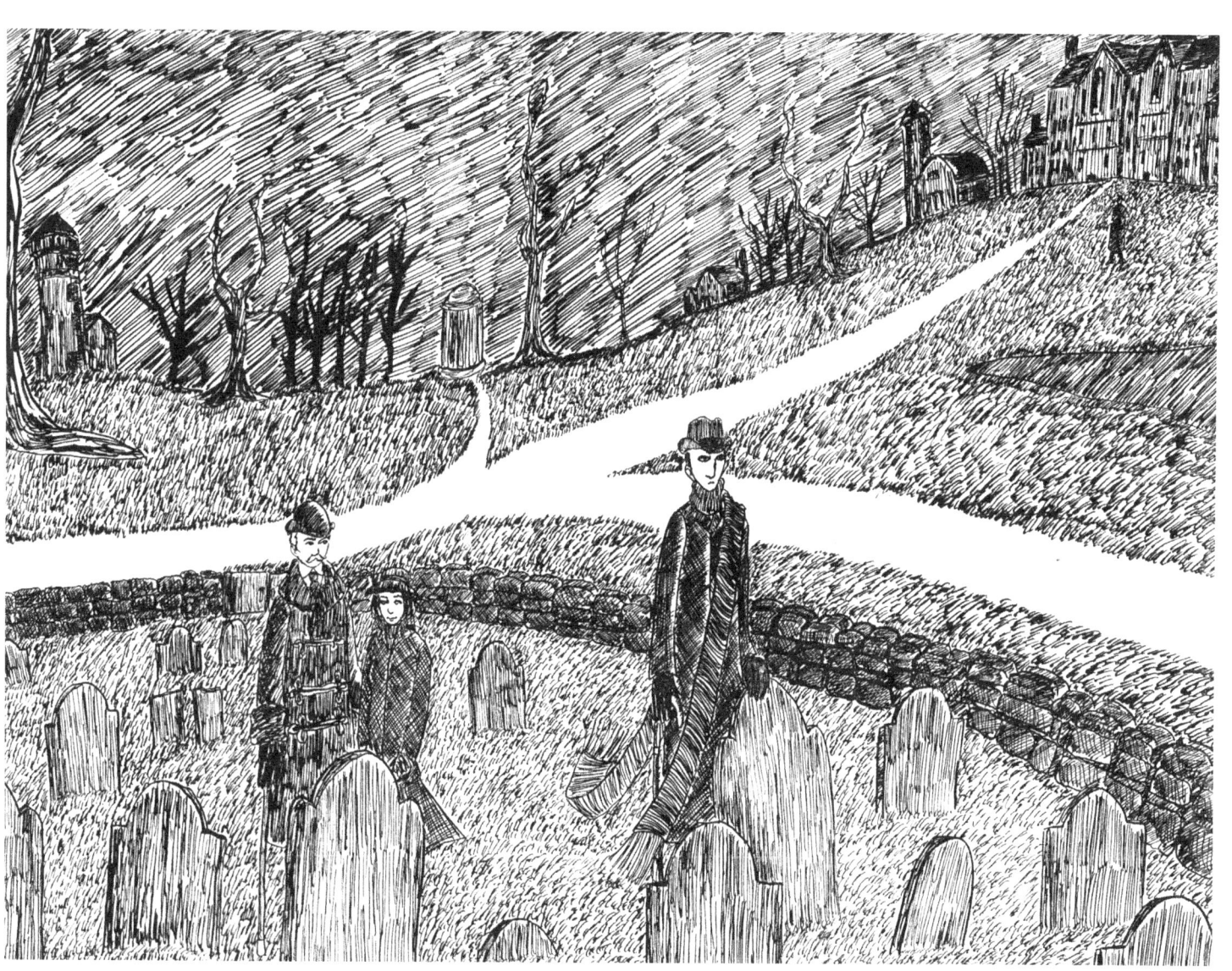

Untitled 2000

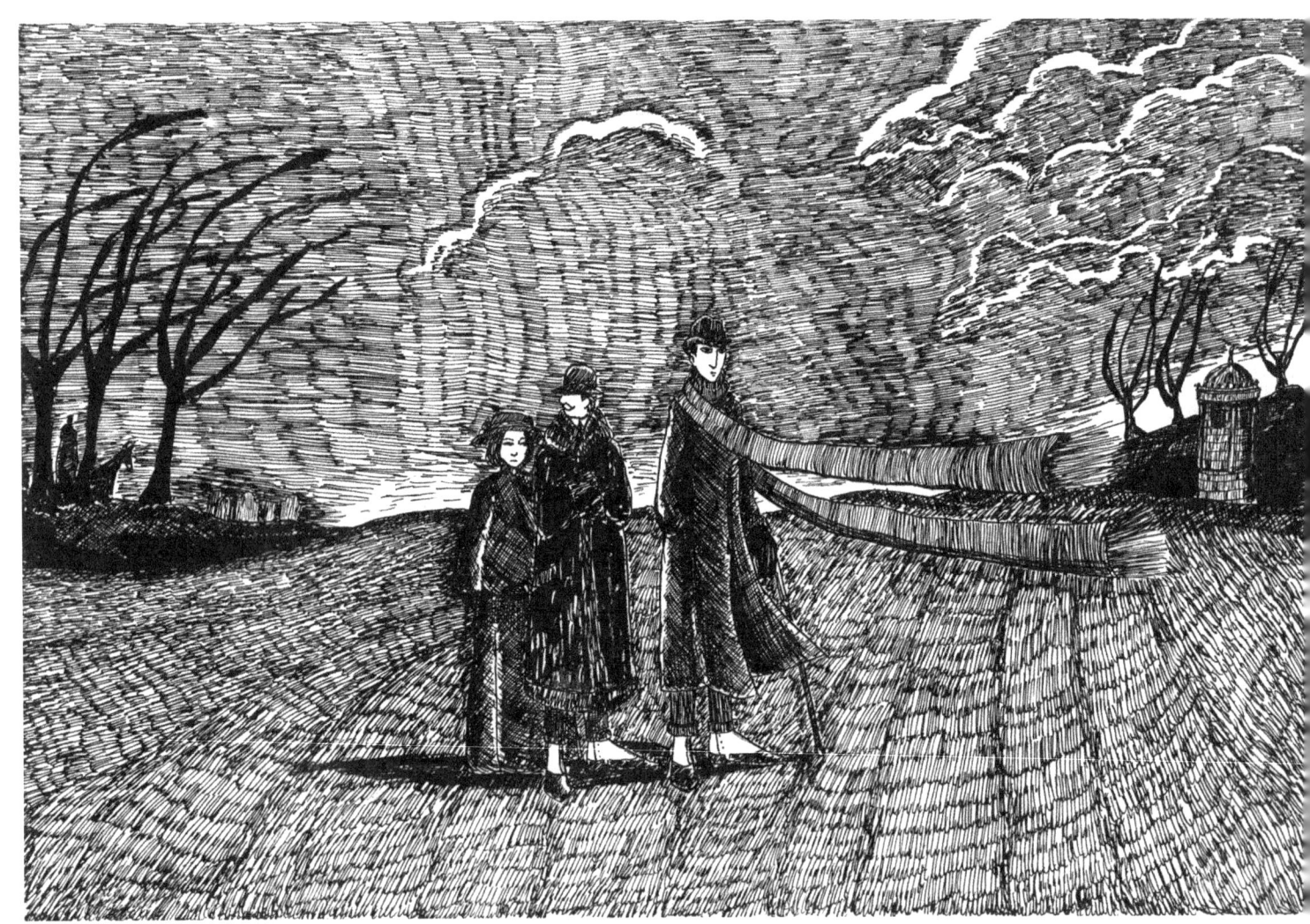

Untitled 2001

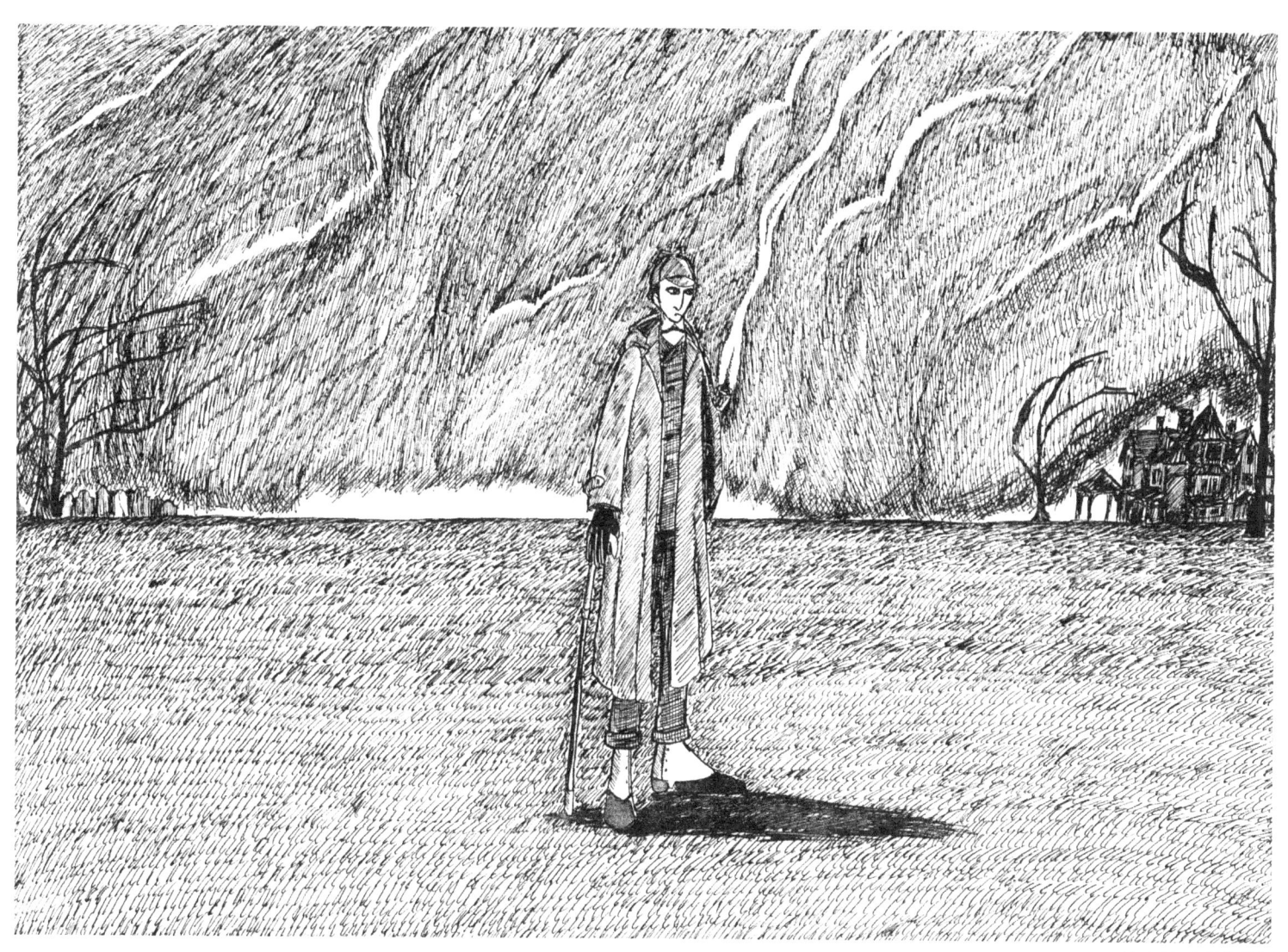

Untitled 2001

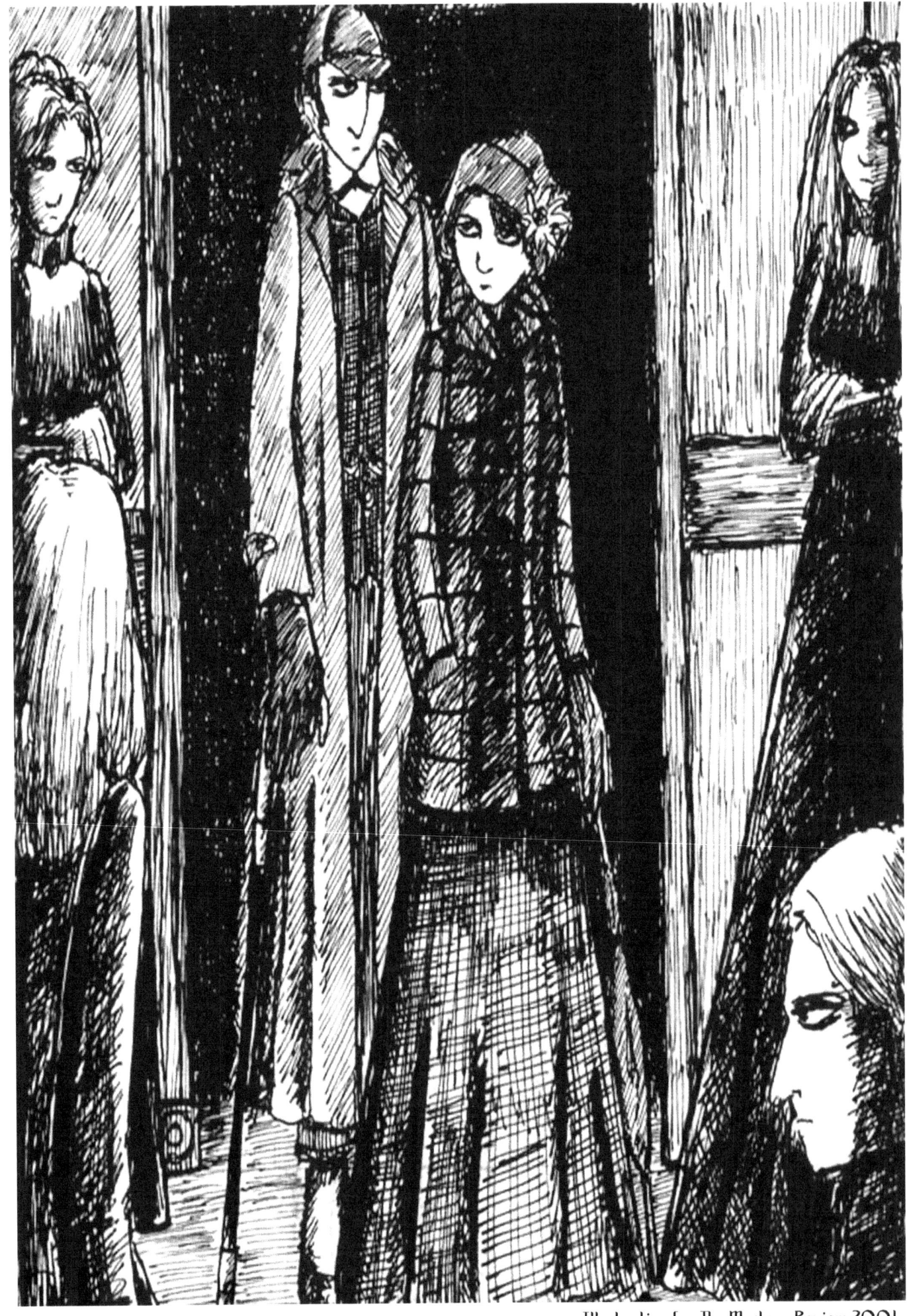

Illustration for The Mystery Review 2001

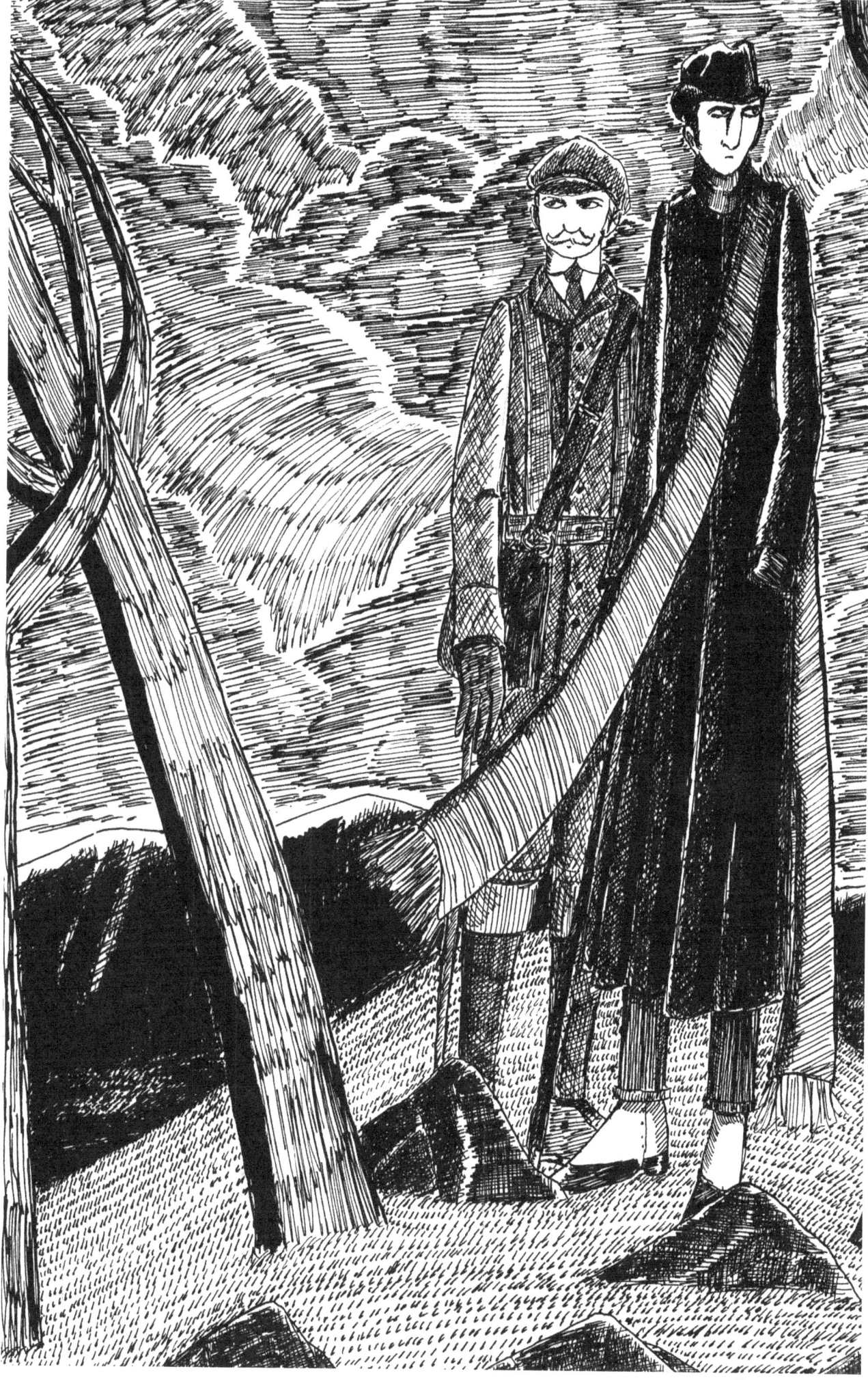

The Moor 2002

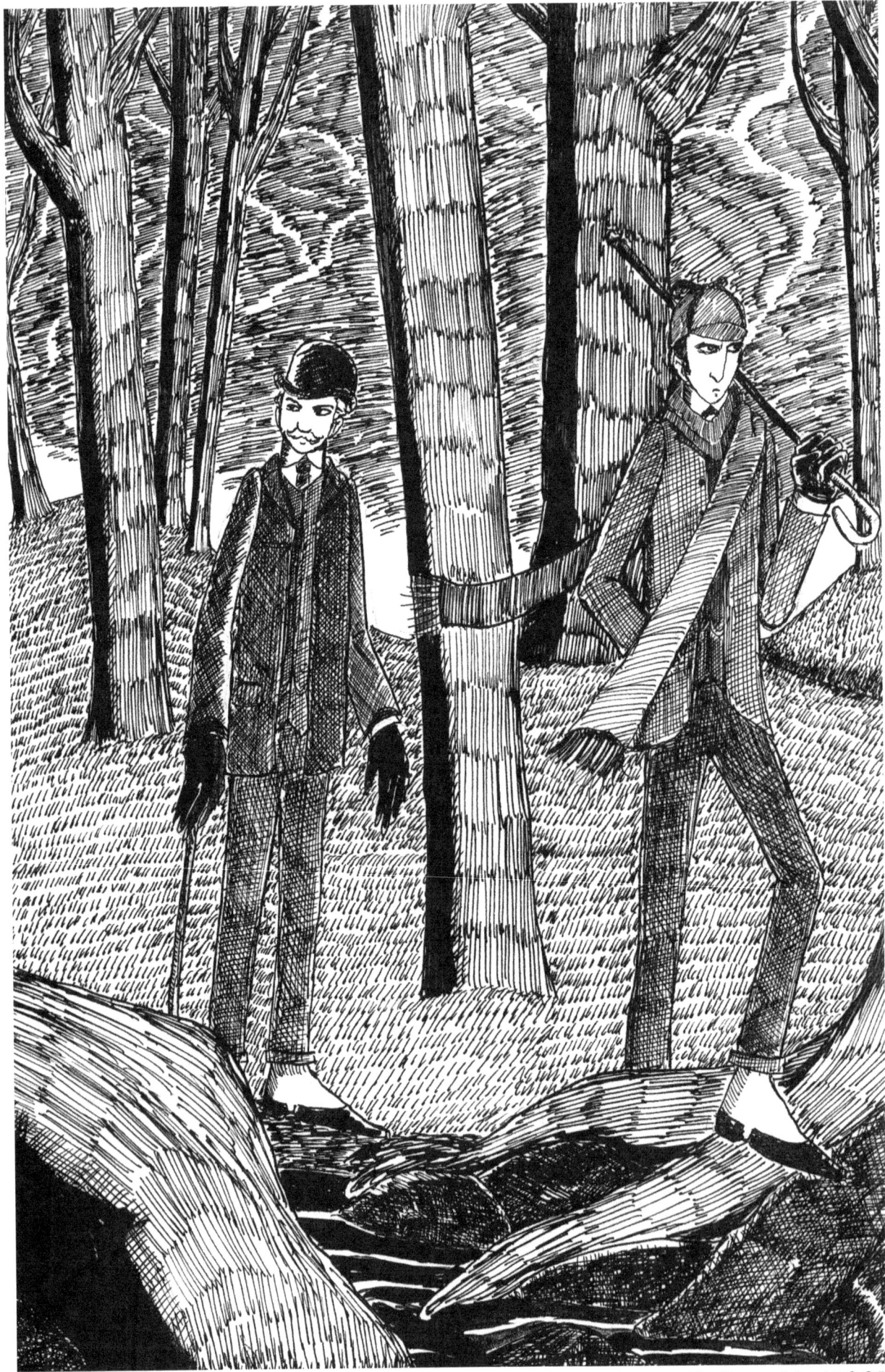

The Priory School 2002

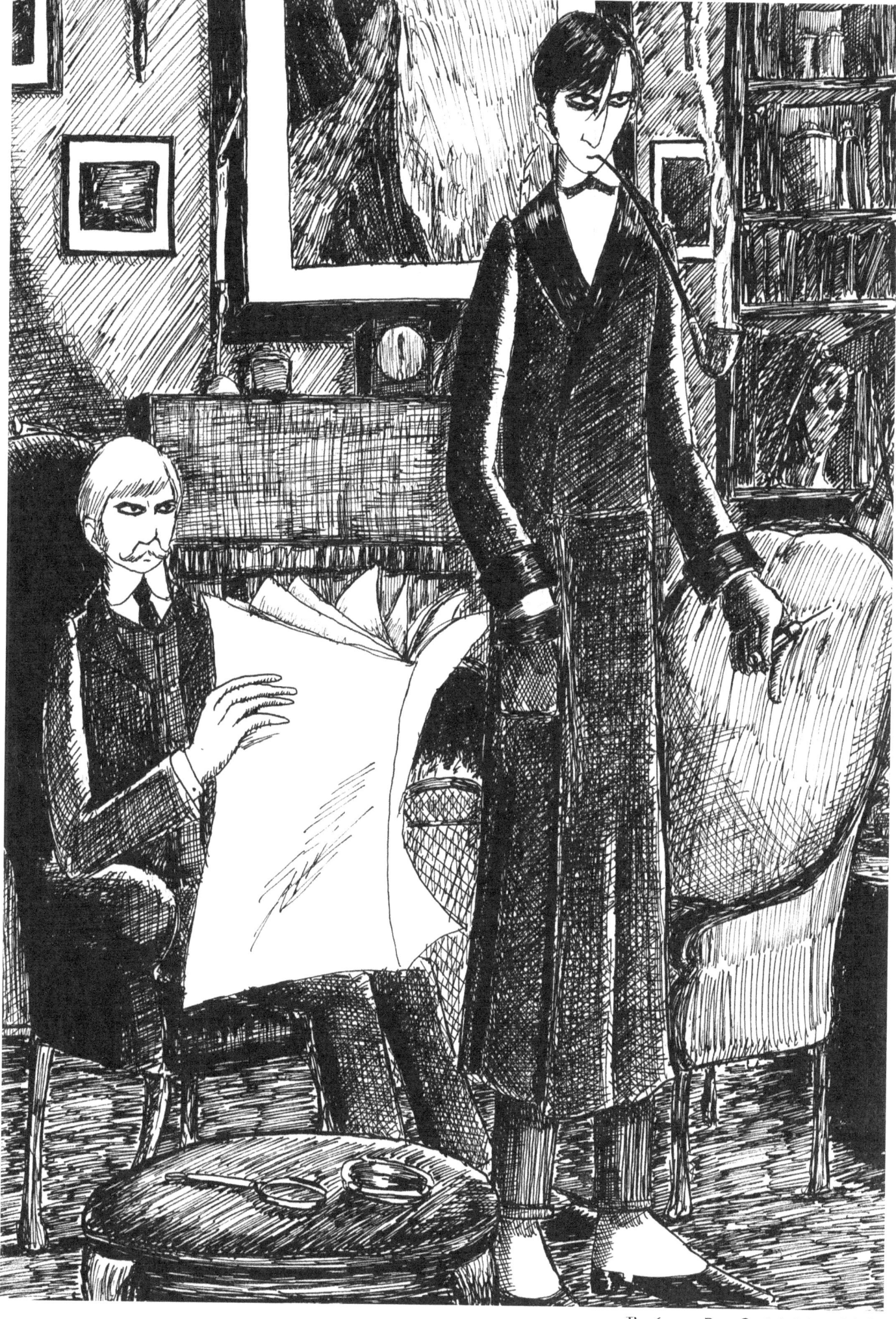

The Seven-Per-Cent Solution 2002

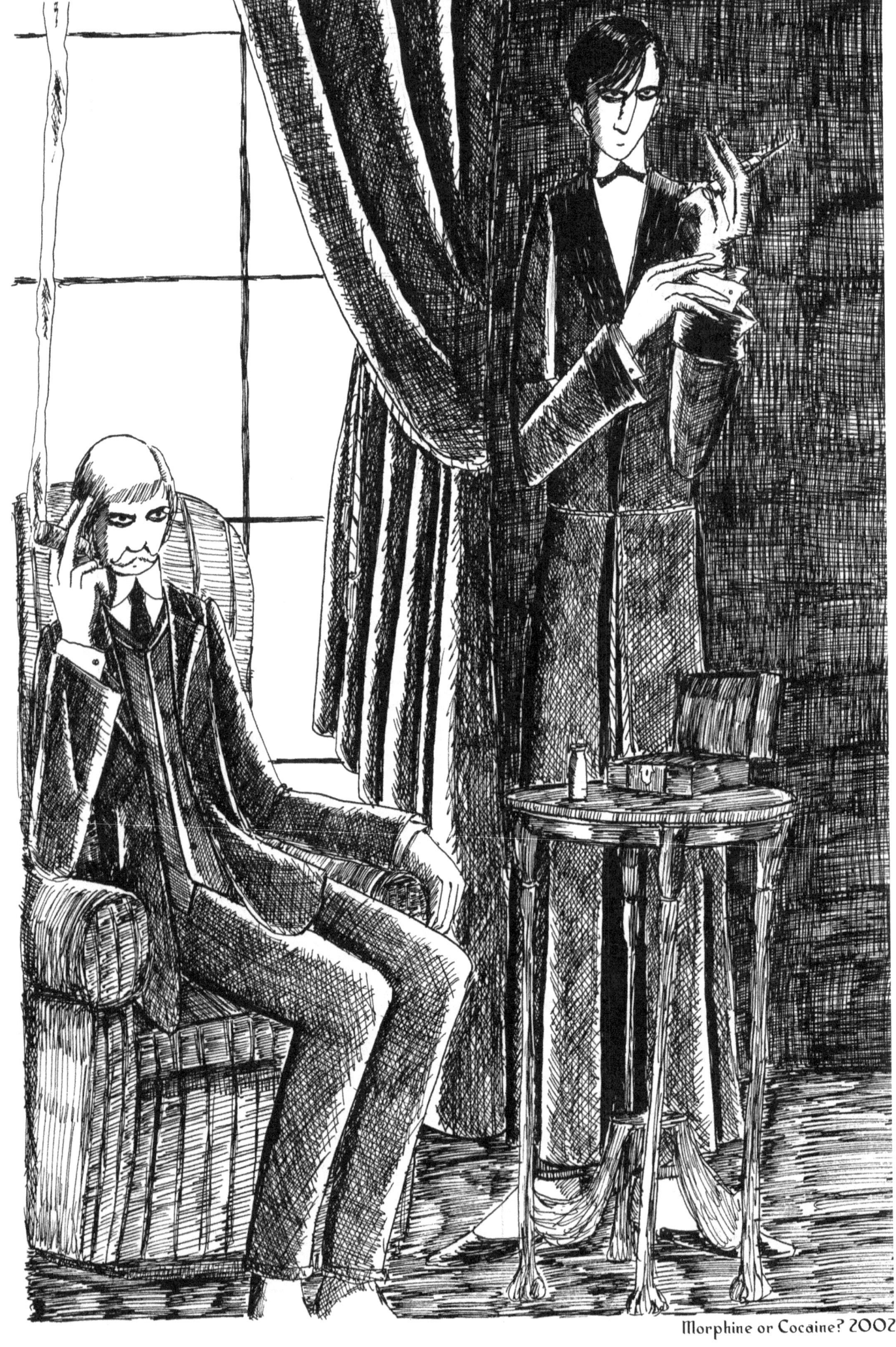

Morphine or Cocaine? 2002

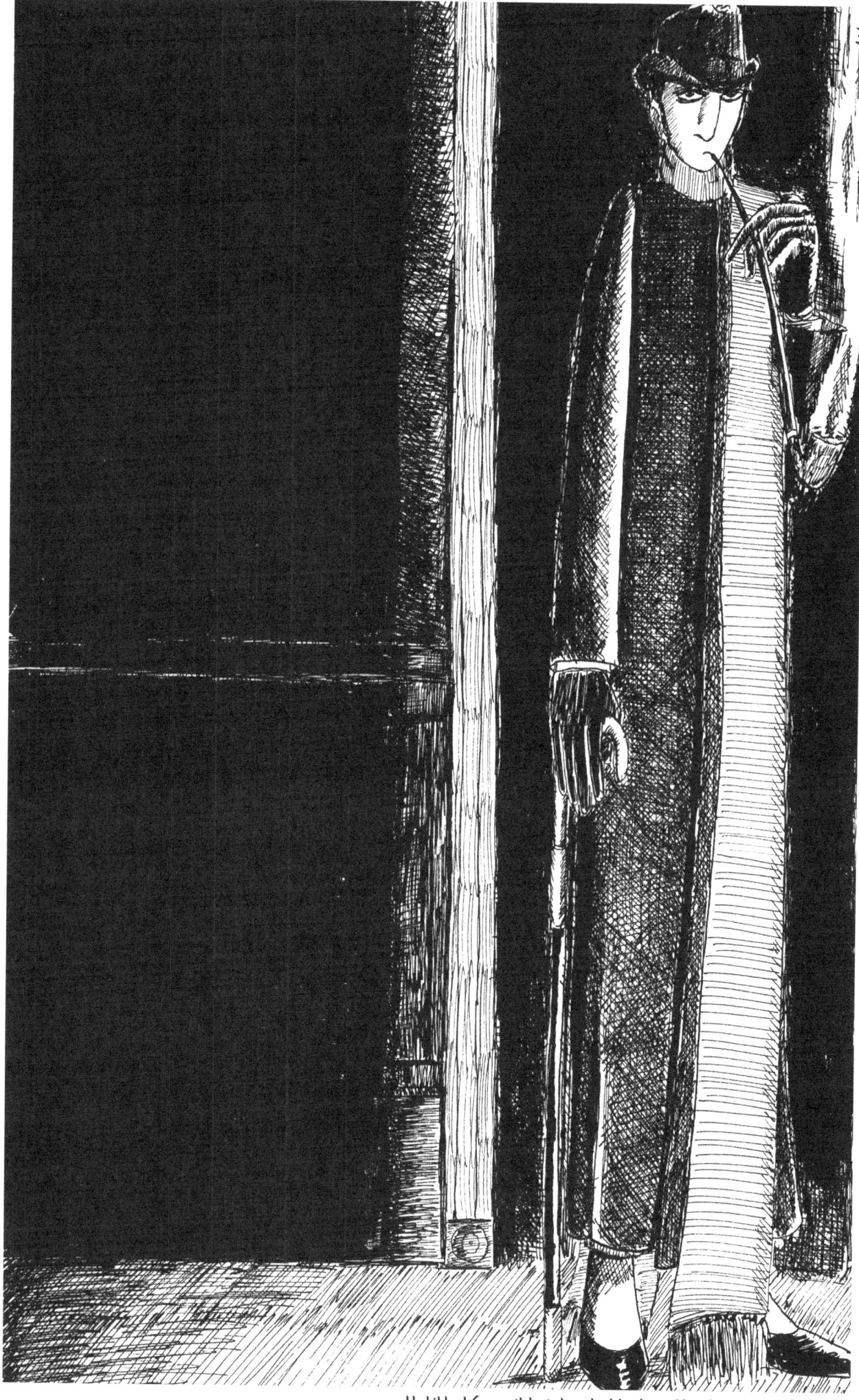

Untitled (possibly intended to be a theatre poster) 2003

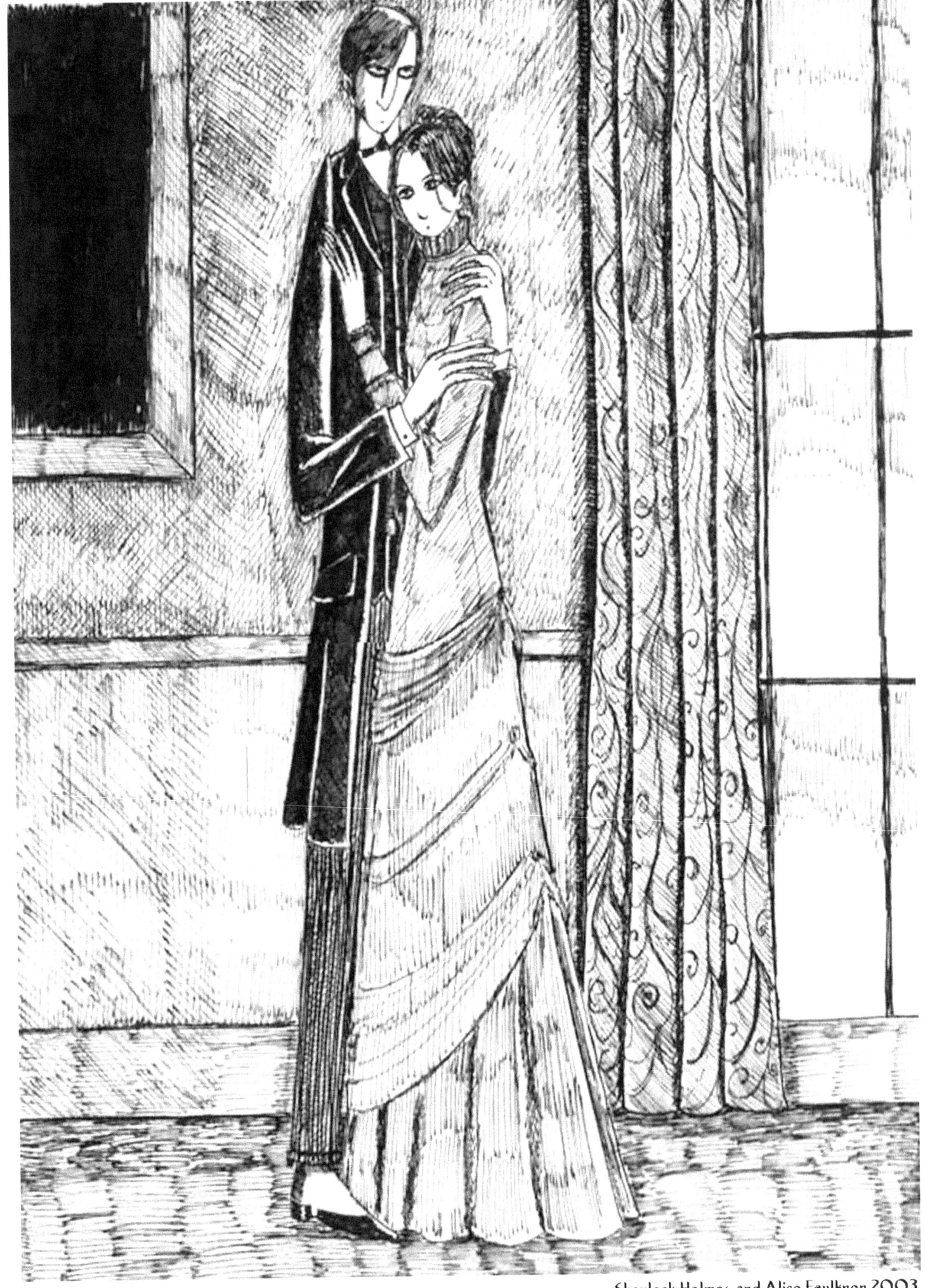

Sherlock Holmes and Alice Faulkner 2003

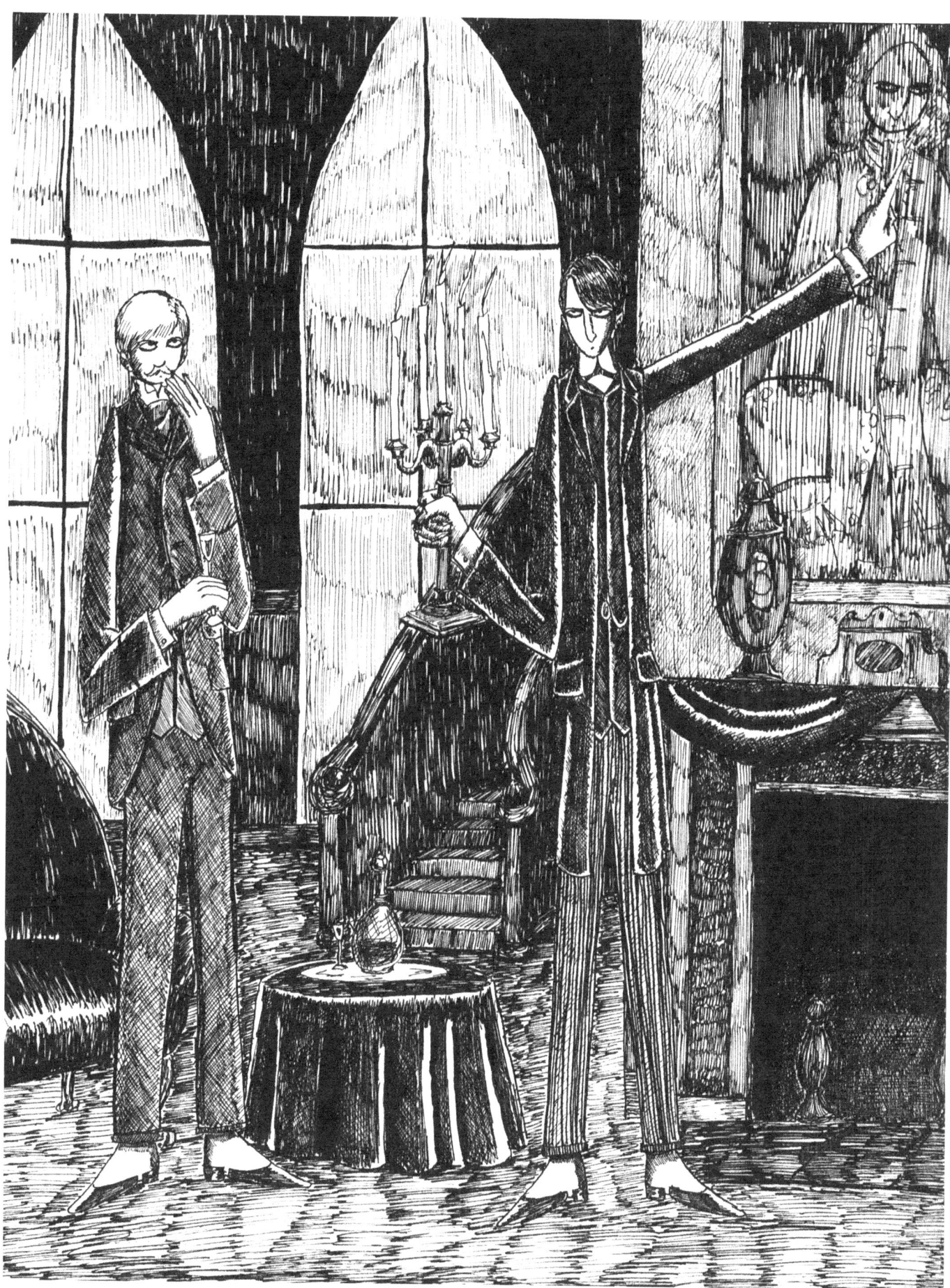

The Hound of the Baskervilles 2004

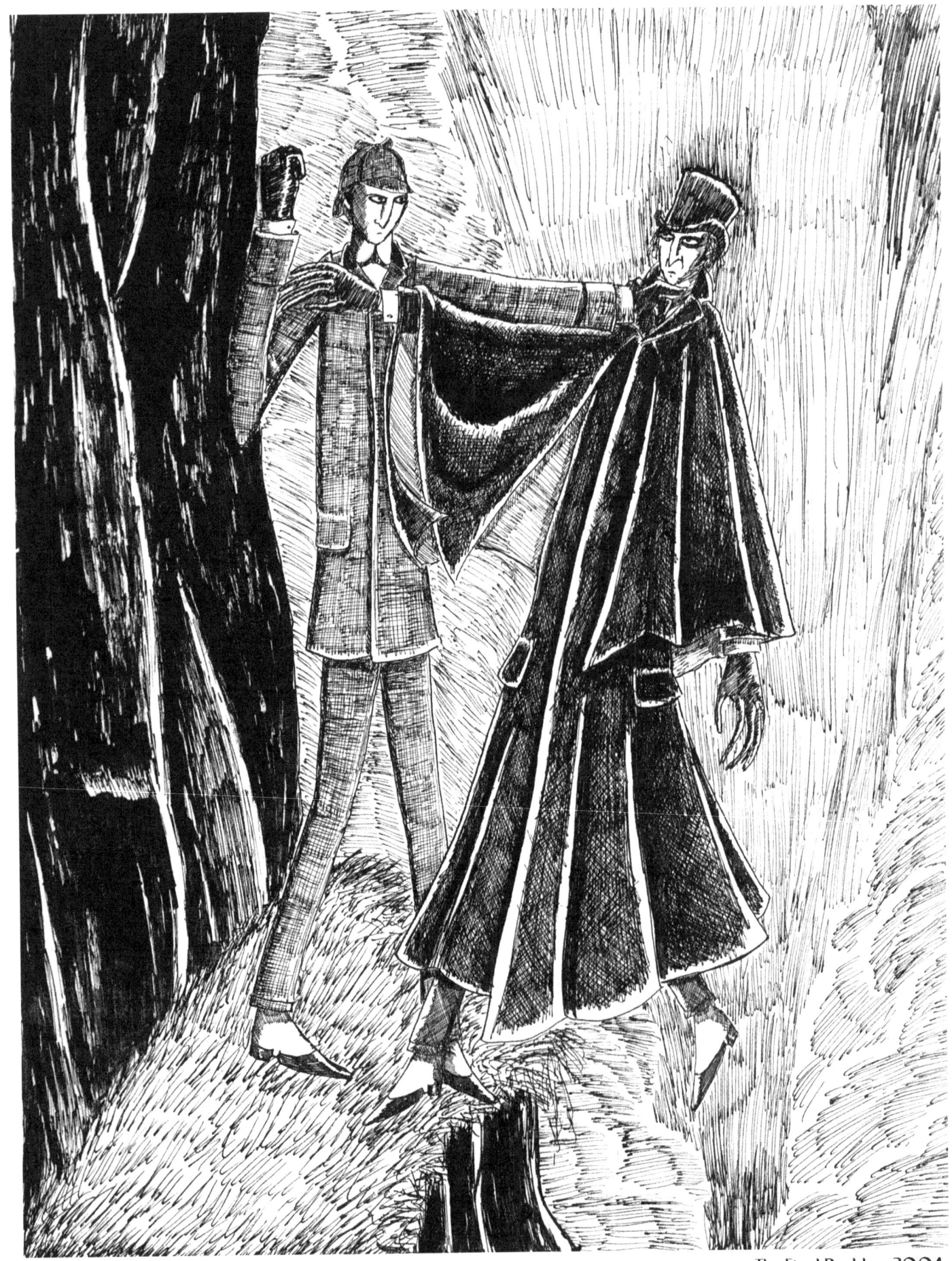

The Final Problem 2004

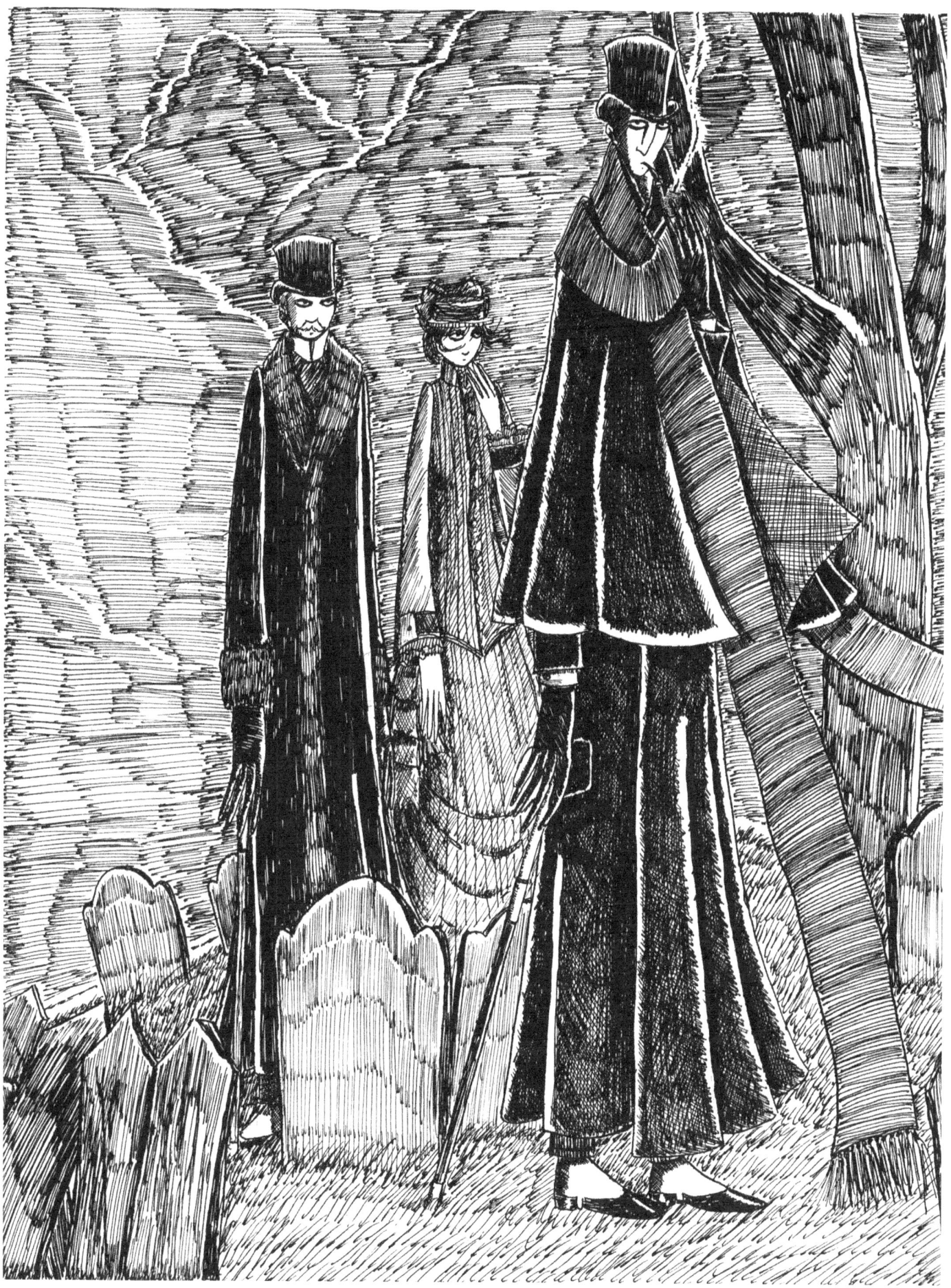

The Adventures of Sherlock Holmes 2004

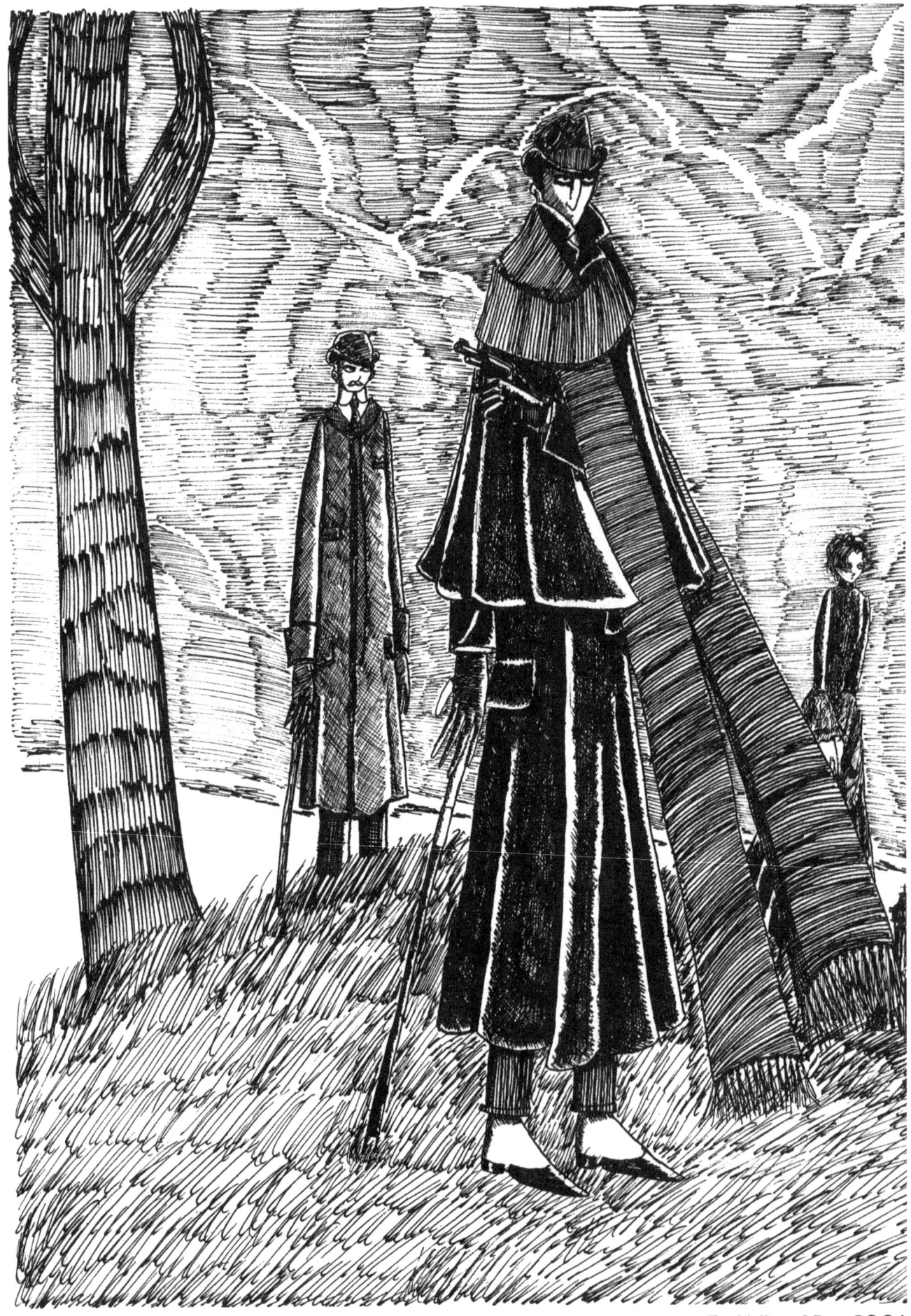

The Valley of Fear 2004

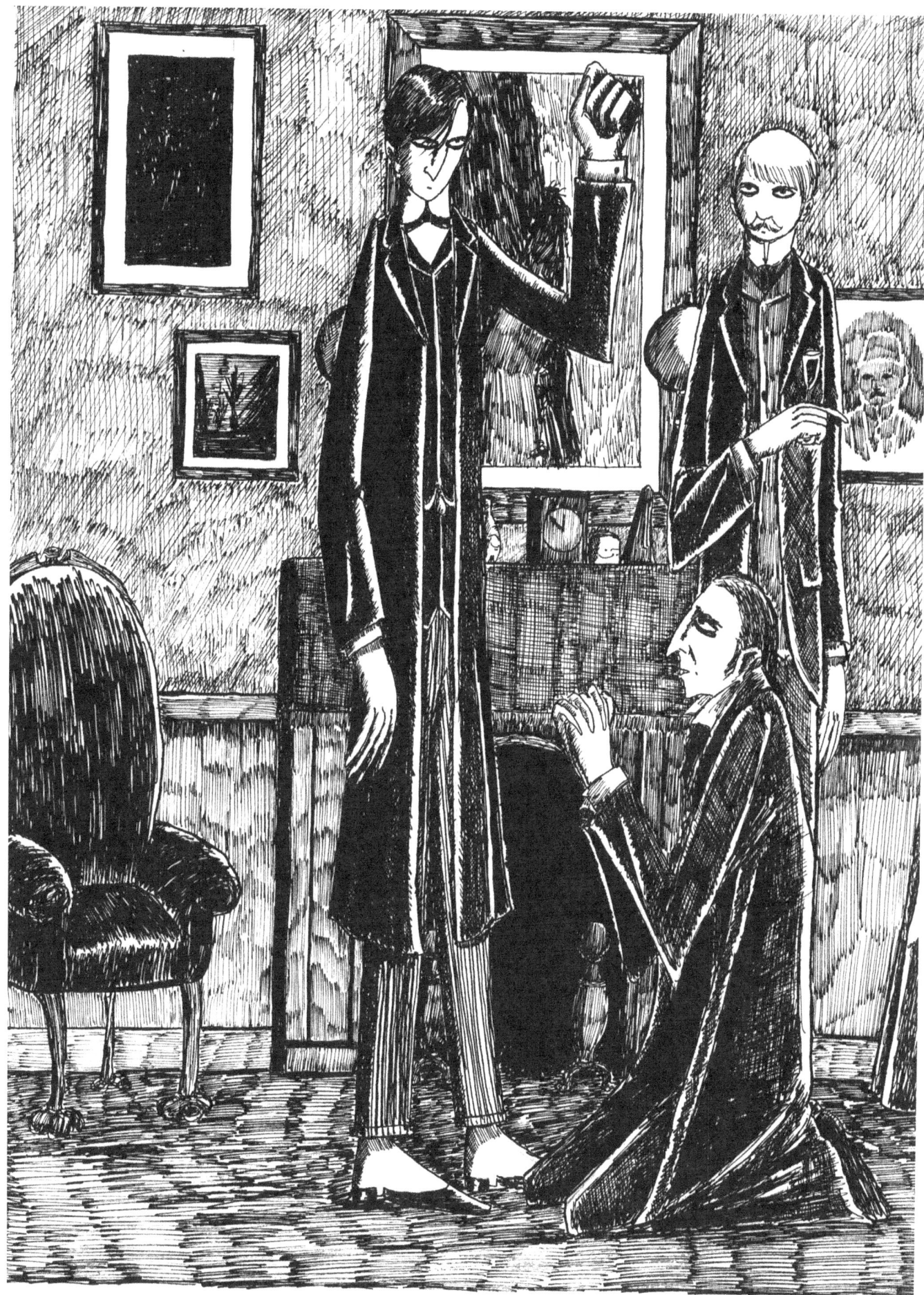

The Blue Carbuncle 2004

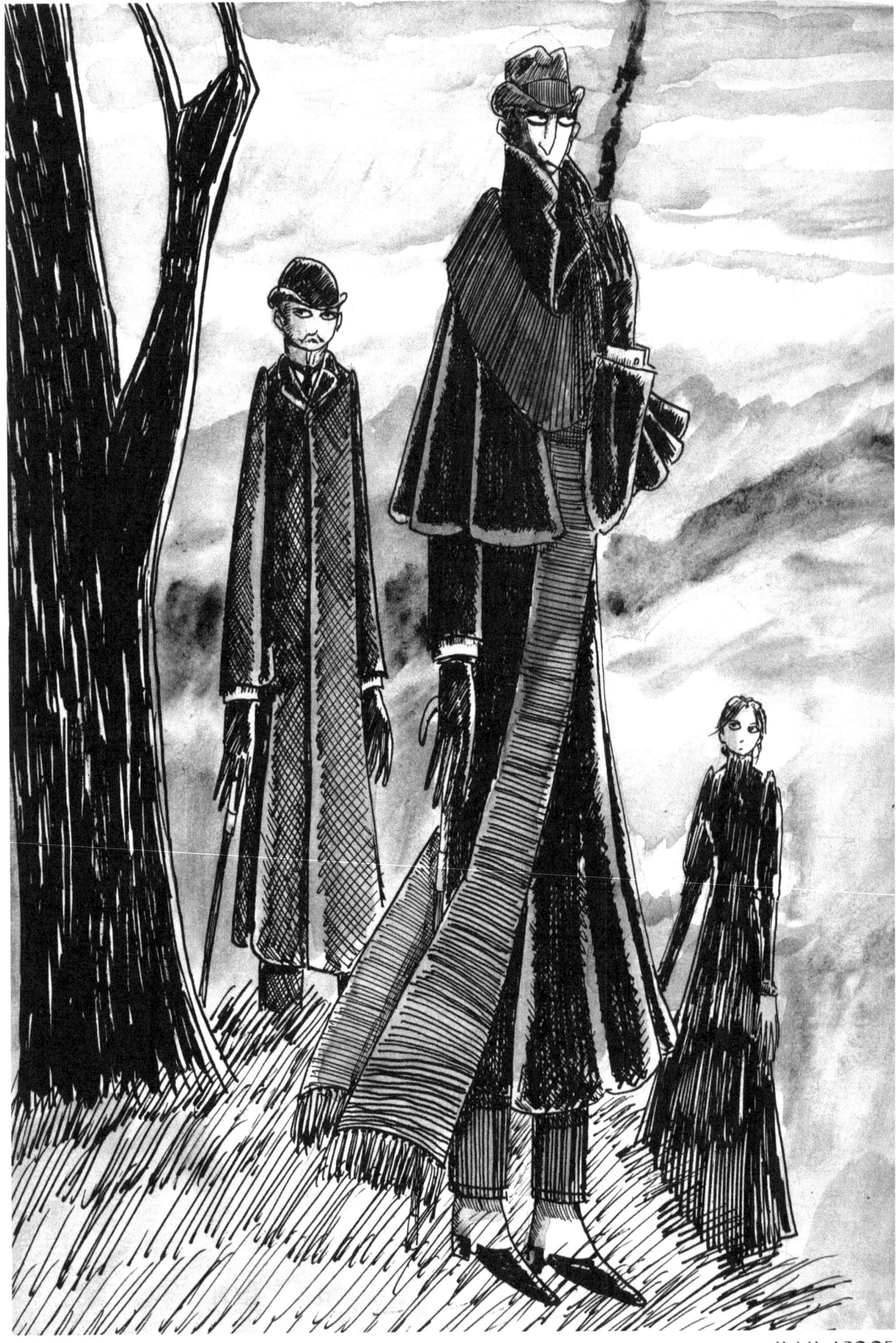

Untitled 2005

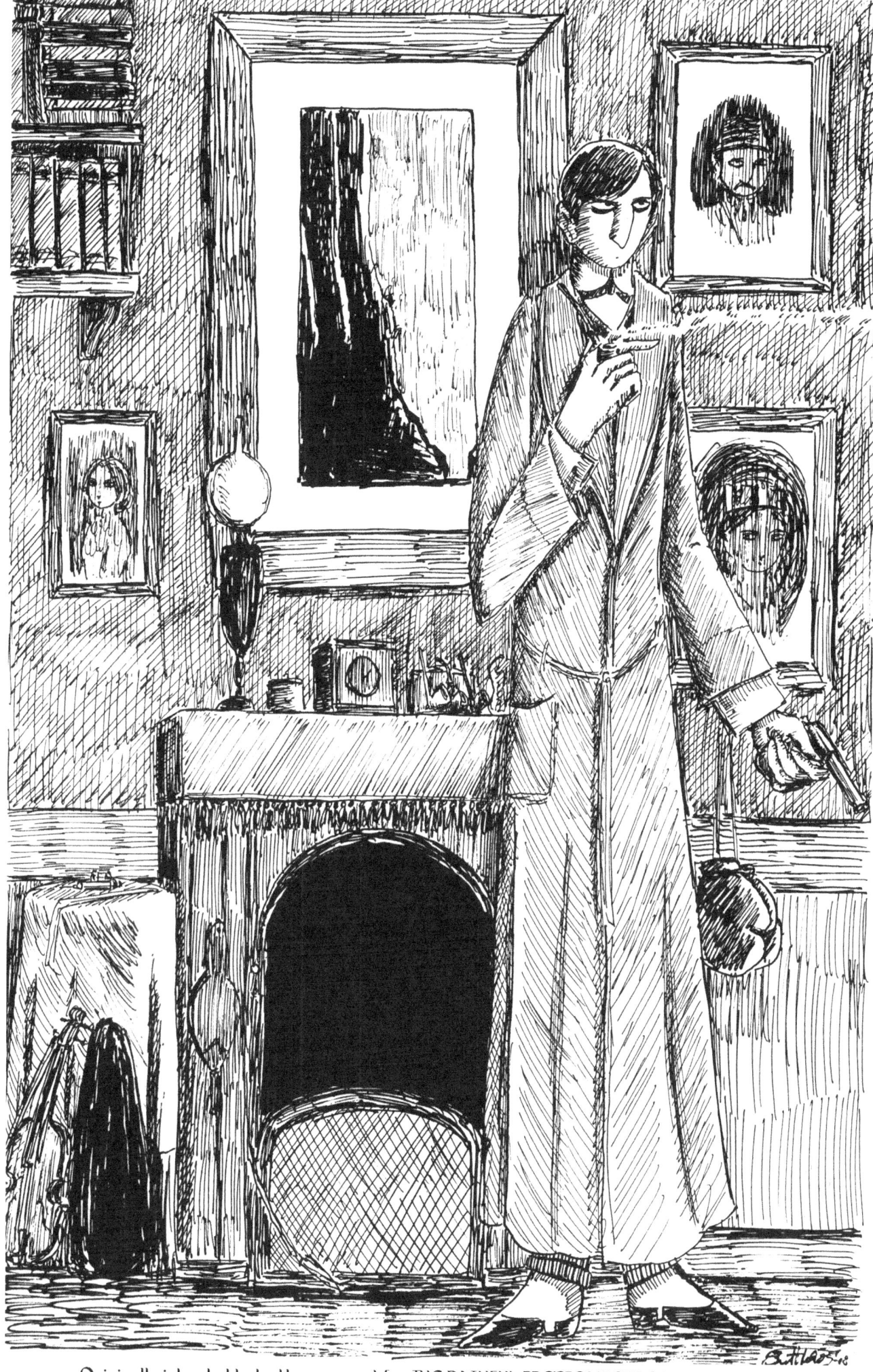

Originally intended to be the cover art for THE PAINFUL PREDICAMENT OF ALICE FAULKNER 2008

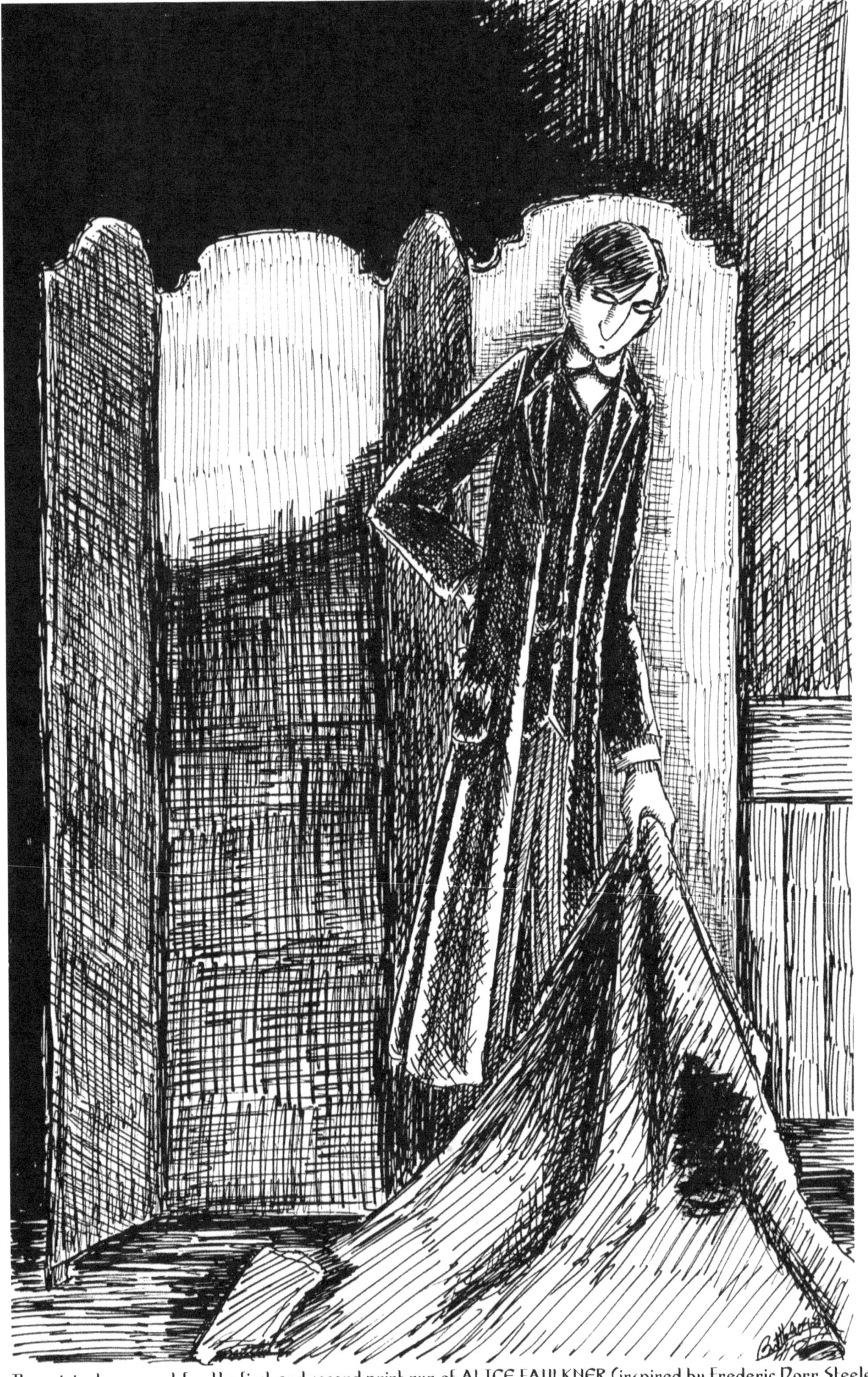

The original cover art for the first and second print run of ALICE FAULKNER (inspired by Frederic Dorr Steele's artwork for The Second Stain) 2008

SMALL WORKS

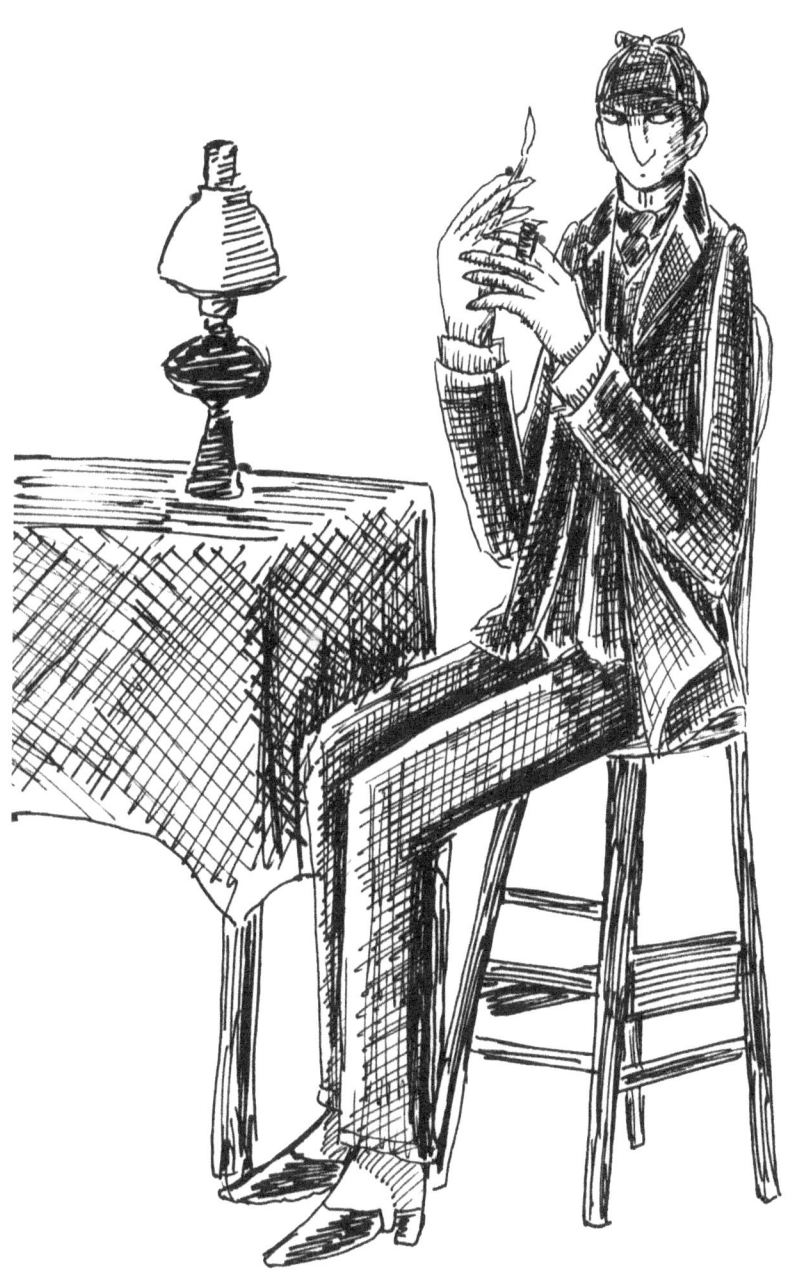

A Selection of smaller illustrations

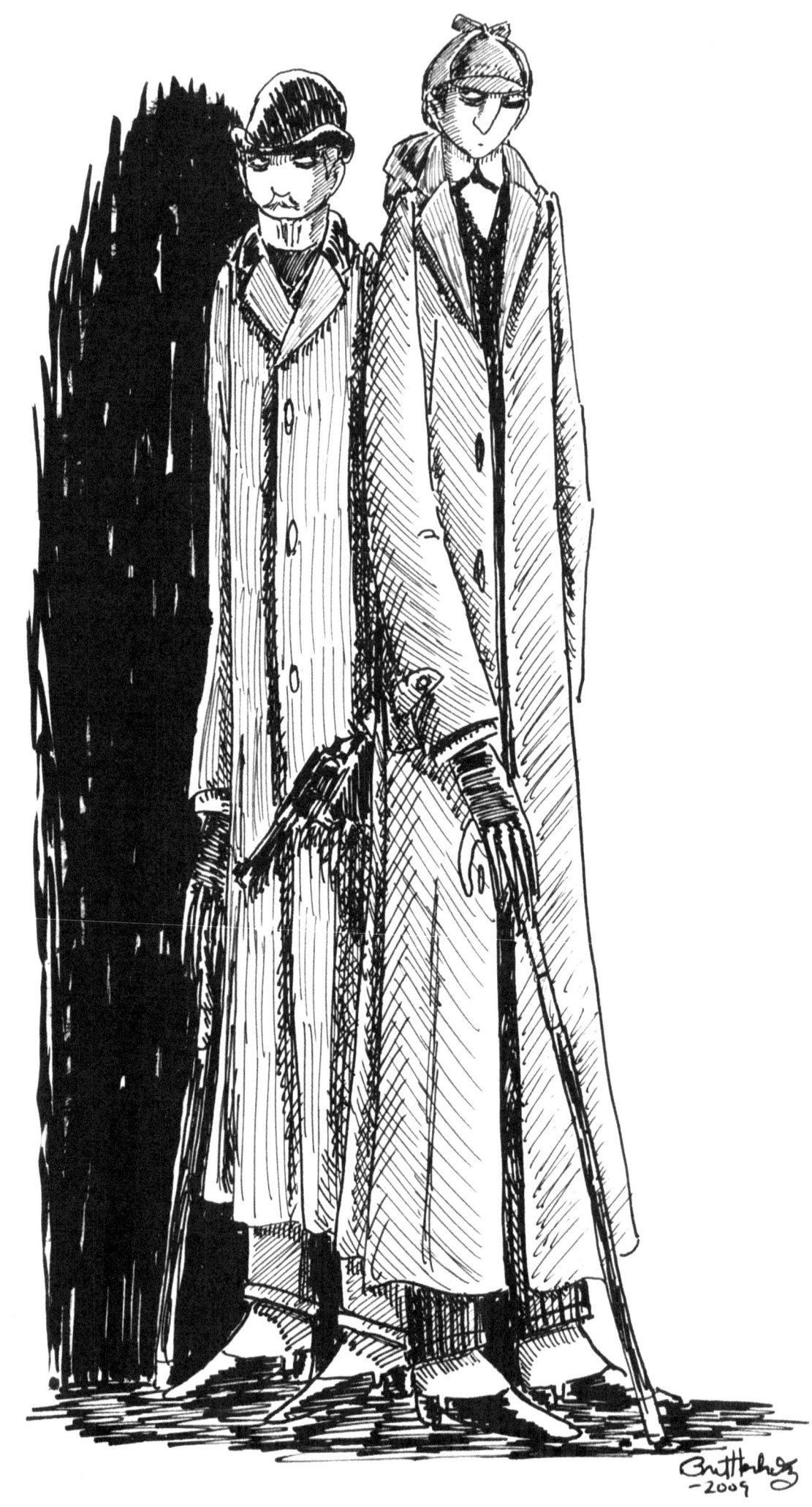

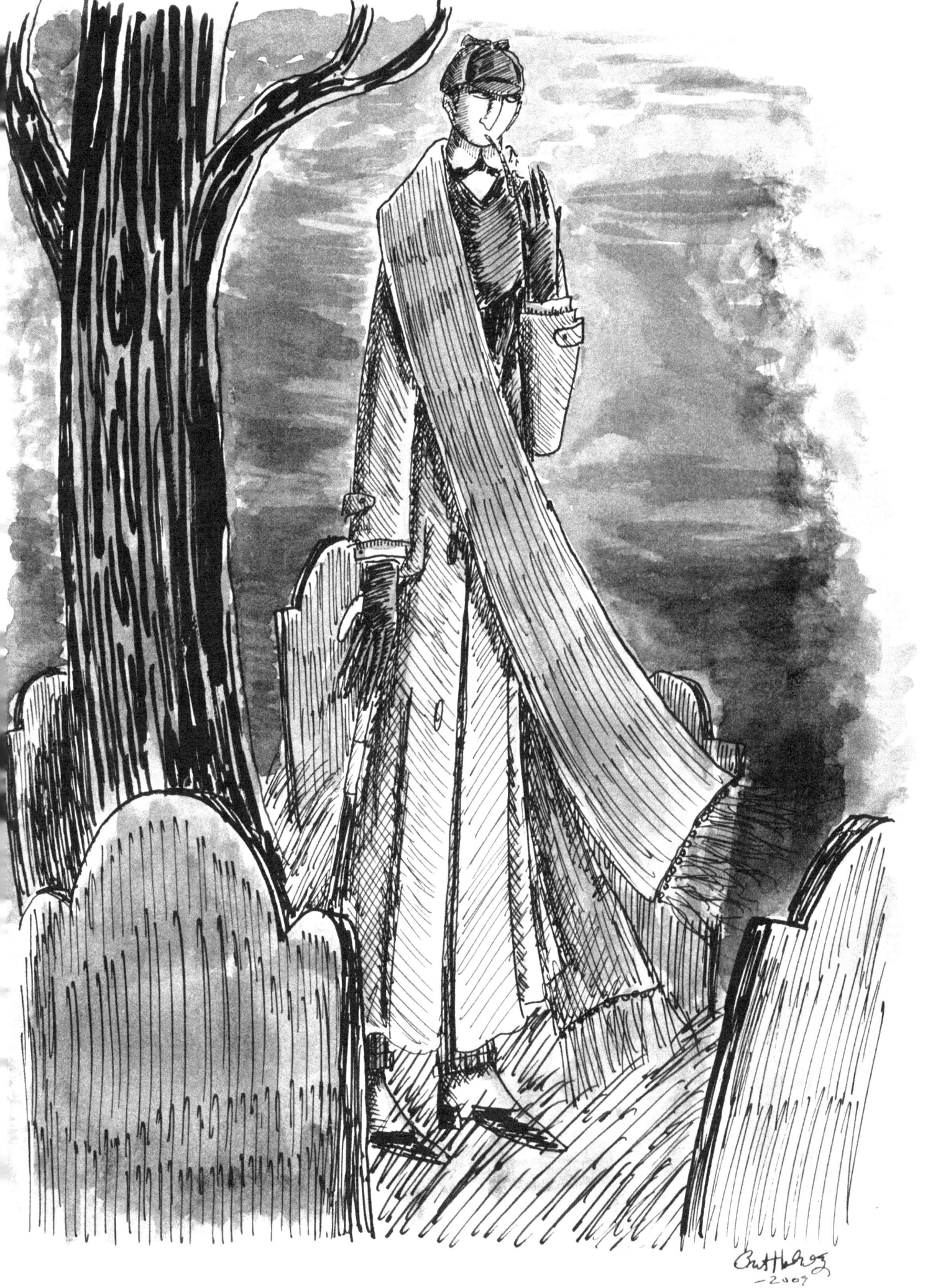

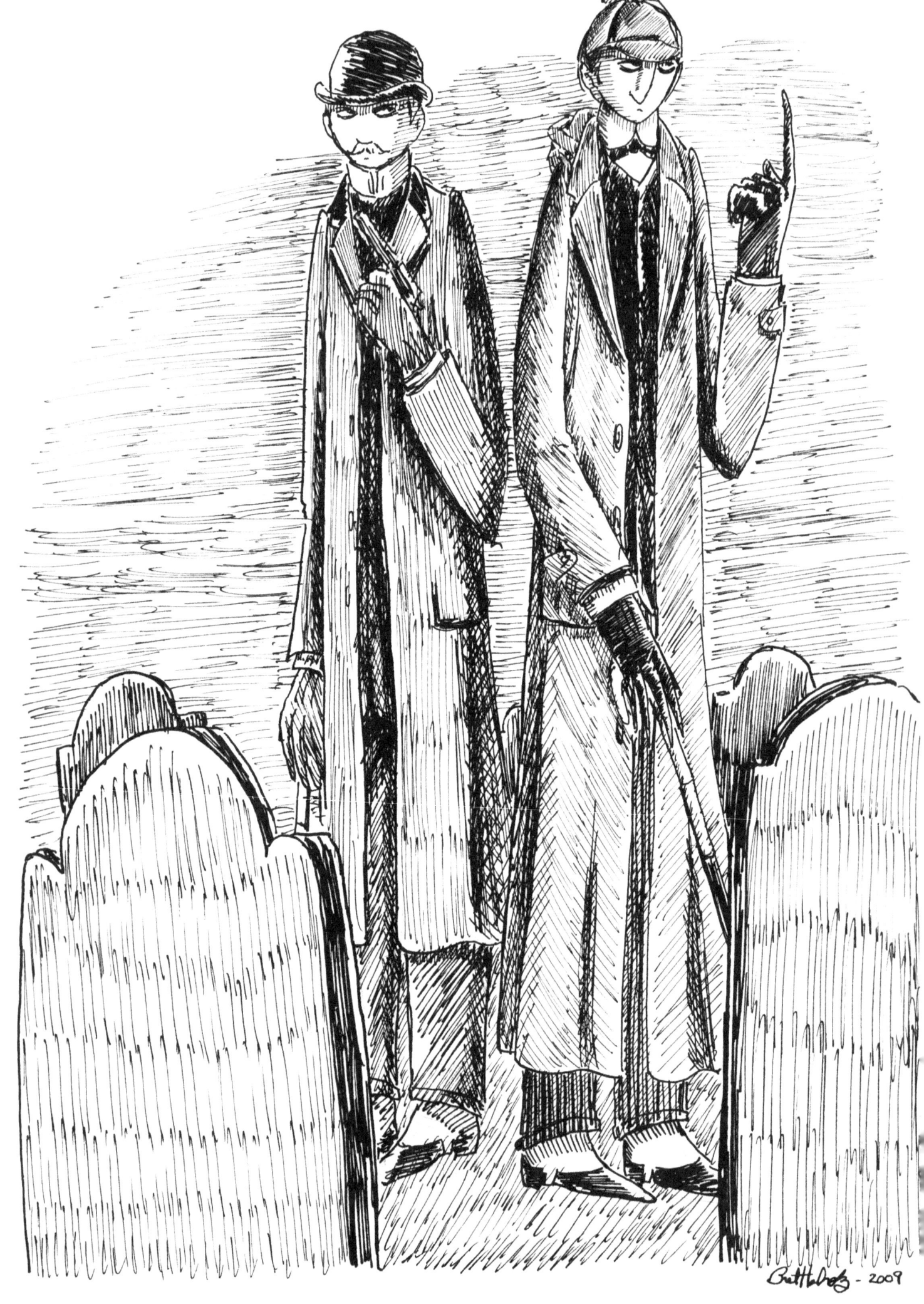

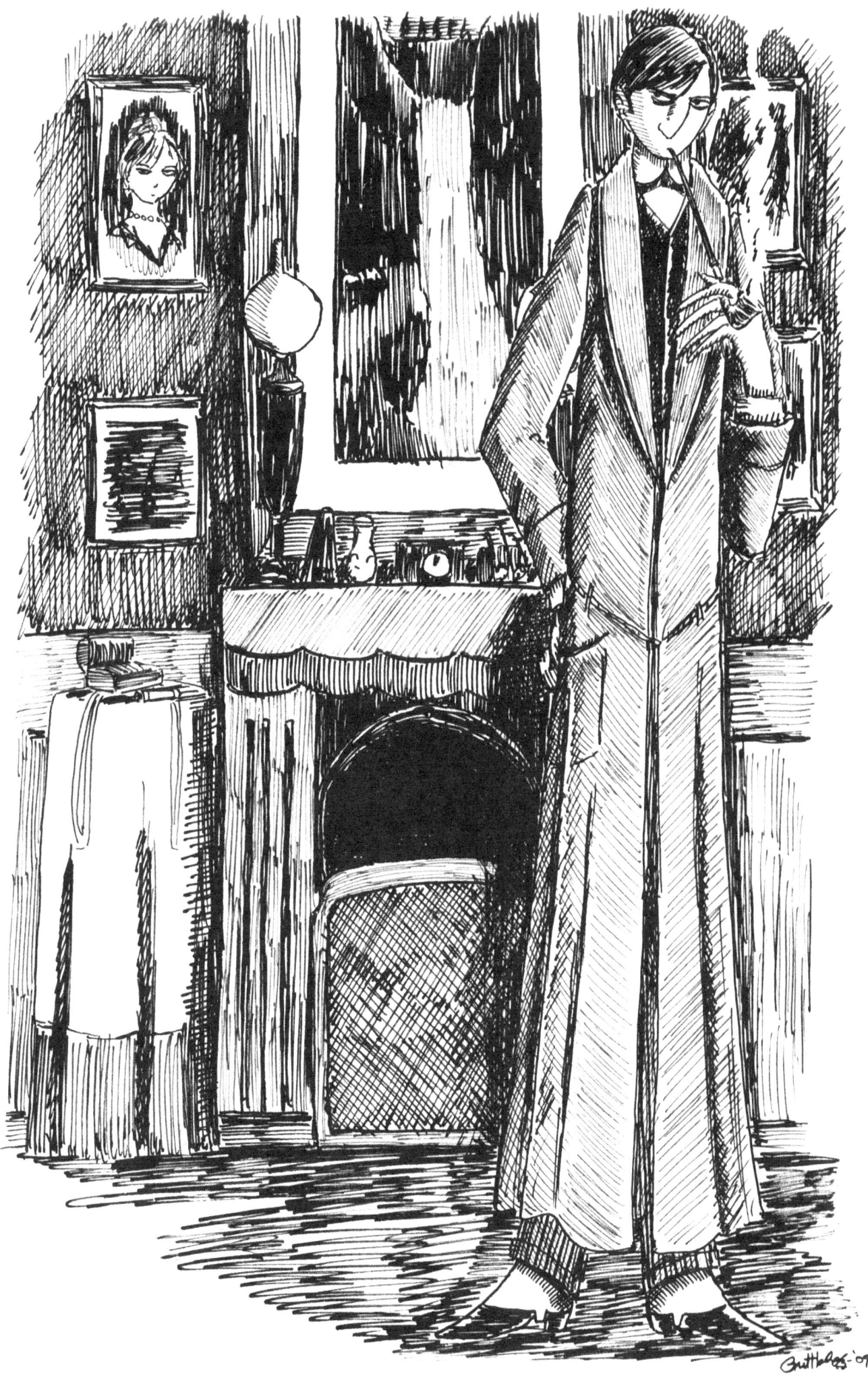

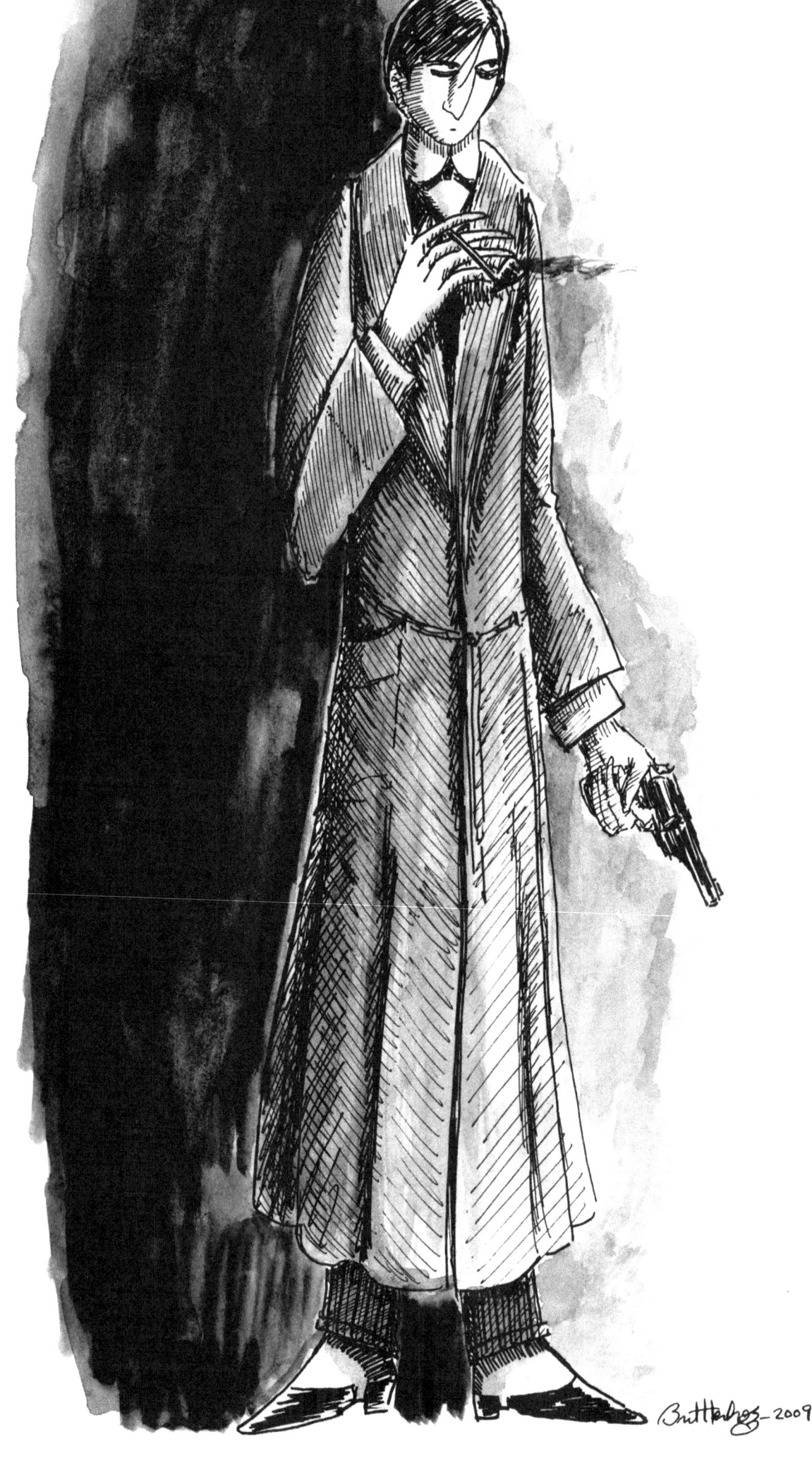

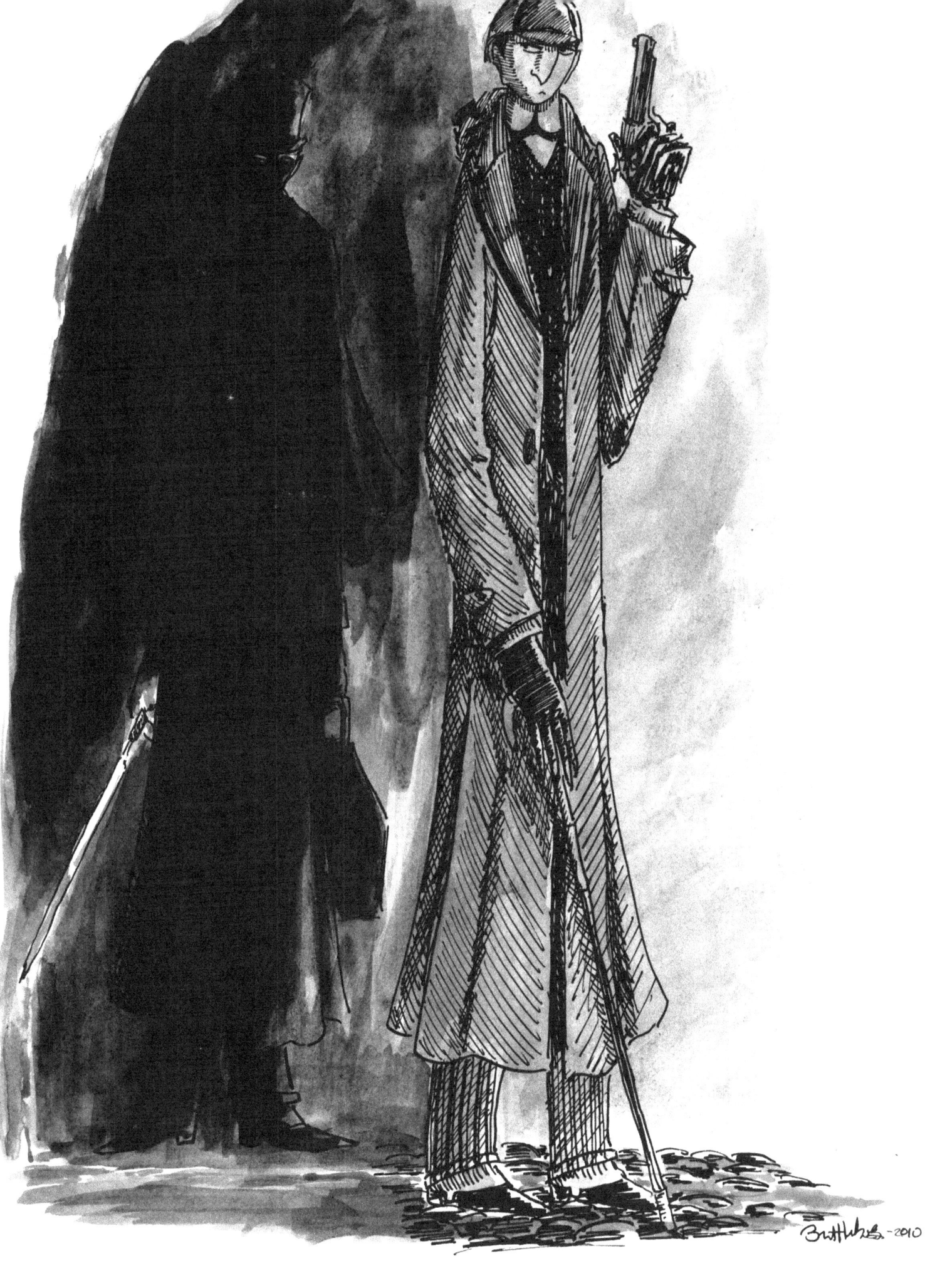

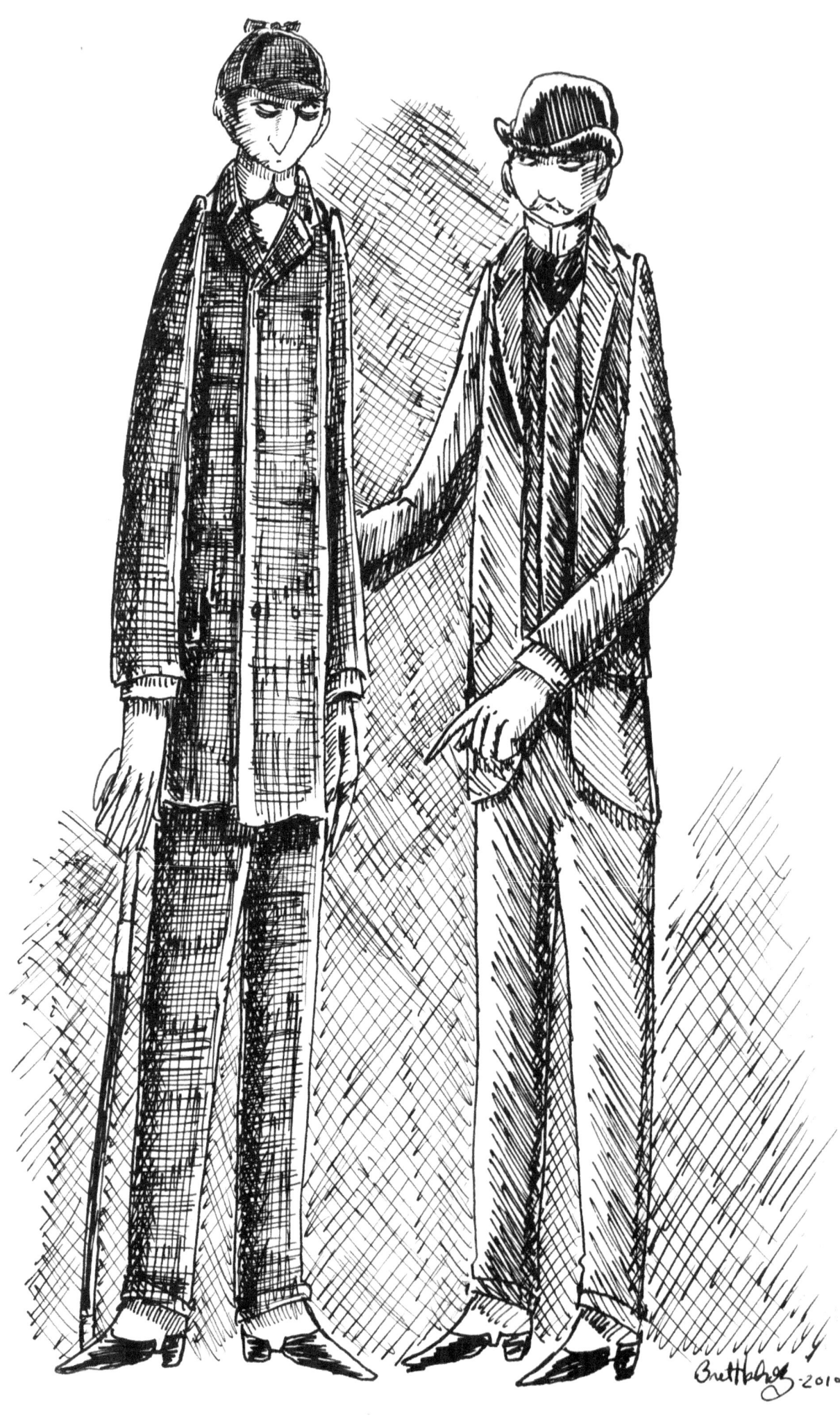

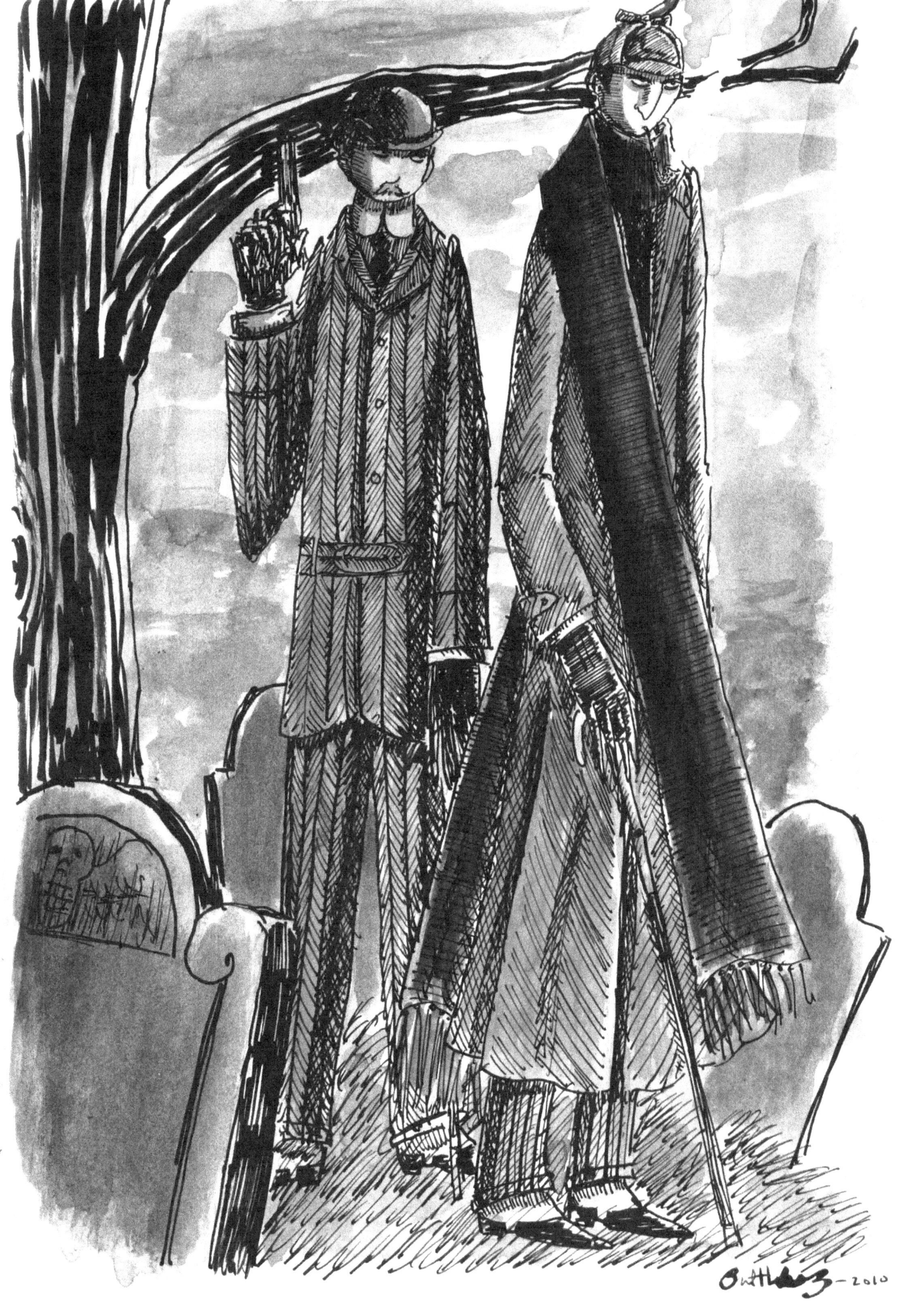

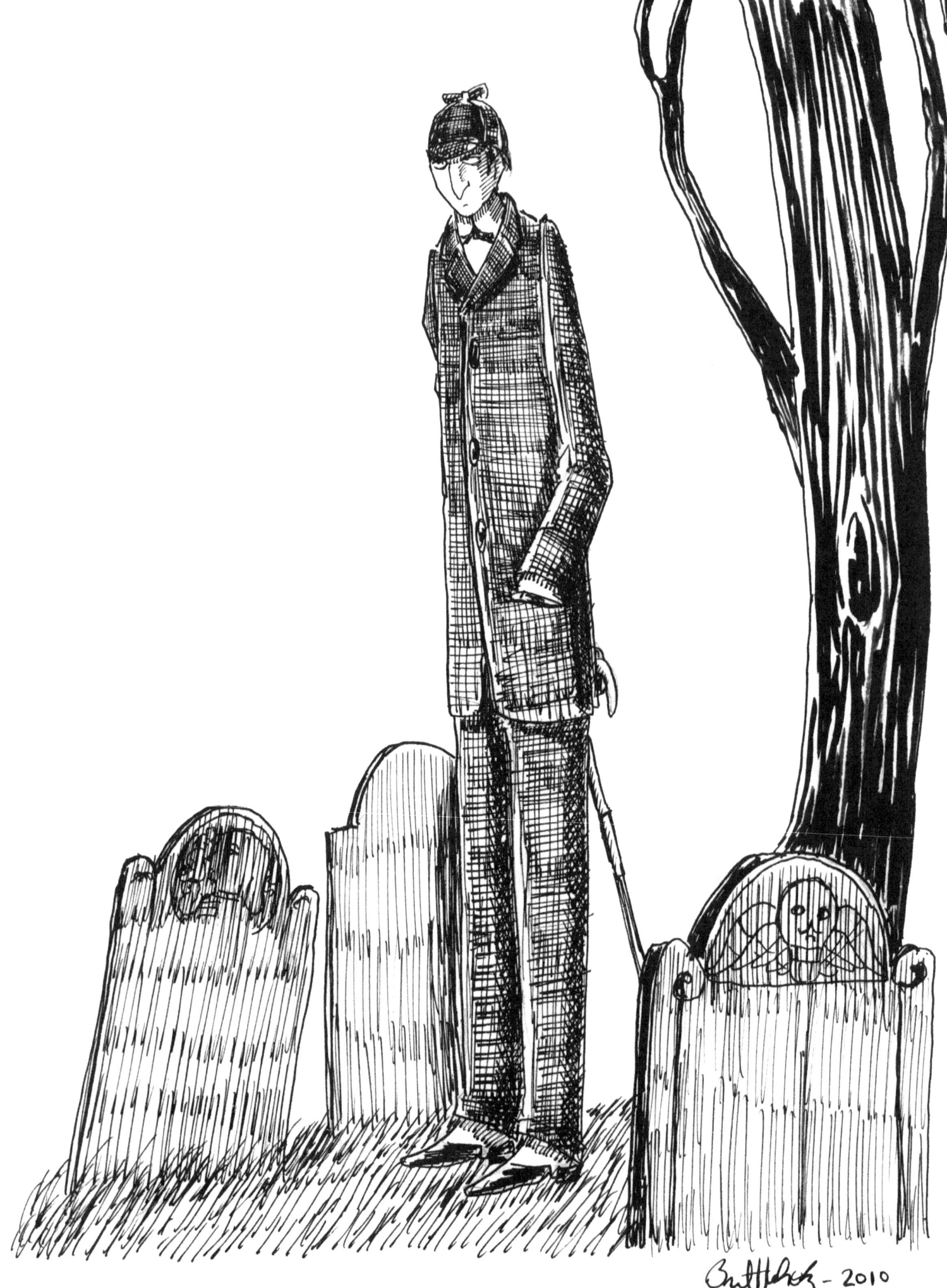

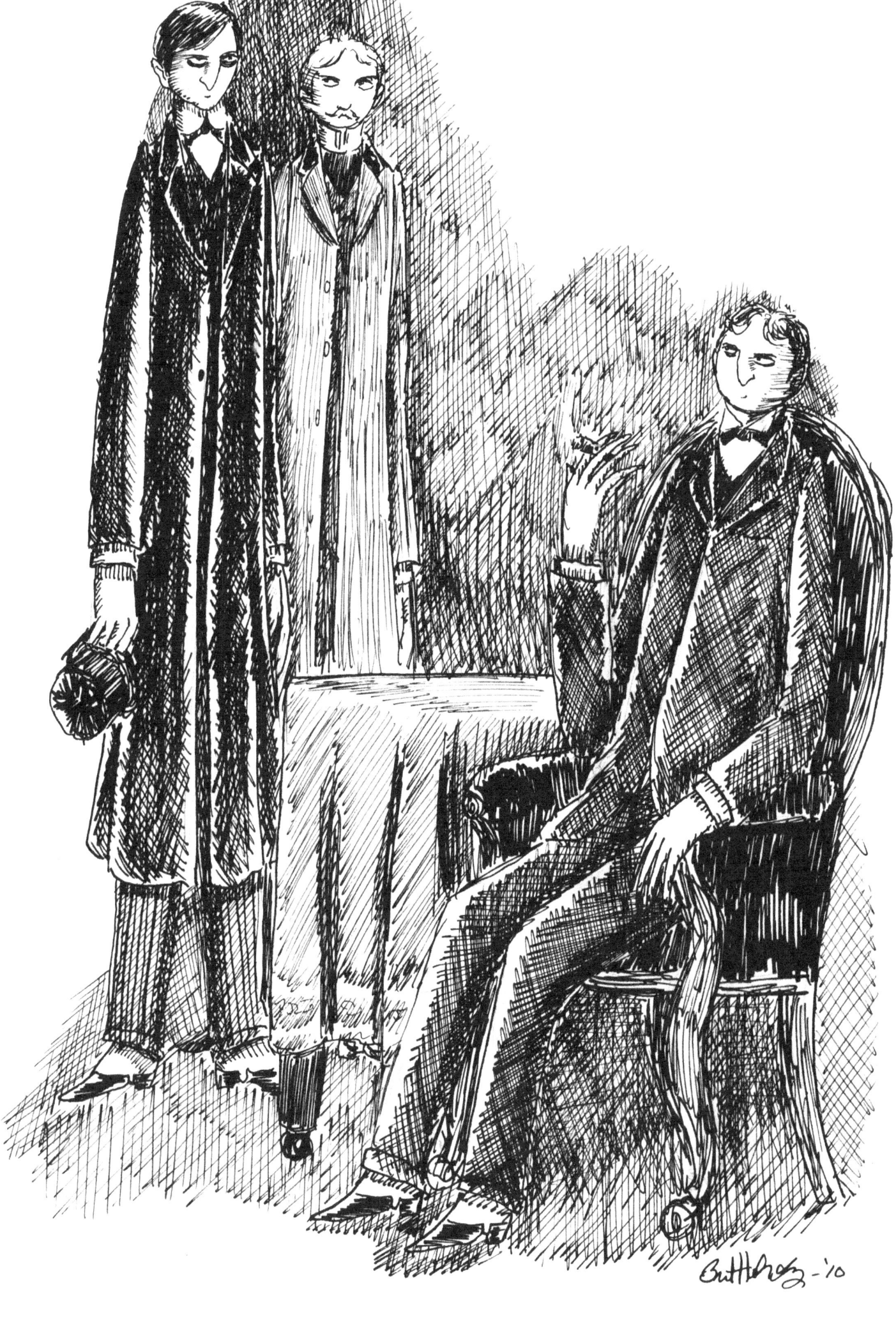

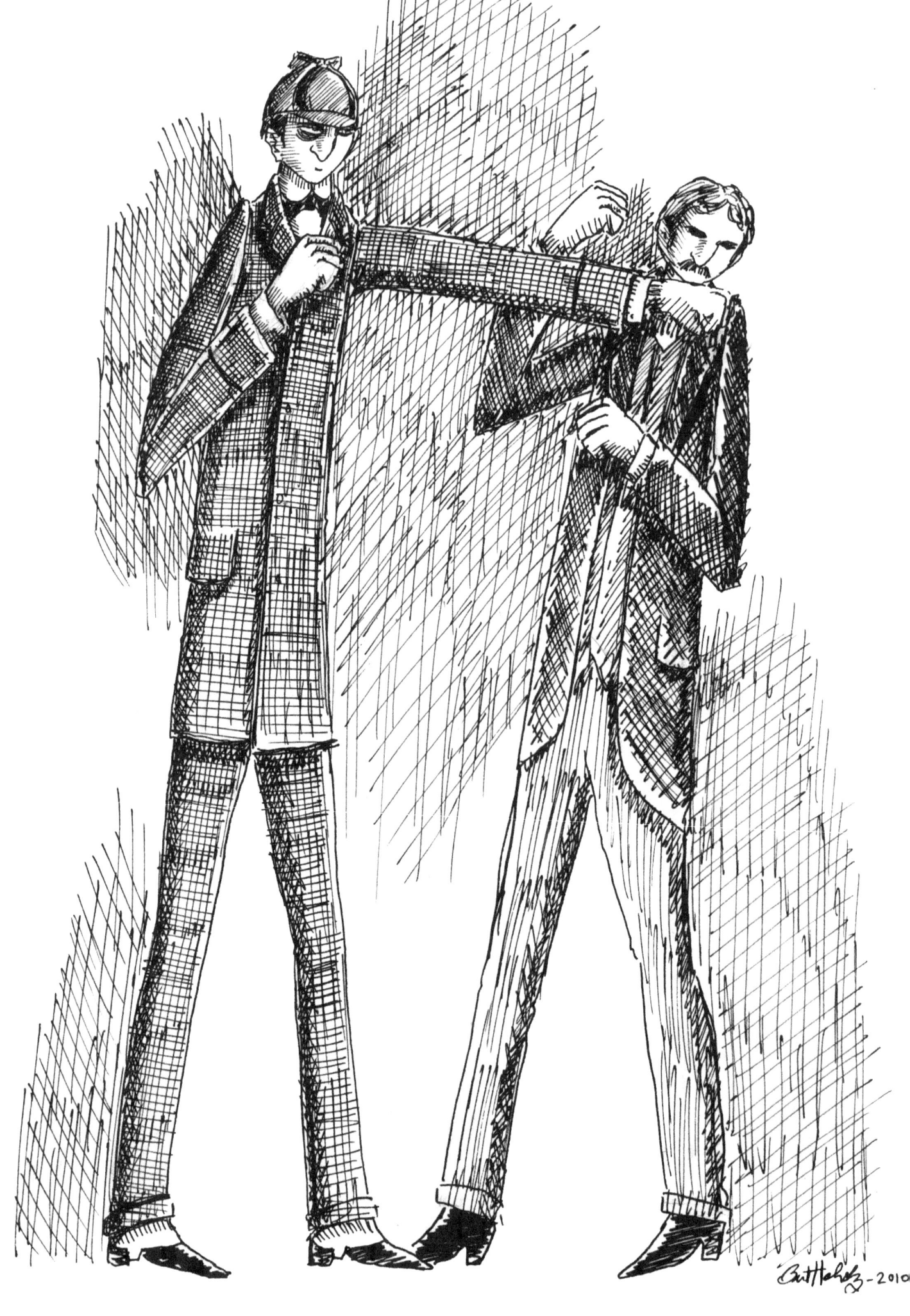

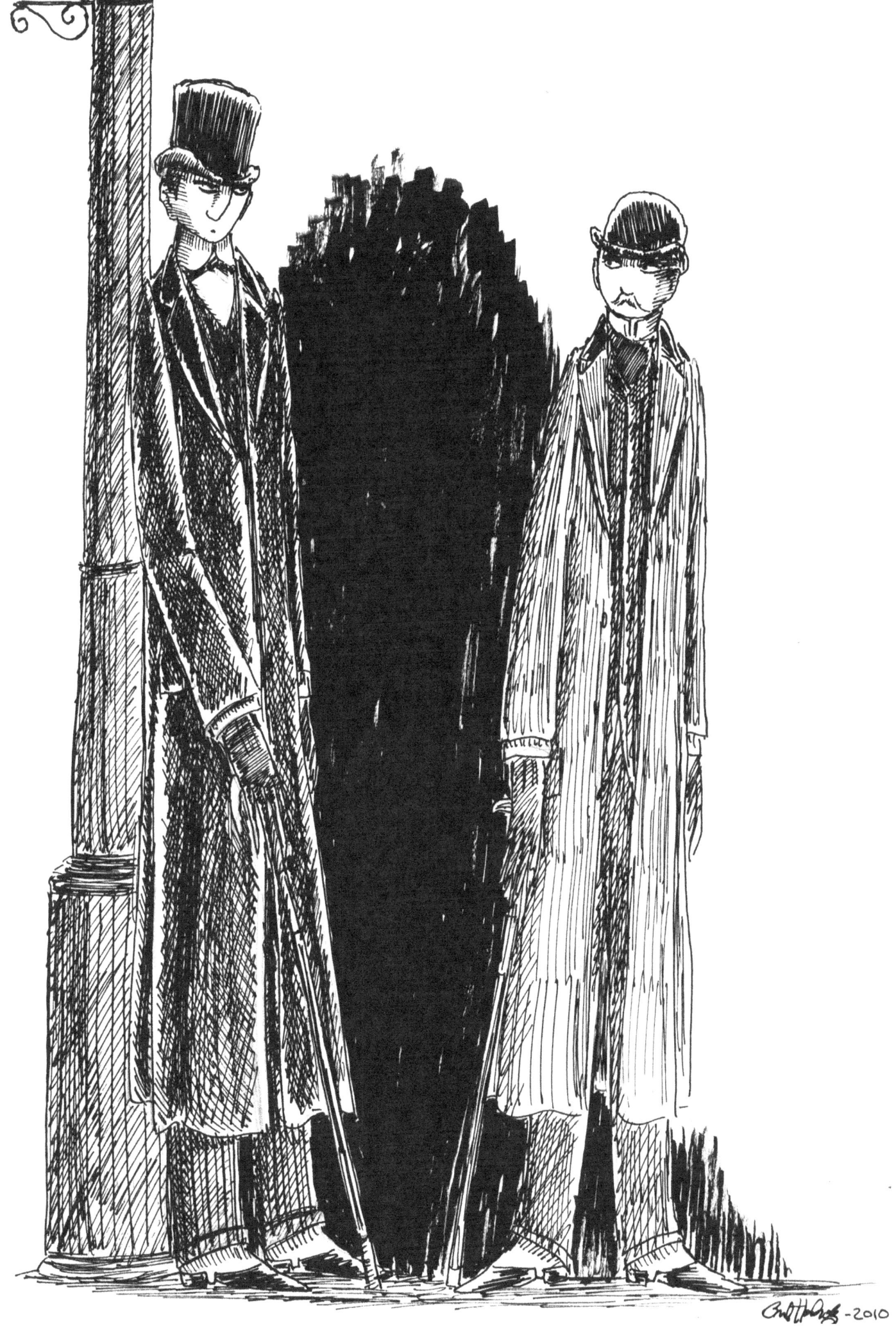

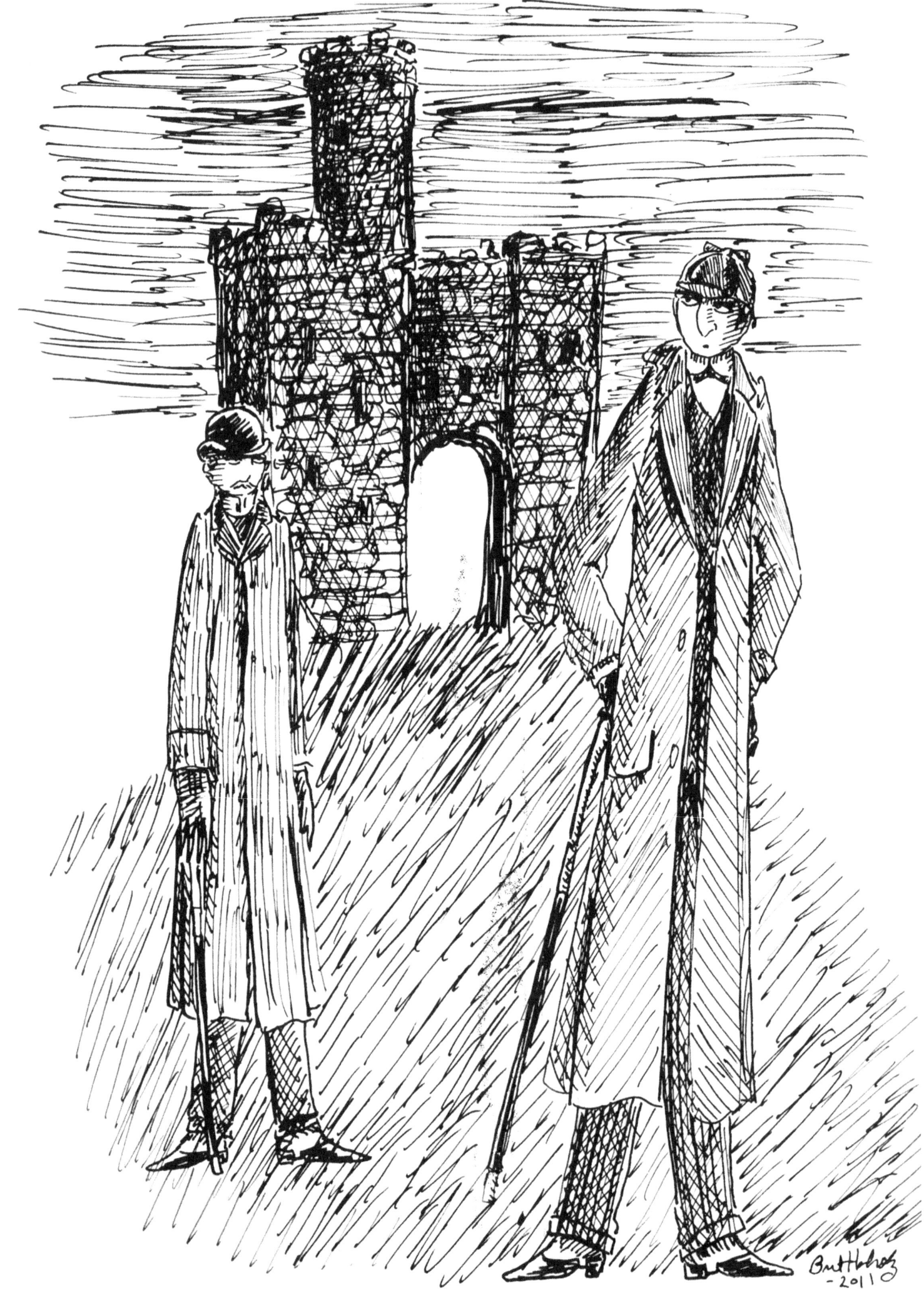

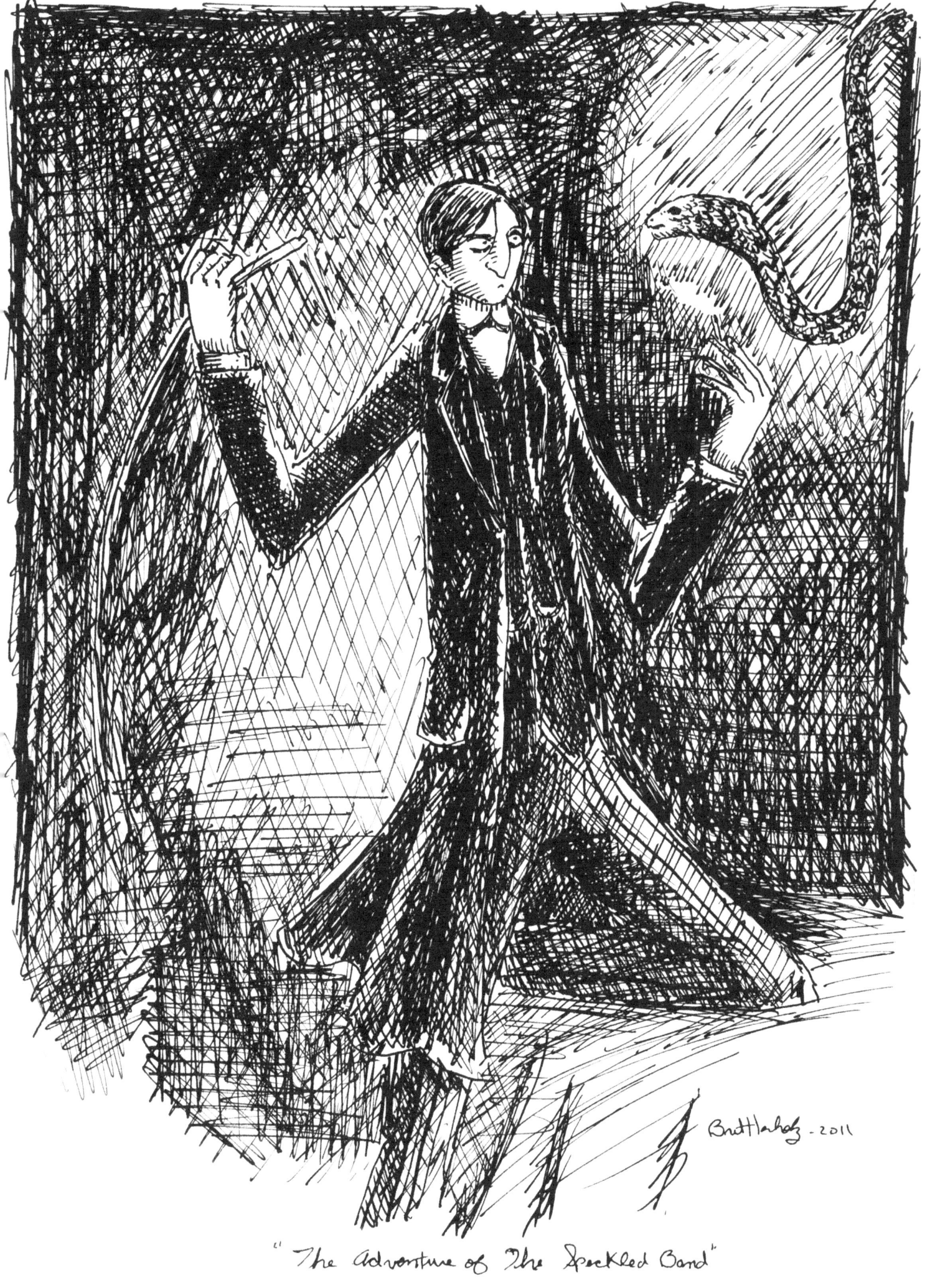

"The Adventure of The Speckled Band"

COMIC ART

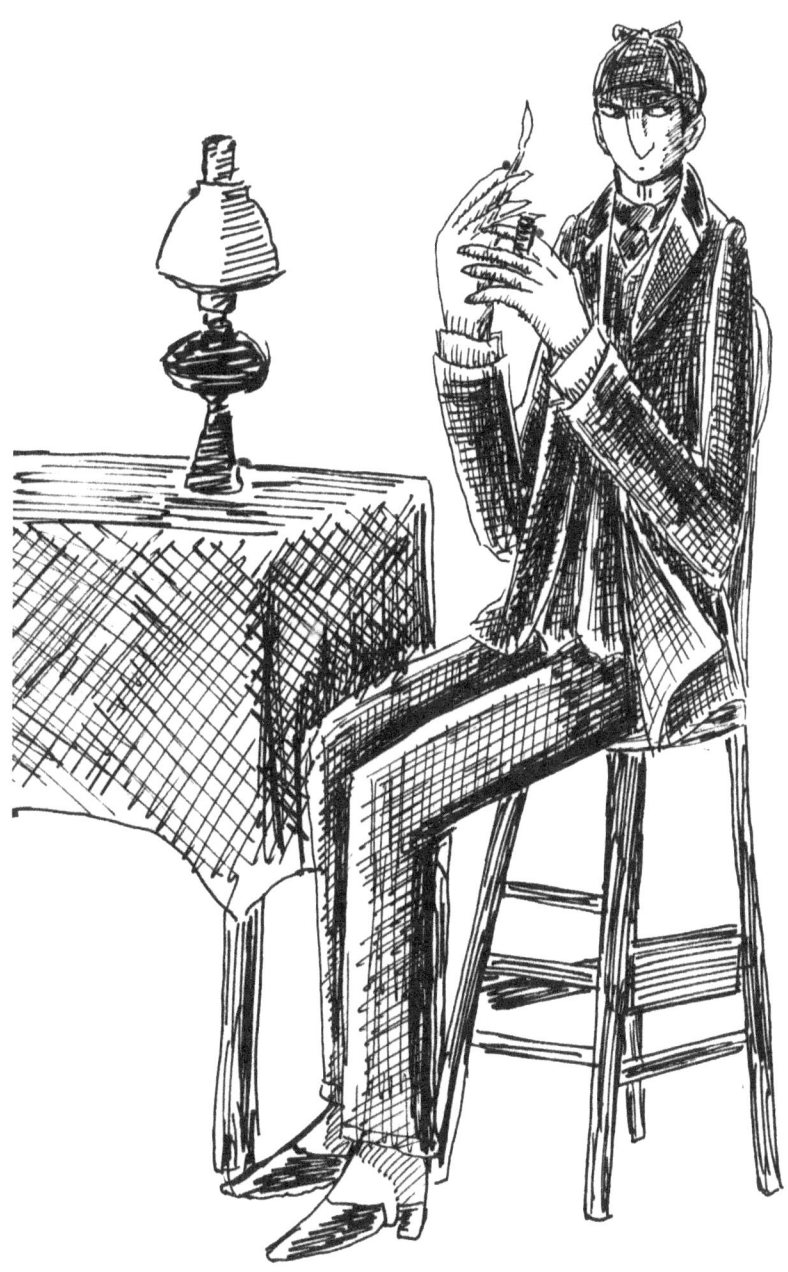

Pages from projects unpublished and works in progress. Since a
number of these projects are unfinished, the pages remained unlettered.
Most of the dialogue would have been added later on the computer.

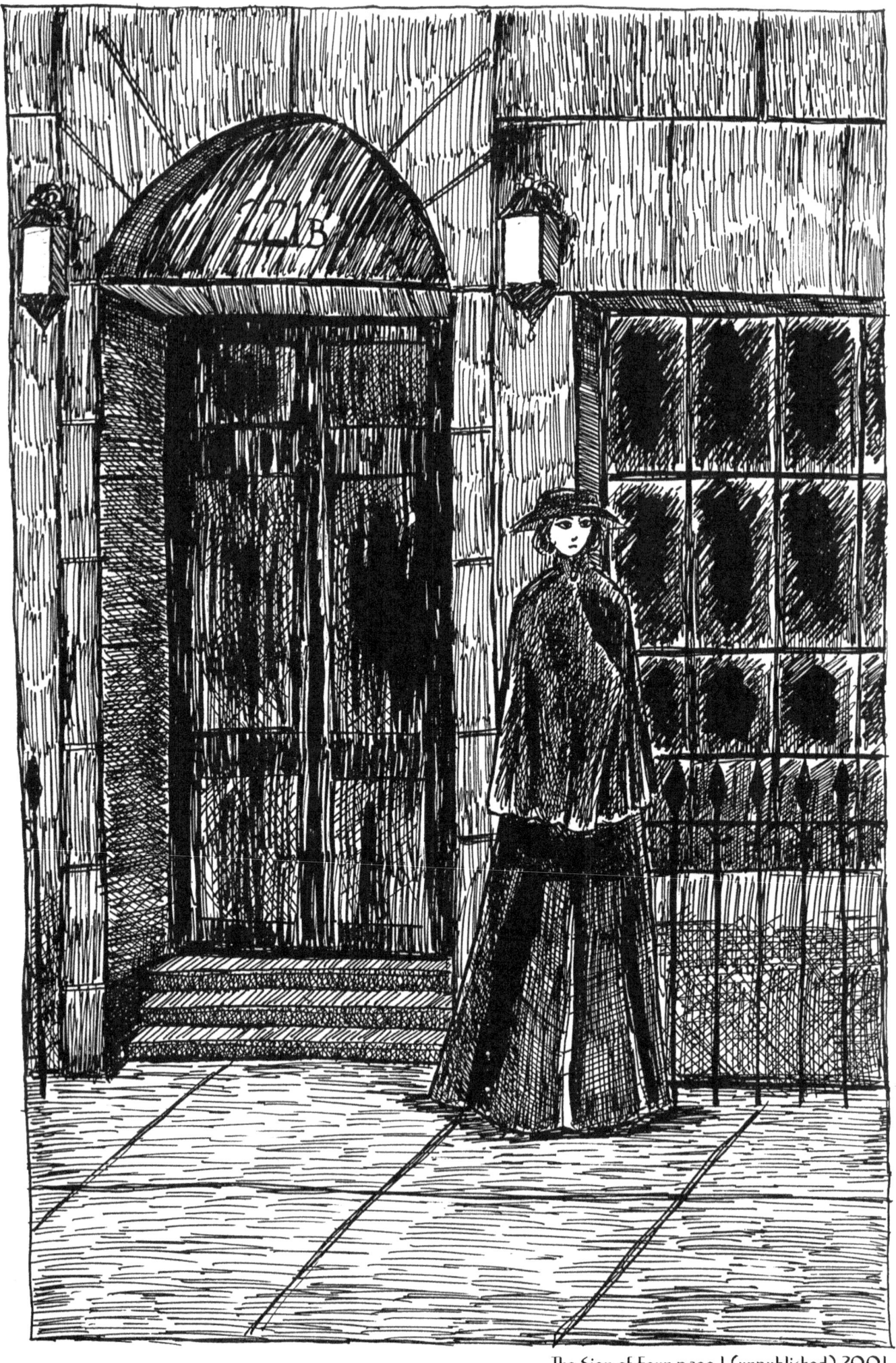

The Sign of Four page 1 (unpublished) 2001

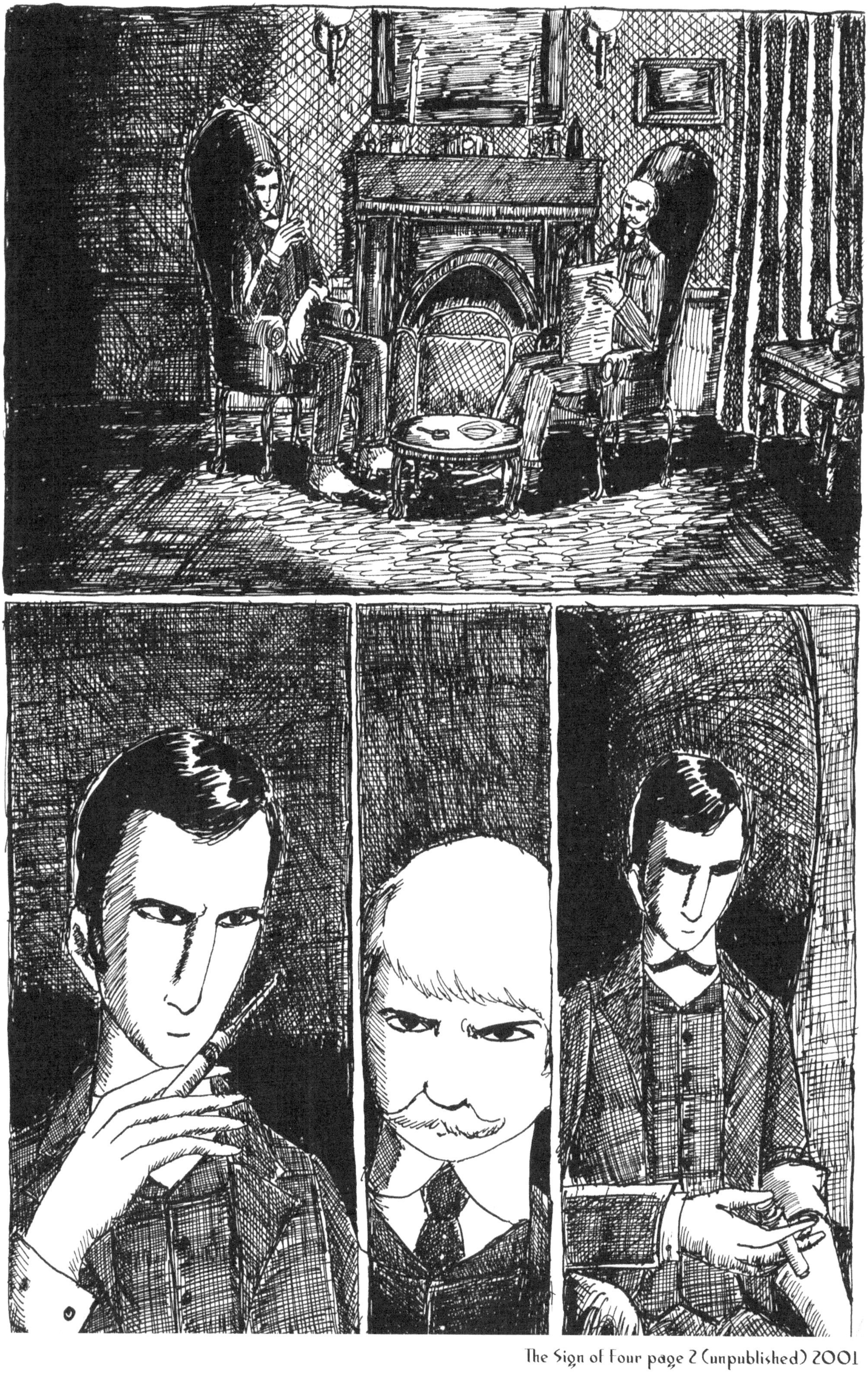

The Sign of Four page 2 (unpublished) 2001

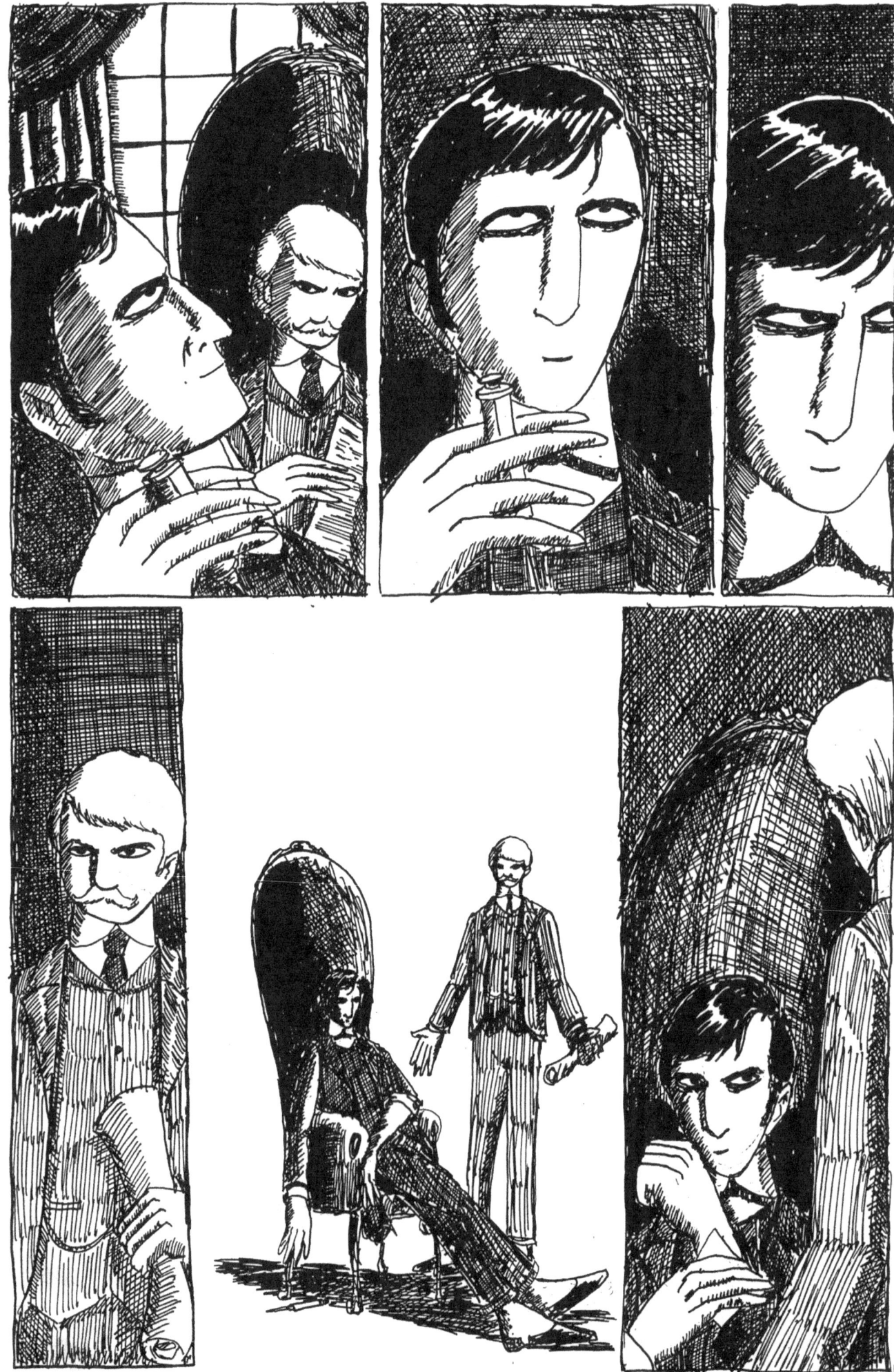

The Sign of Four page 3 (unpublished) 2001

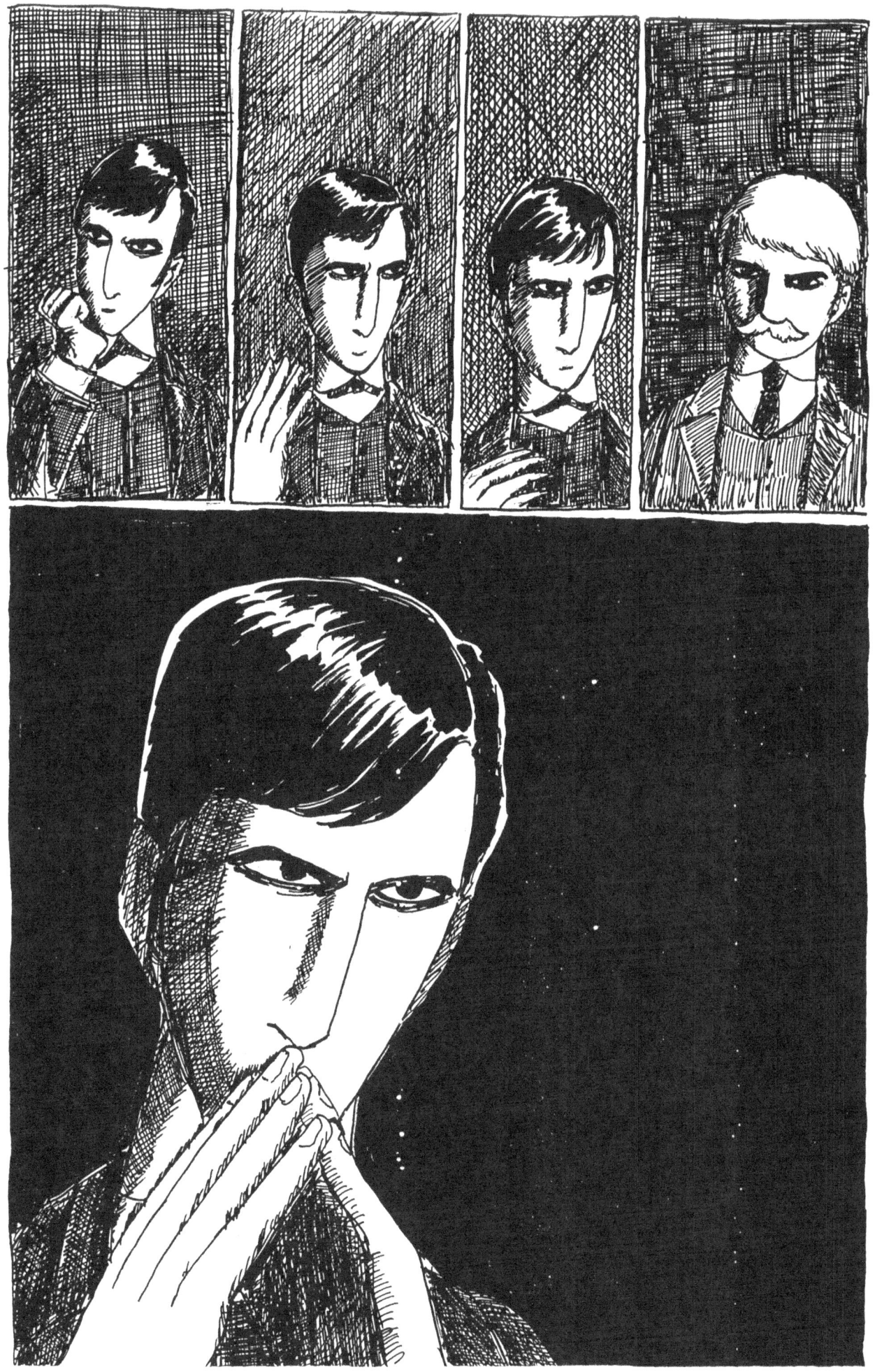

The Sign of Four page 3 (unpublished) 2001

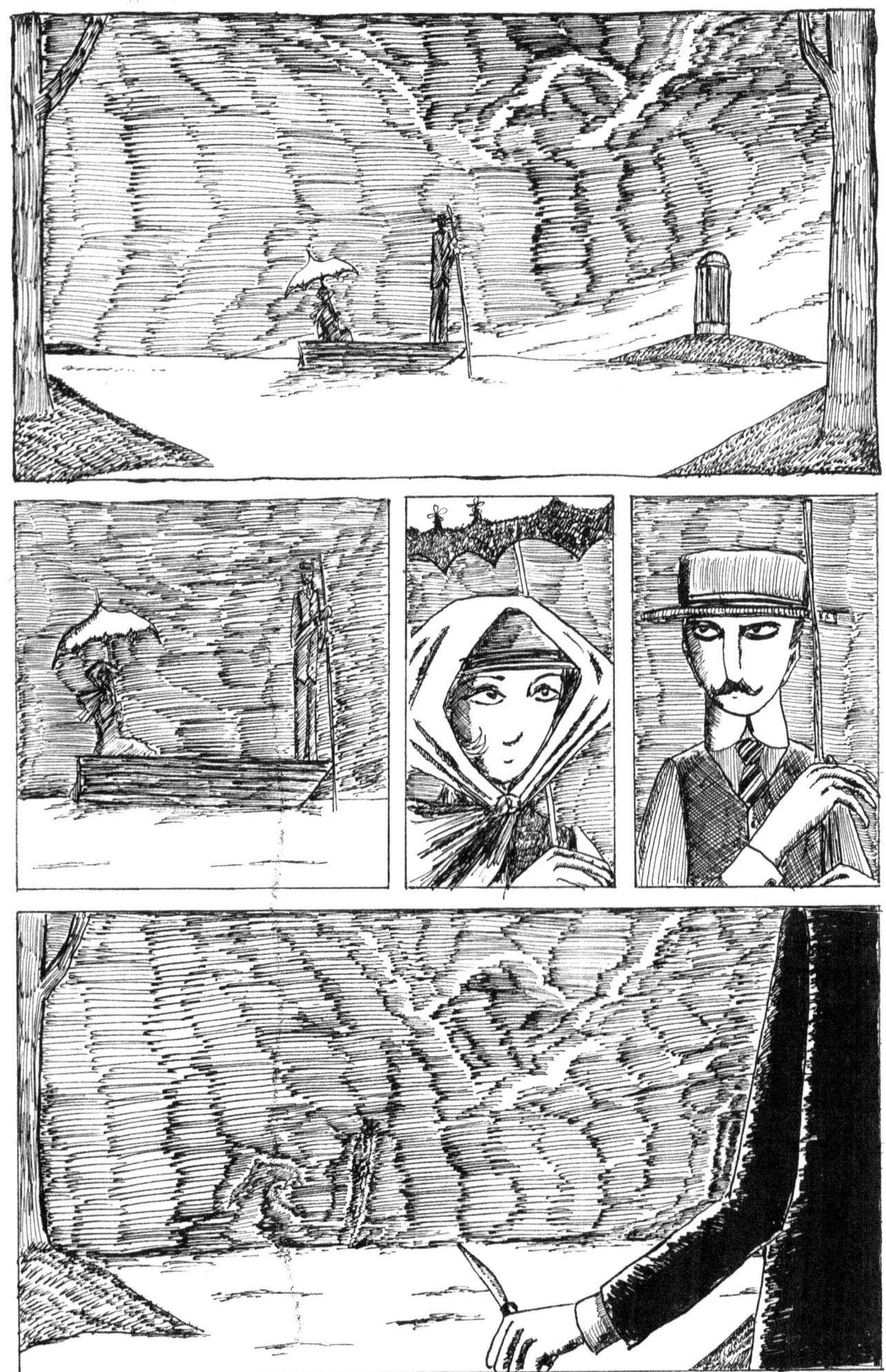

The Adventure of the Cardboard Box page 1 (unpublished) 2004

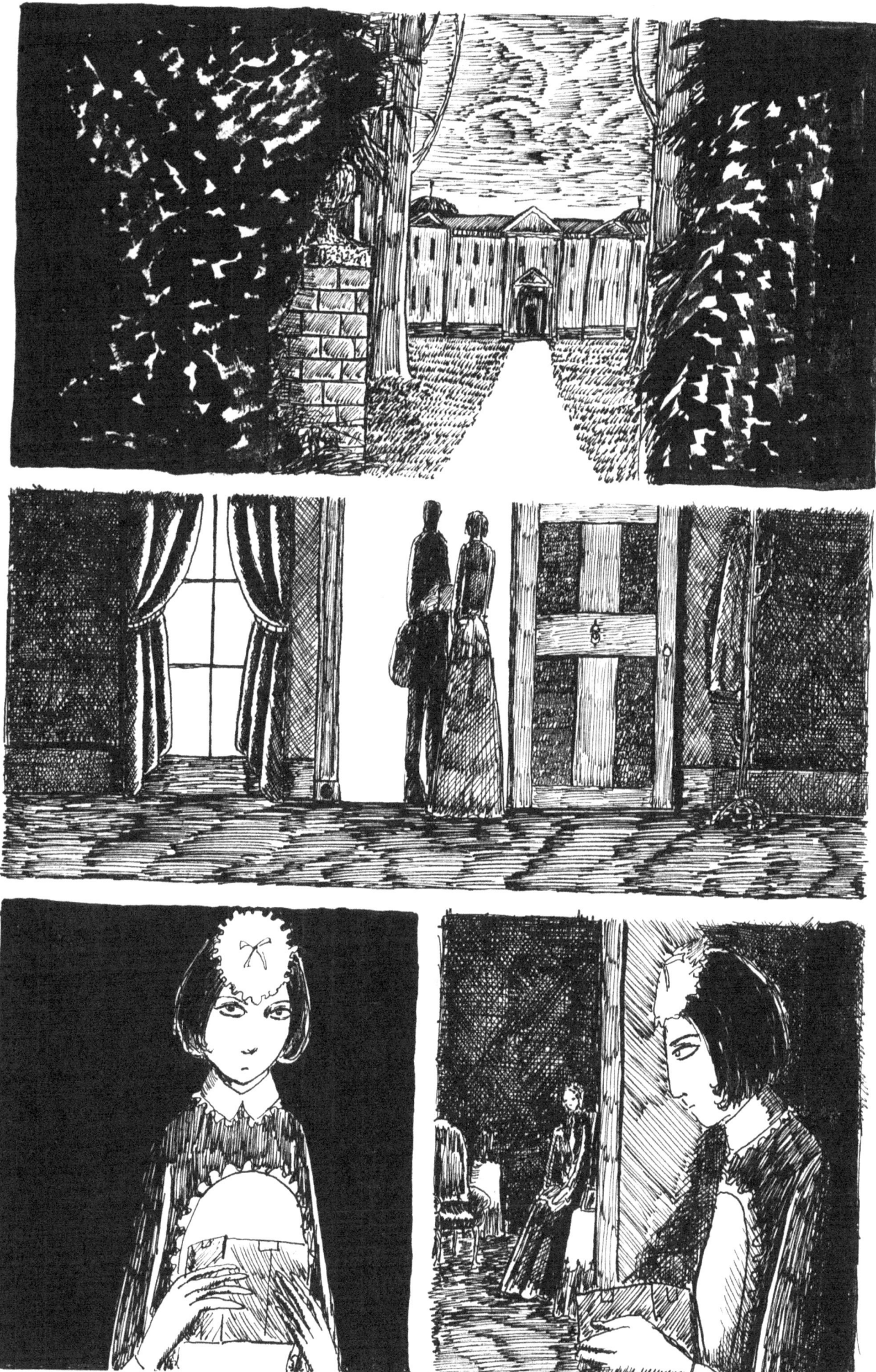

The Adventure of the Cardboard Box page 2 (unpublished) 2004

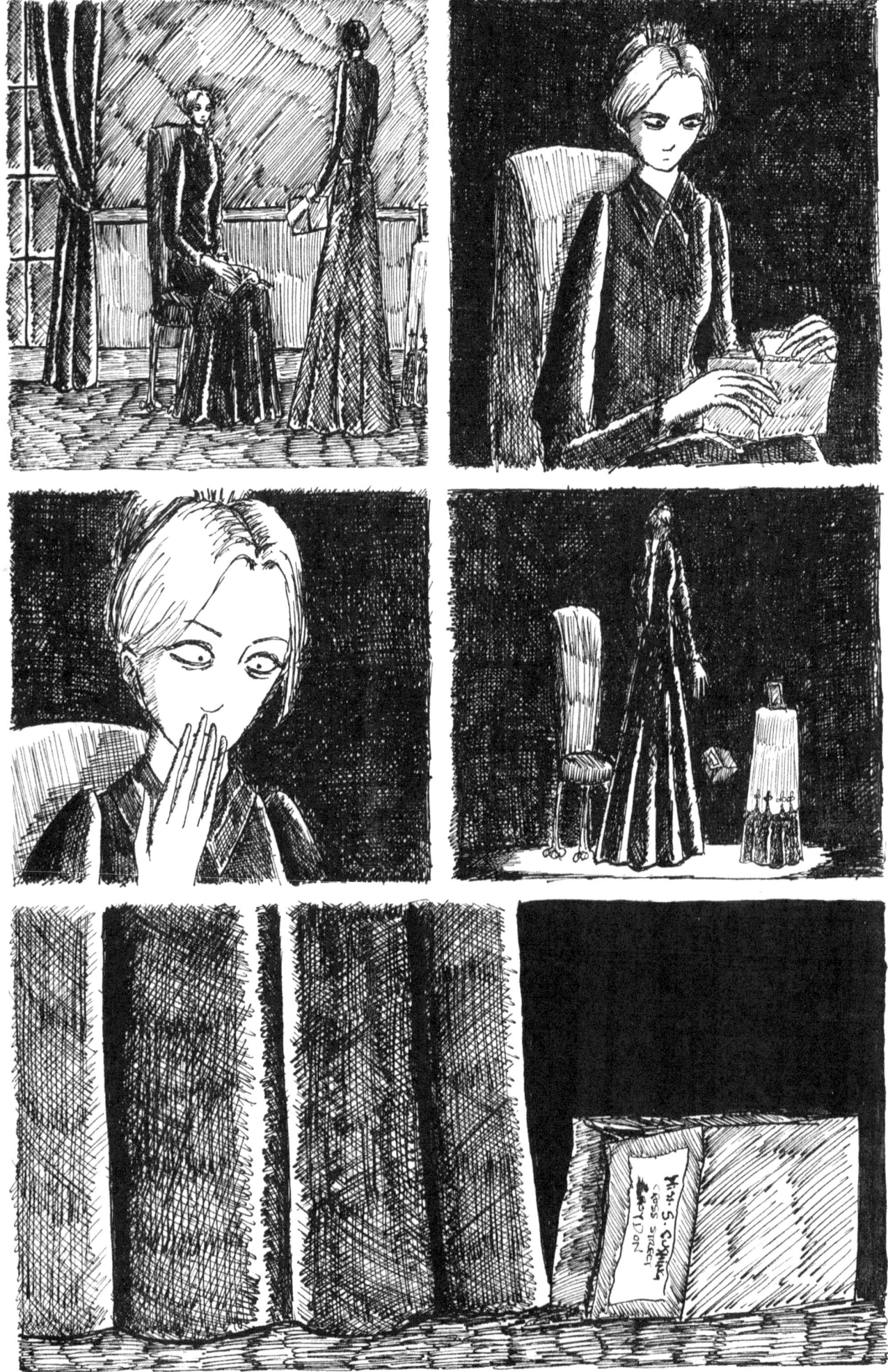

The Adventure of the Cardboard Box page 3 (unpublished) 2004

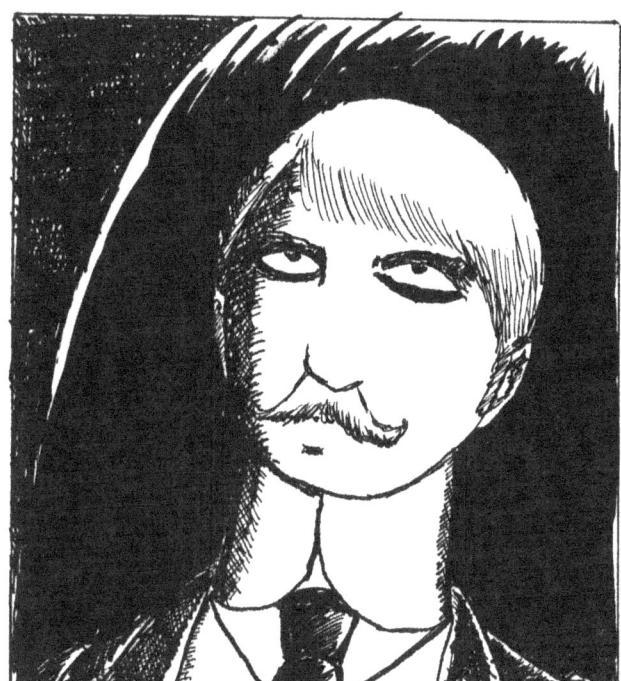
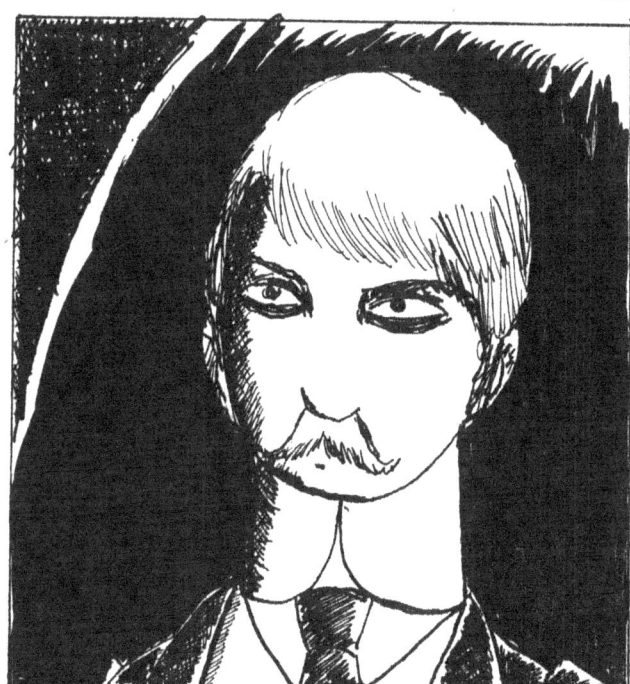

The Adventure of the Cardboard Box page 4 (unpublished) 2004

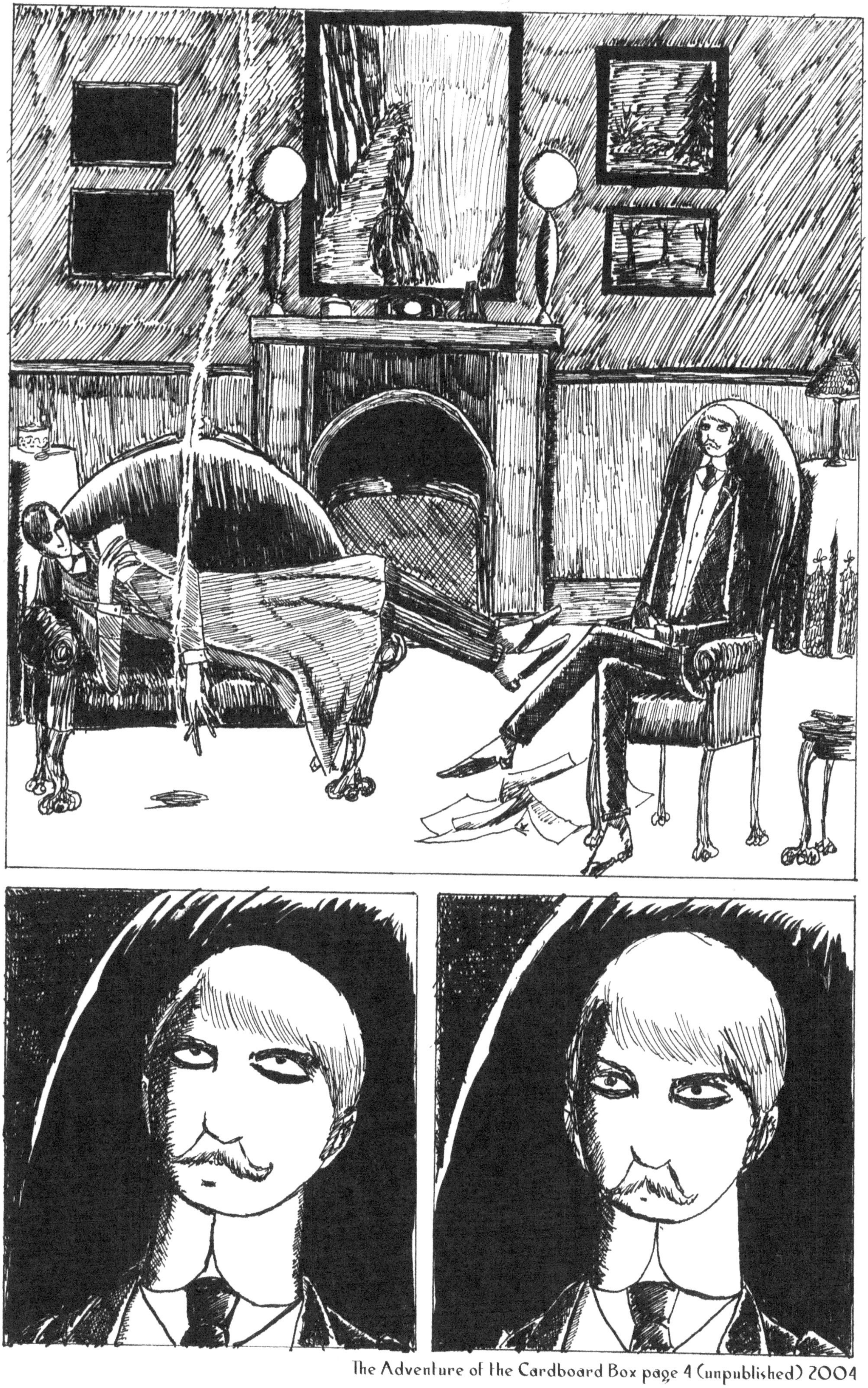

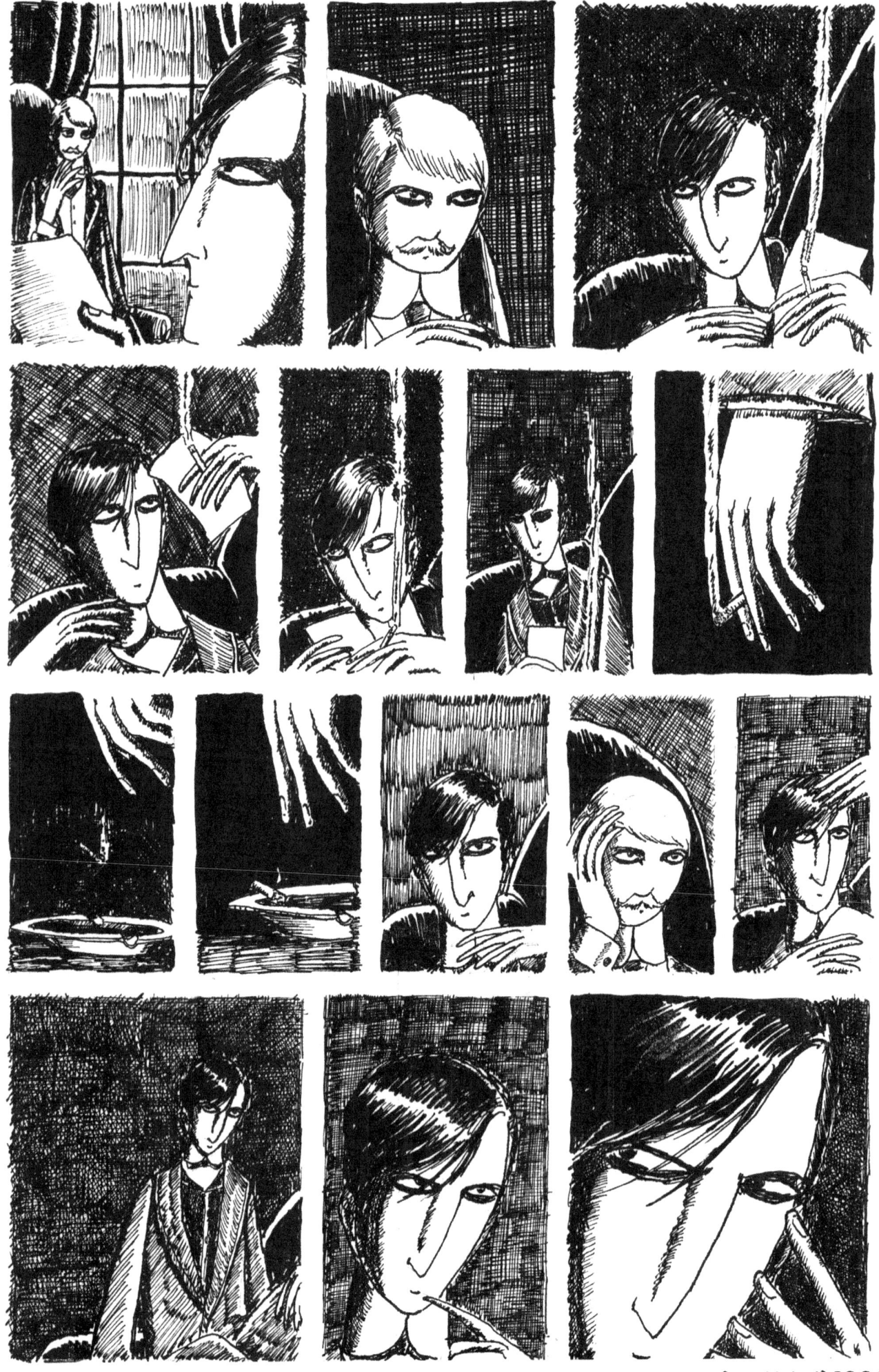

The Adventure of the Cardboard Box page 5 (unpublished) 2004

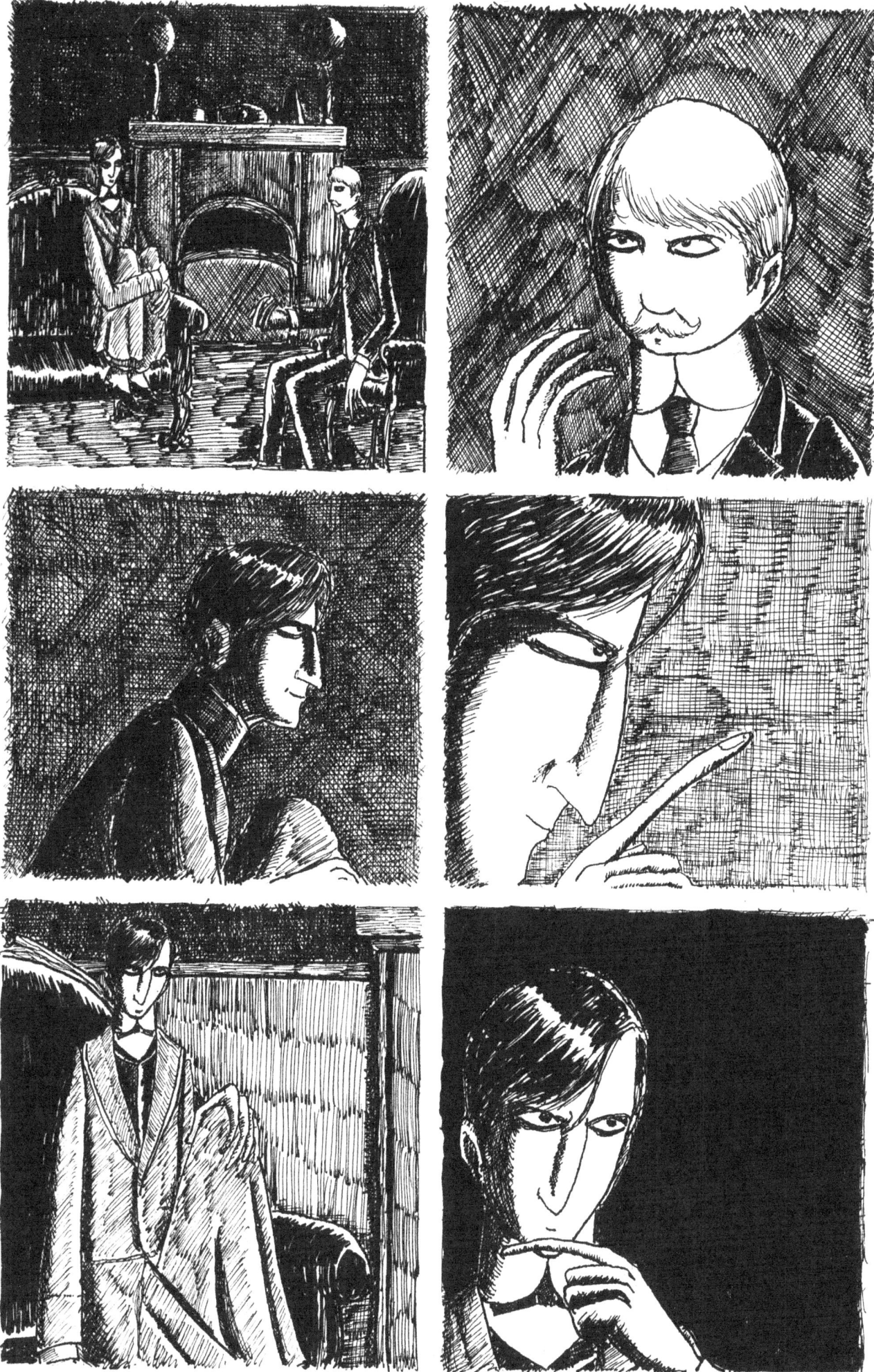

The Adventure of the Cardboard Box page 6 (unpublished) 2004

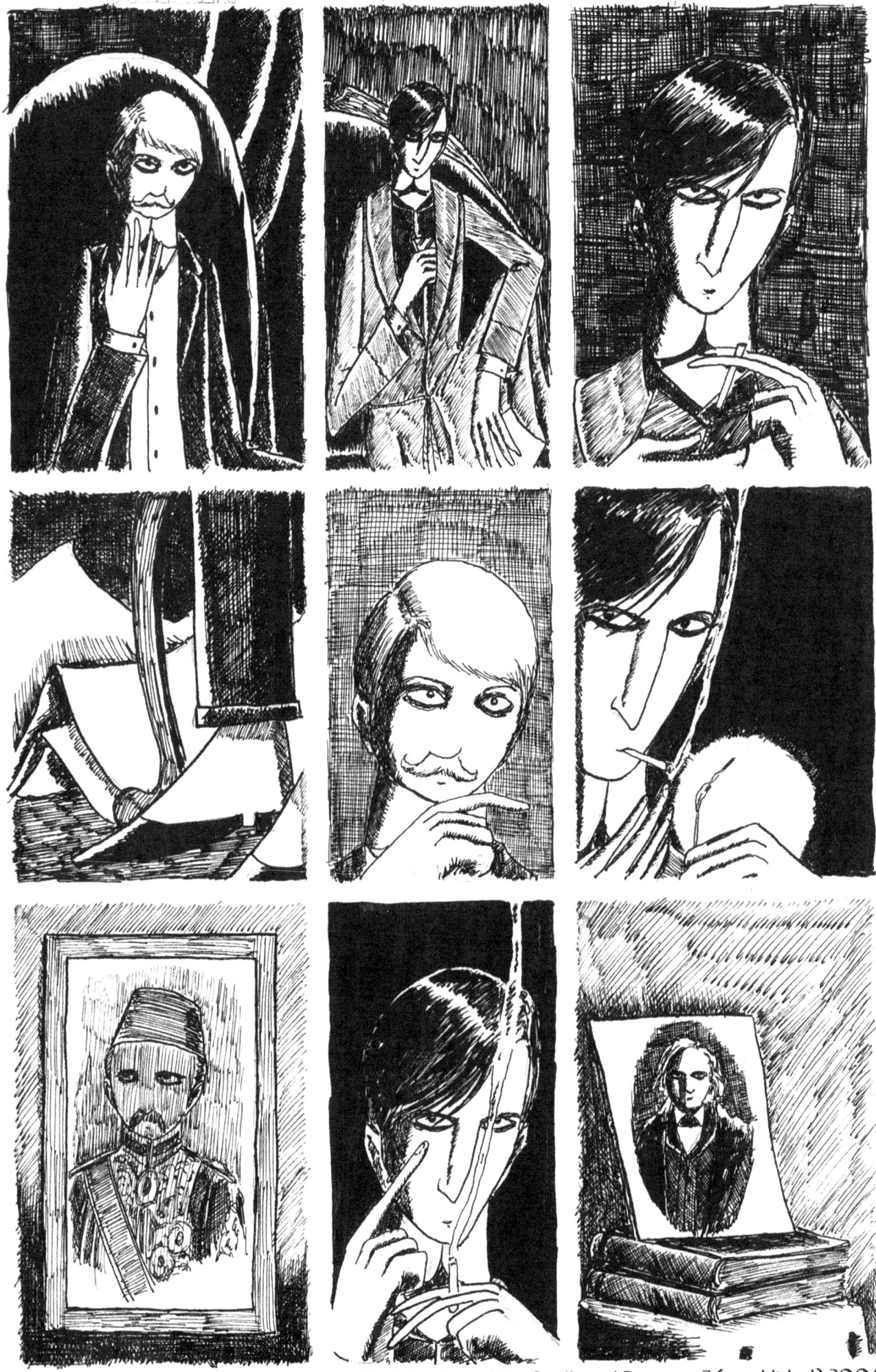

The Adventure of the Cardboard Box page 7 (unpublished) 2004

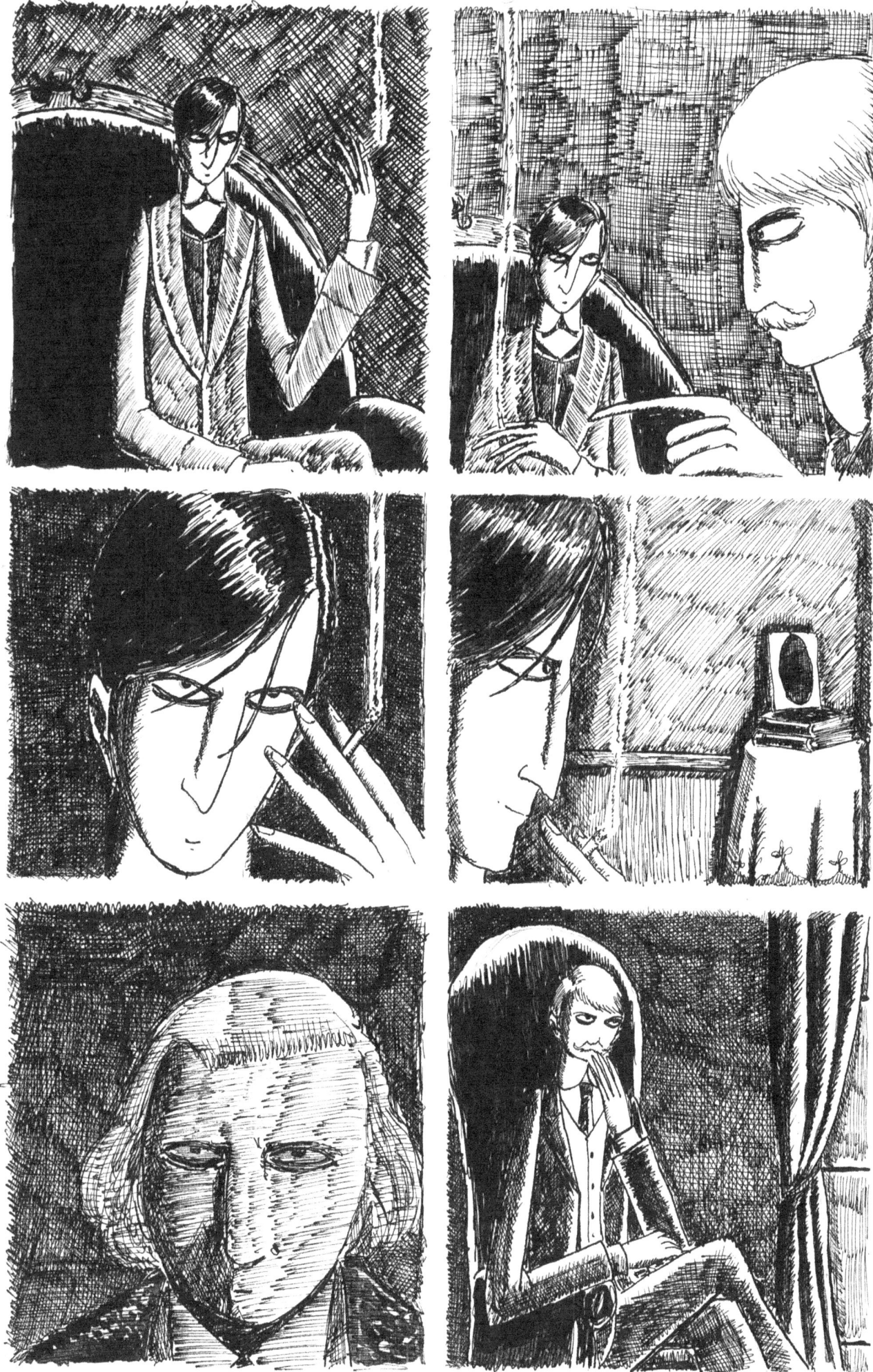

The Adventure of the Cardboard Box page 8 (unpublished) 2004

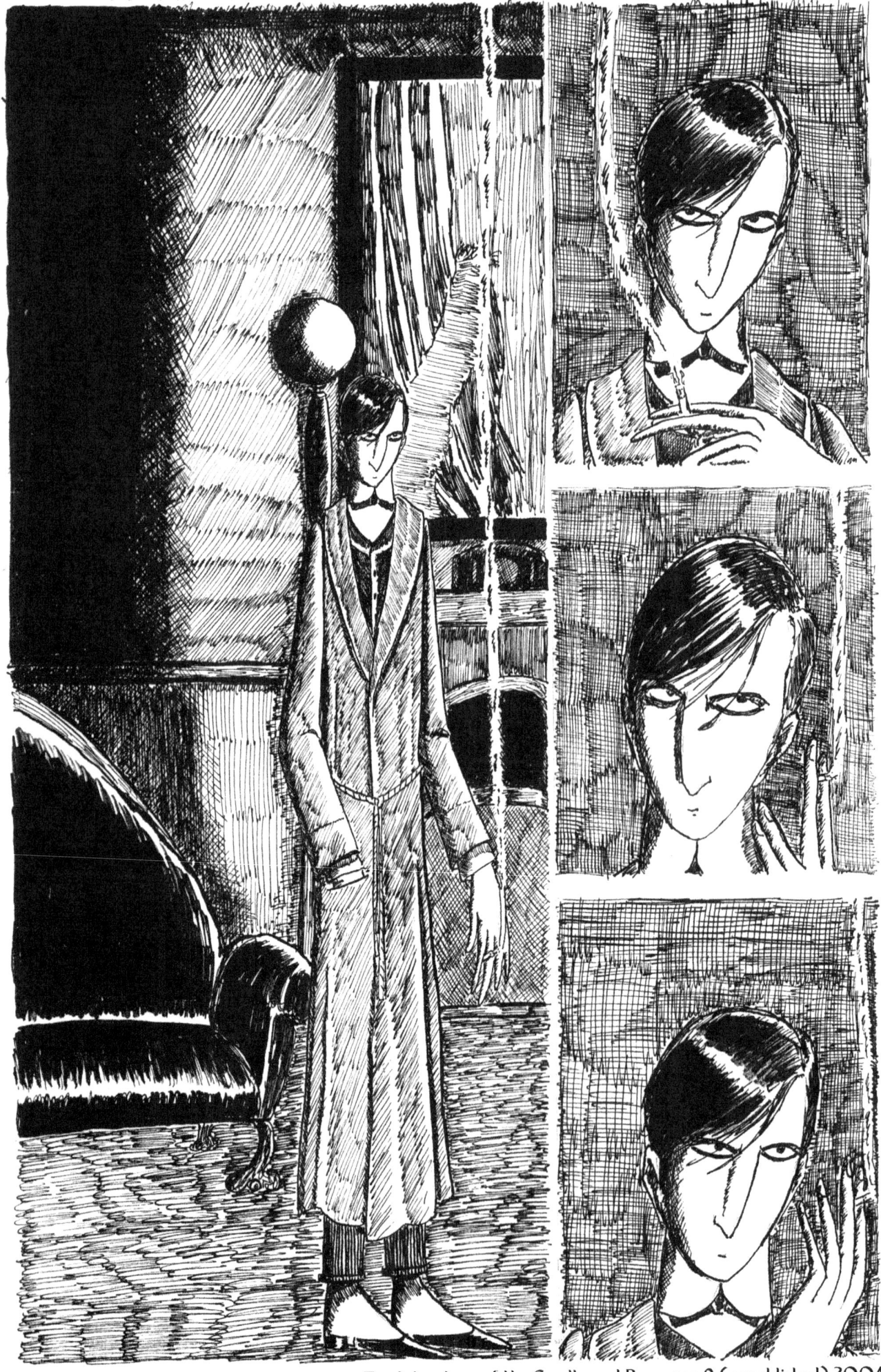

The Adventure of the Cardboard Box page 9 (unpublished) 2004

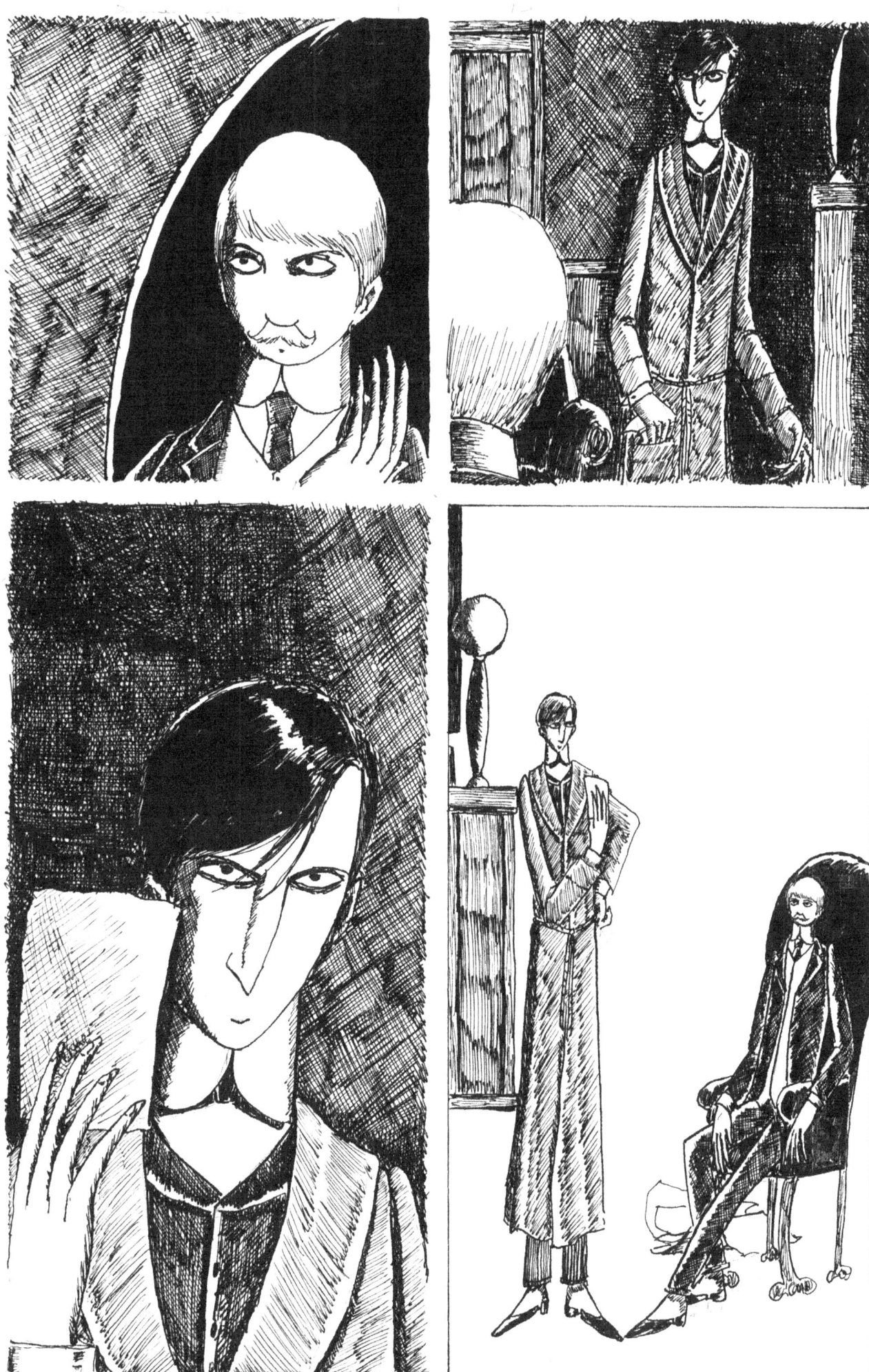

The Adventure of the Cardboard Box page 10 (unpublished) 2004

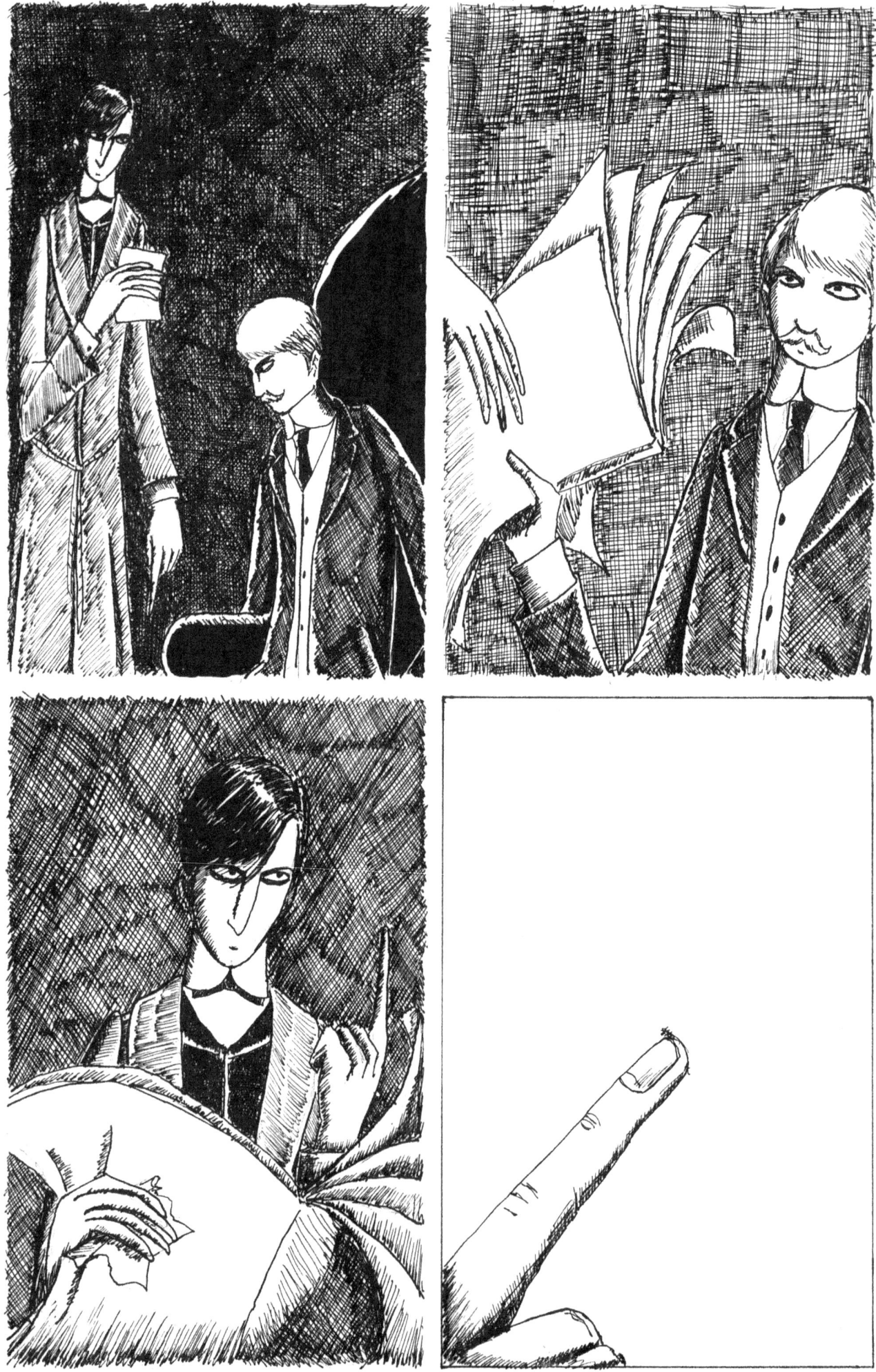

The Adventure of the Cardboard Box page 11 (unpublished) 2004

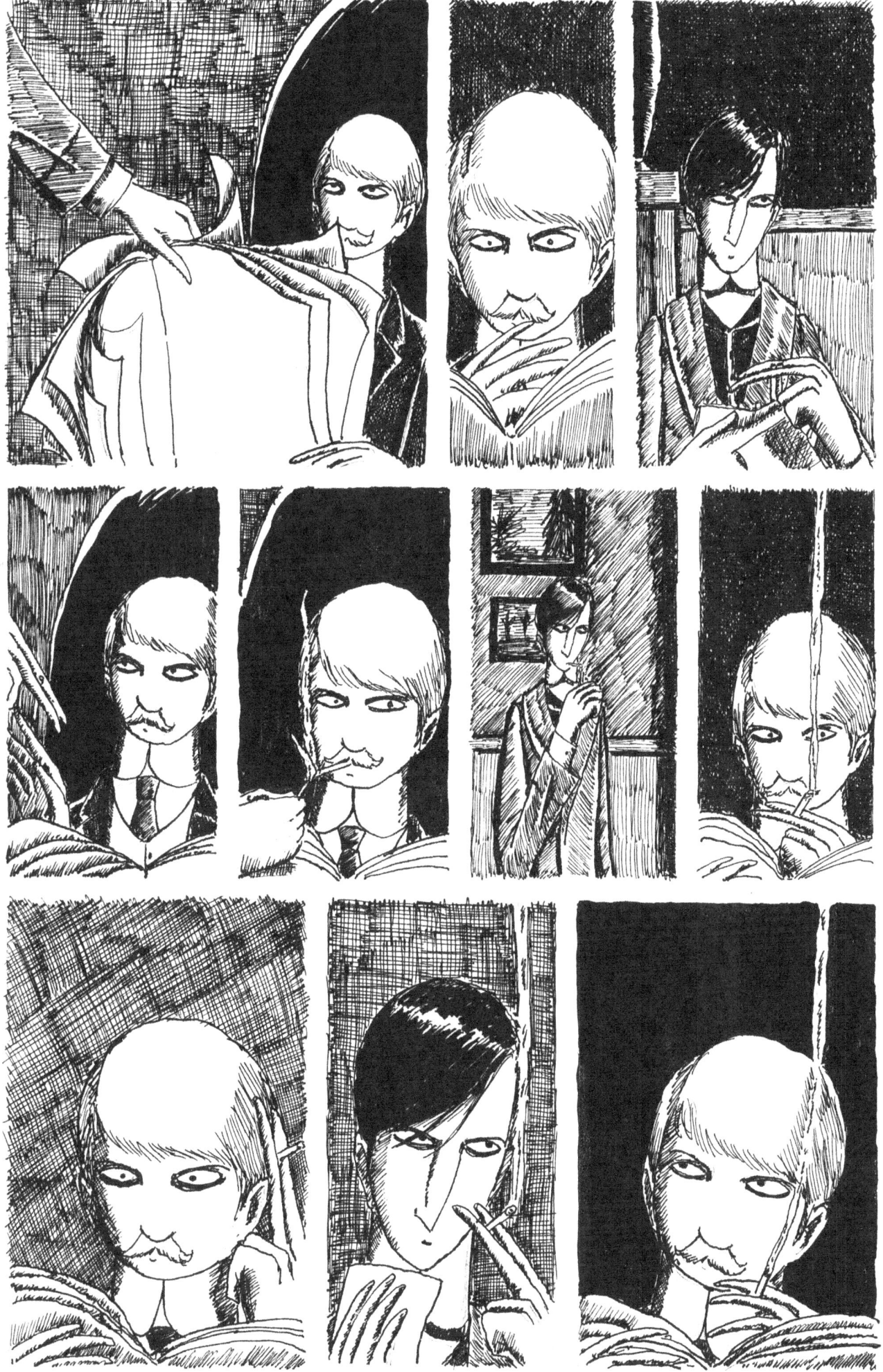

The Adventure of the Cardboard Box page 12 (unpublished) 2004

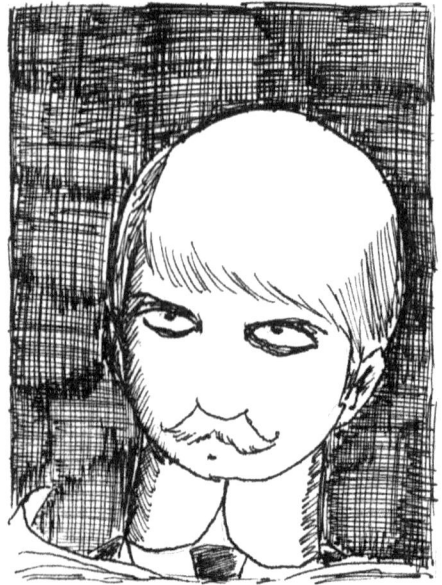
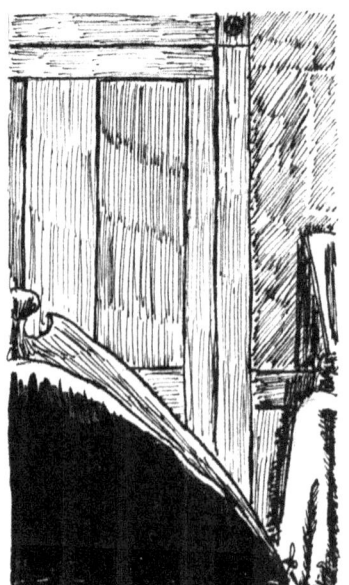
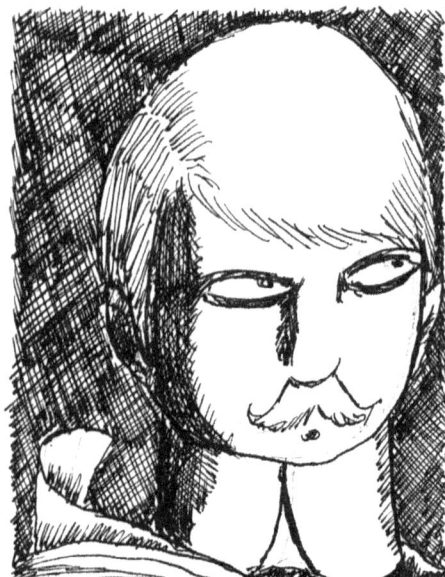

The Adventure of the Cardboard Box page 13 (unpublished) 2004

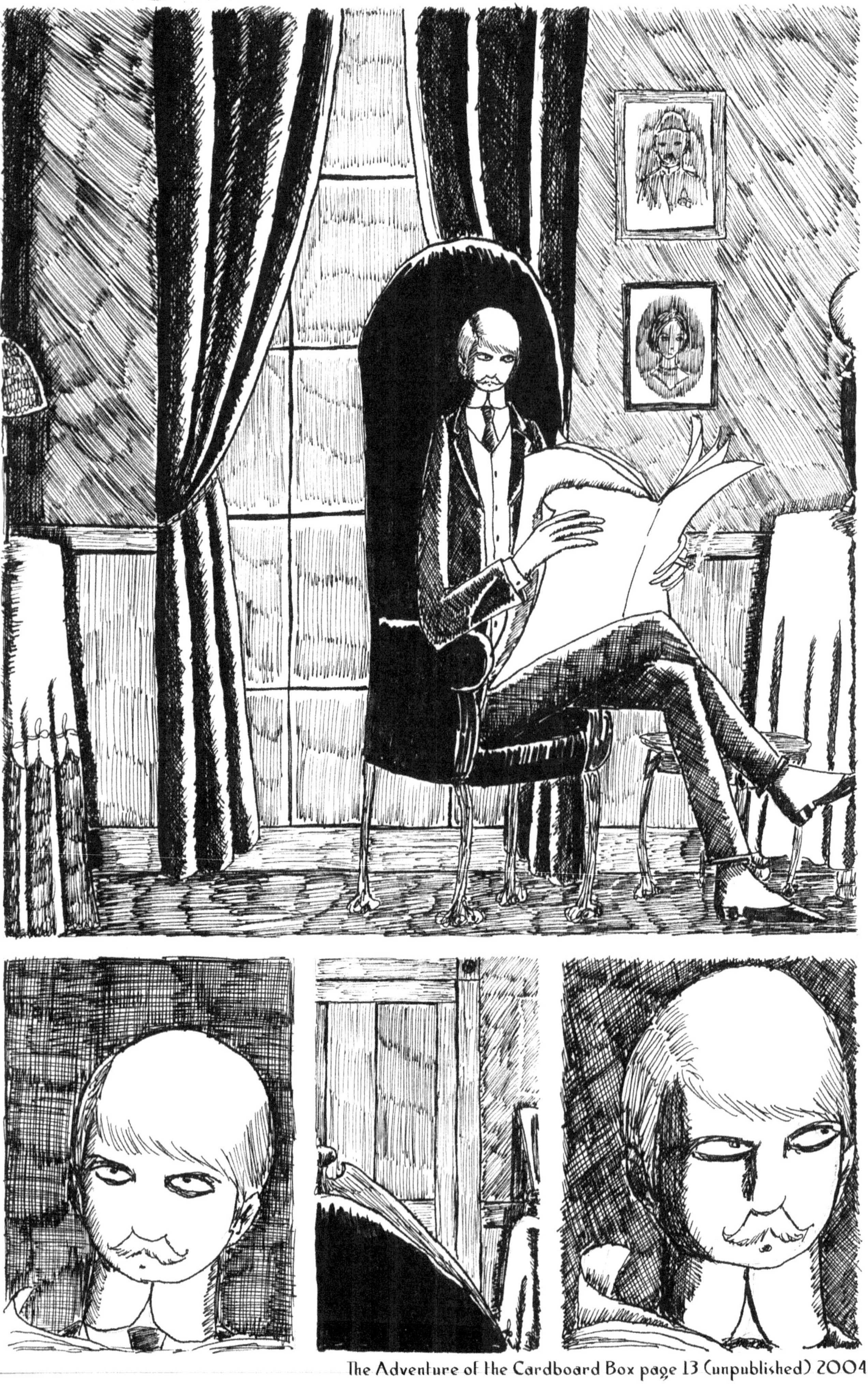

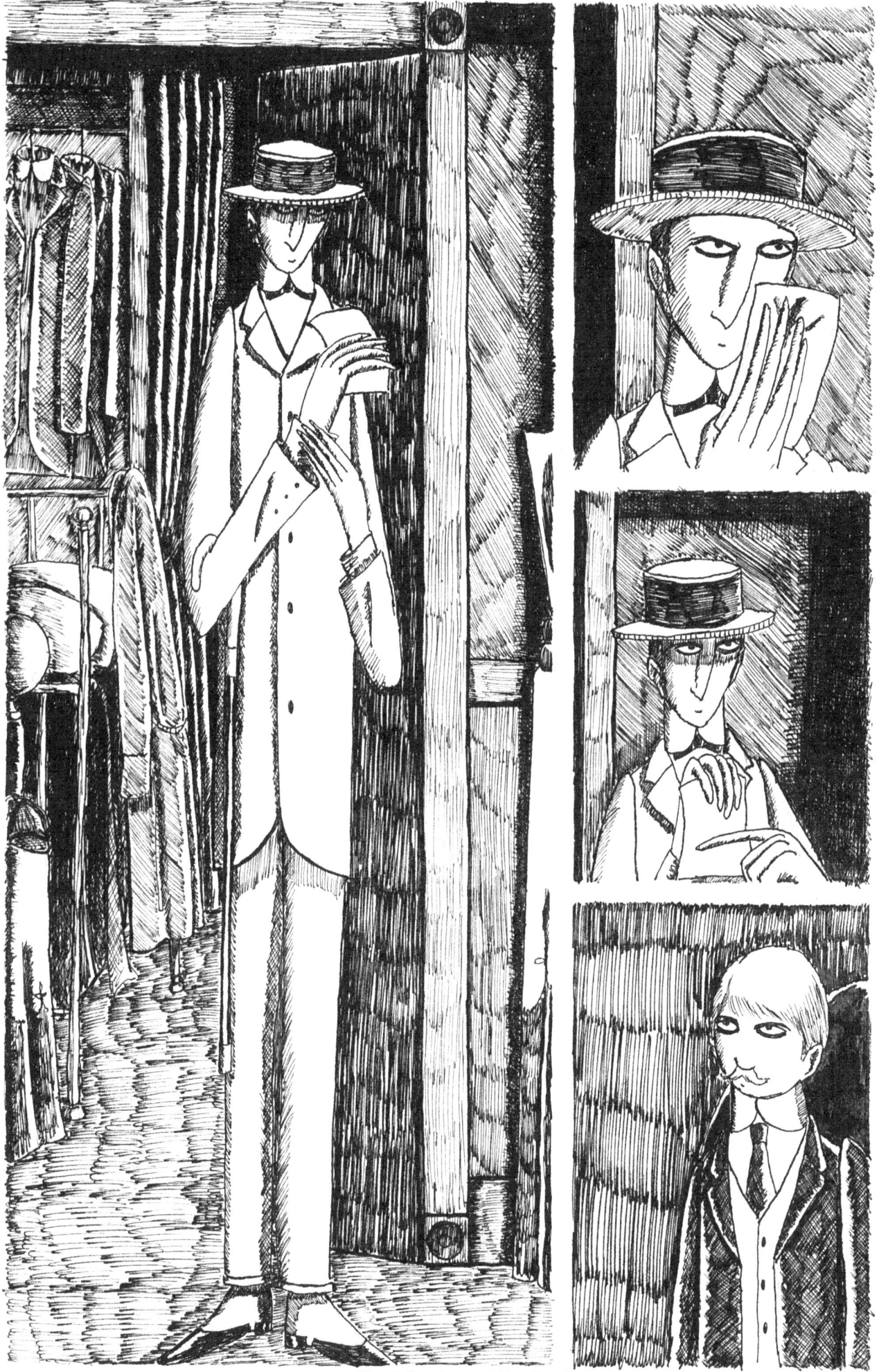

The Adventure of the Cardboard Box page 14 (unpublished) 2004

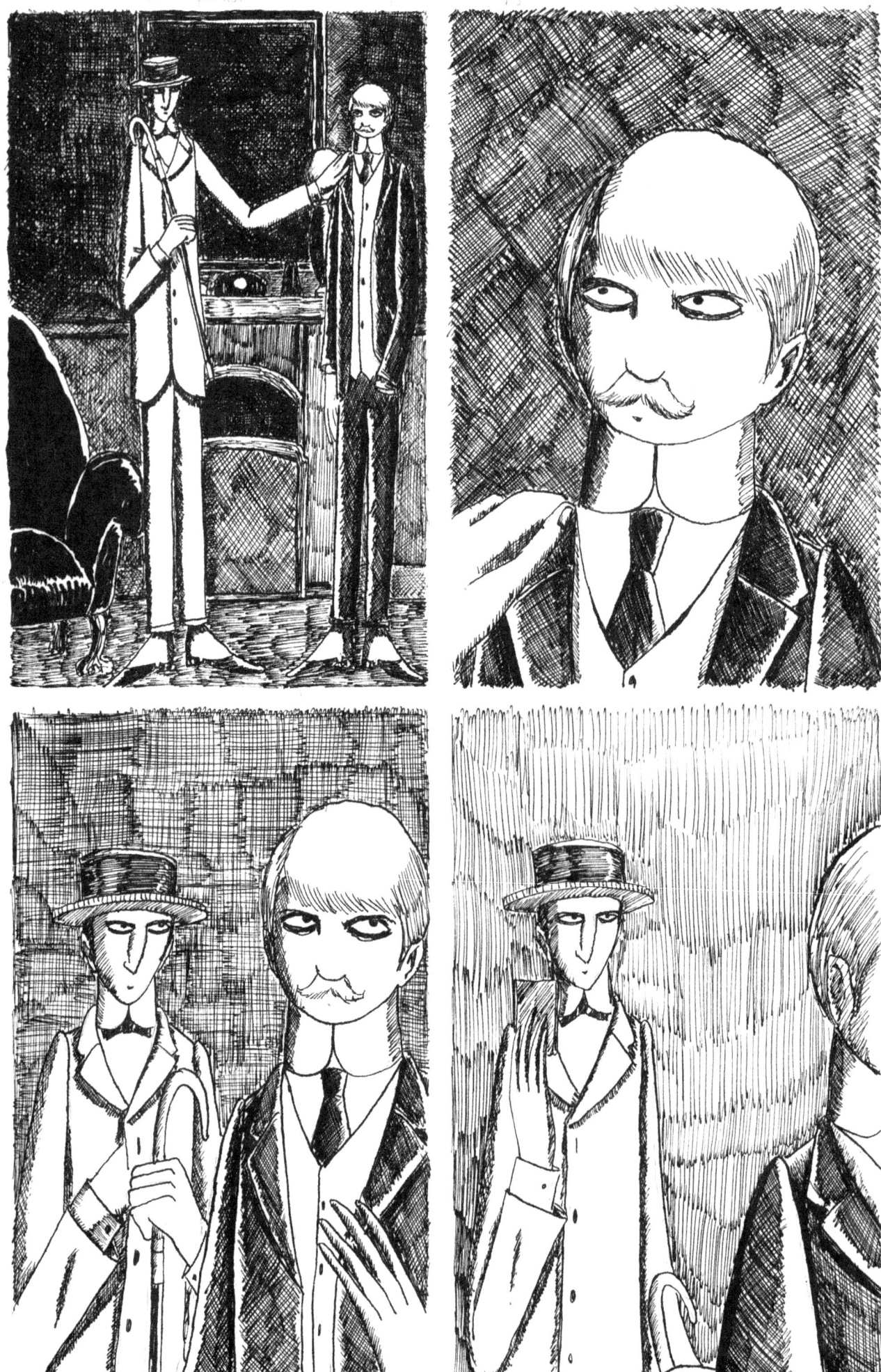

The Adventure of the Cardboard Box page 15 (unpublished) 2004

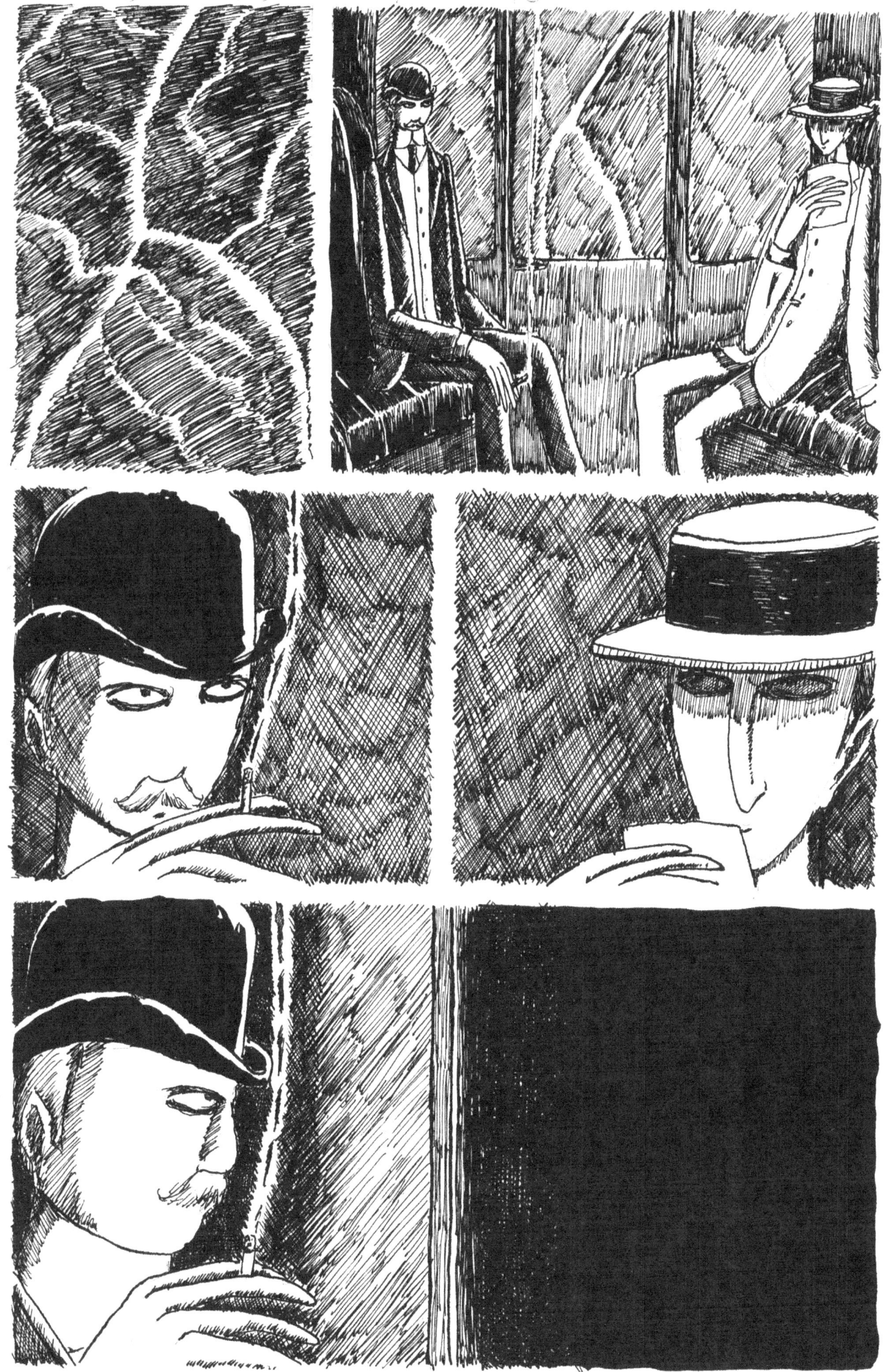

The Adventure of the Cardboard Box page 16 (unpublished) 2004

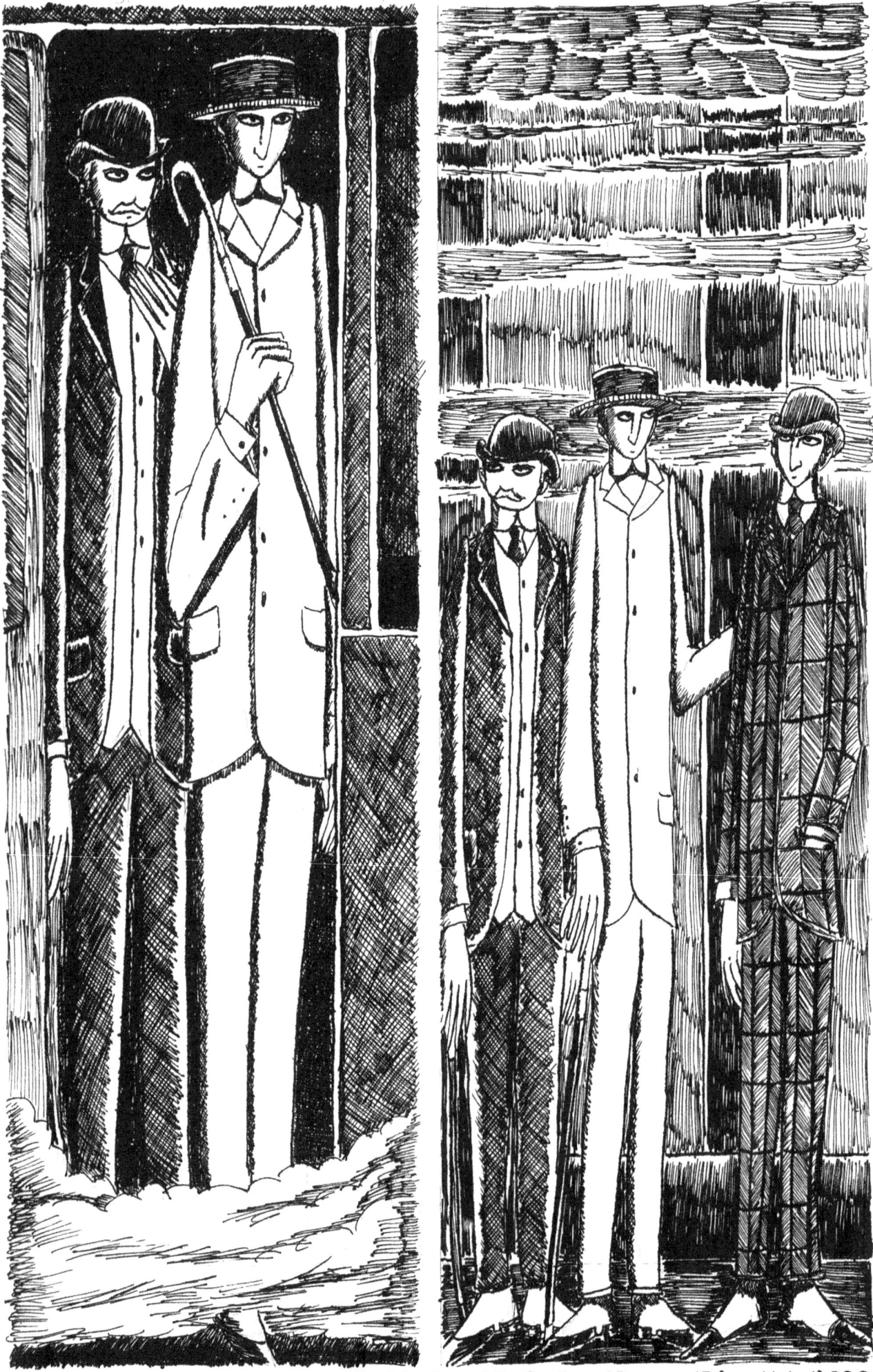

The Adventure of the Cardboard Box page 17 (unpublished) 2004

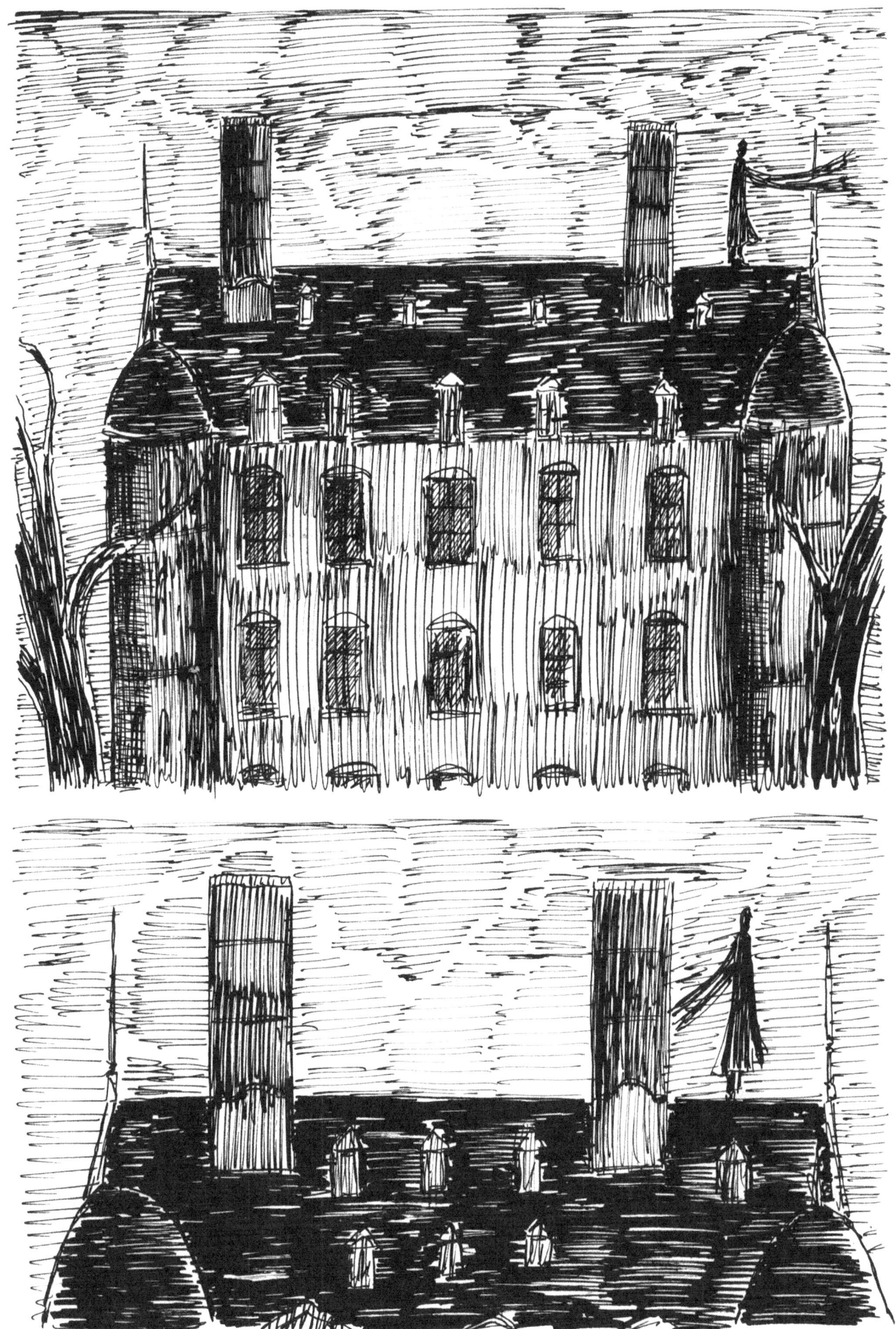

221B Baker Street by Bert Coules page 1 (unpublished) 2010
Bert's story depicts a "Young Sherlock" and re-imagines the whole mythos of Holmes and Watson.

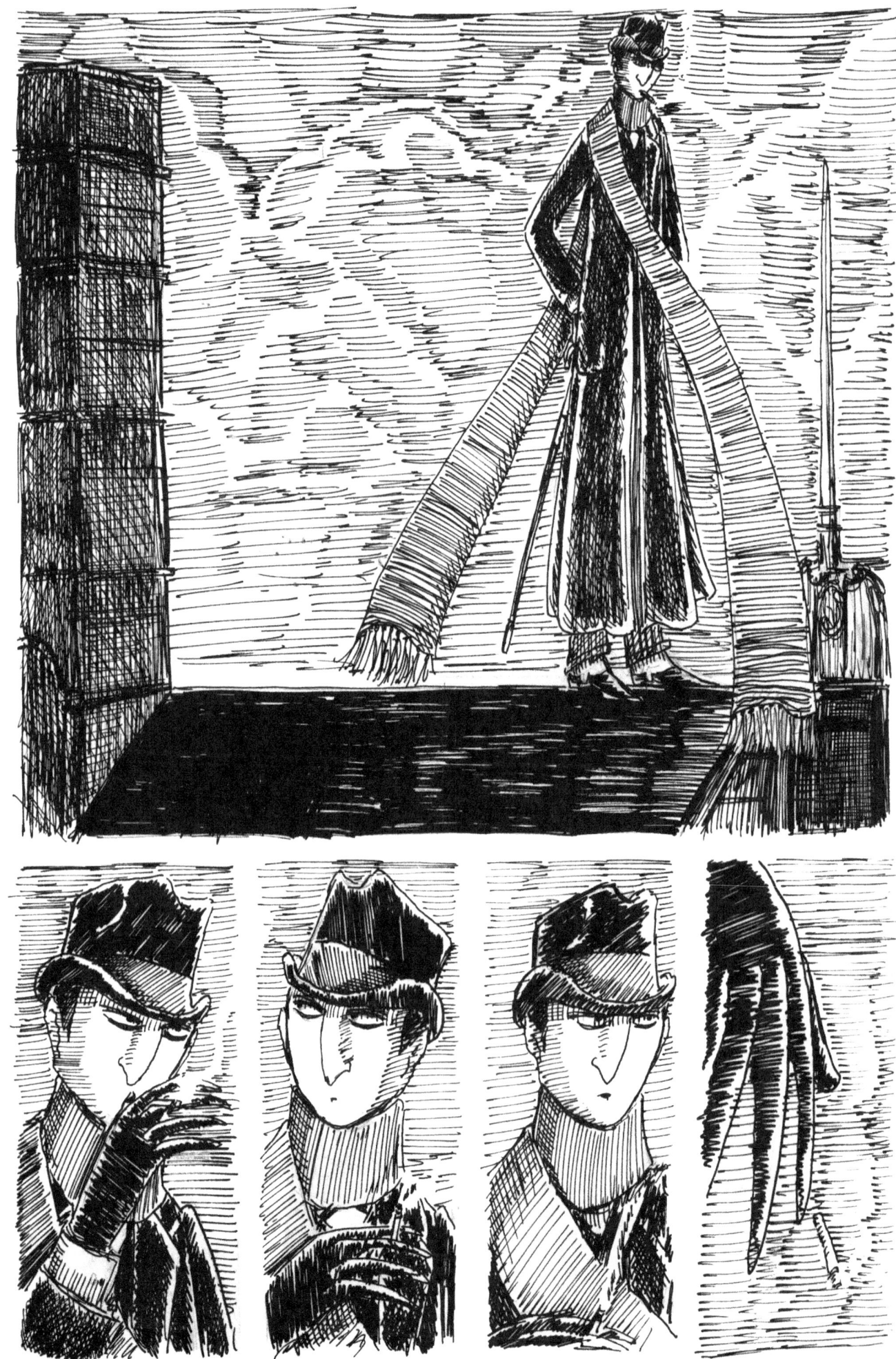

221B Baker Street by Bert Coules page 2 (unpublished) 2010

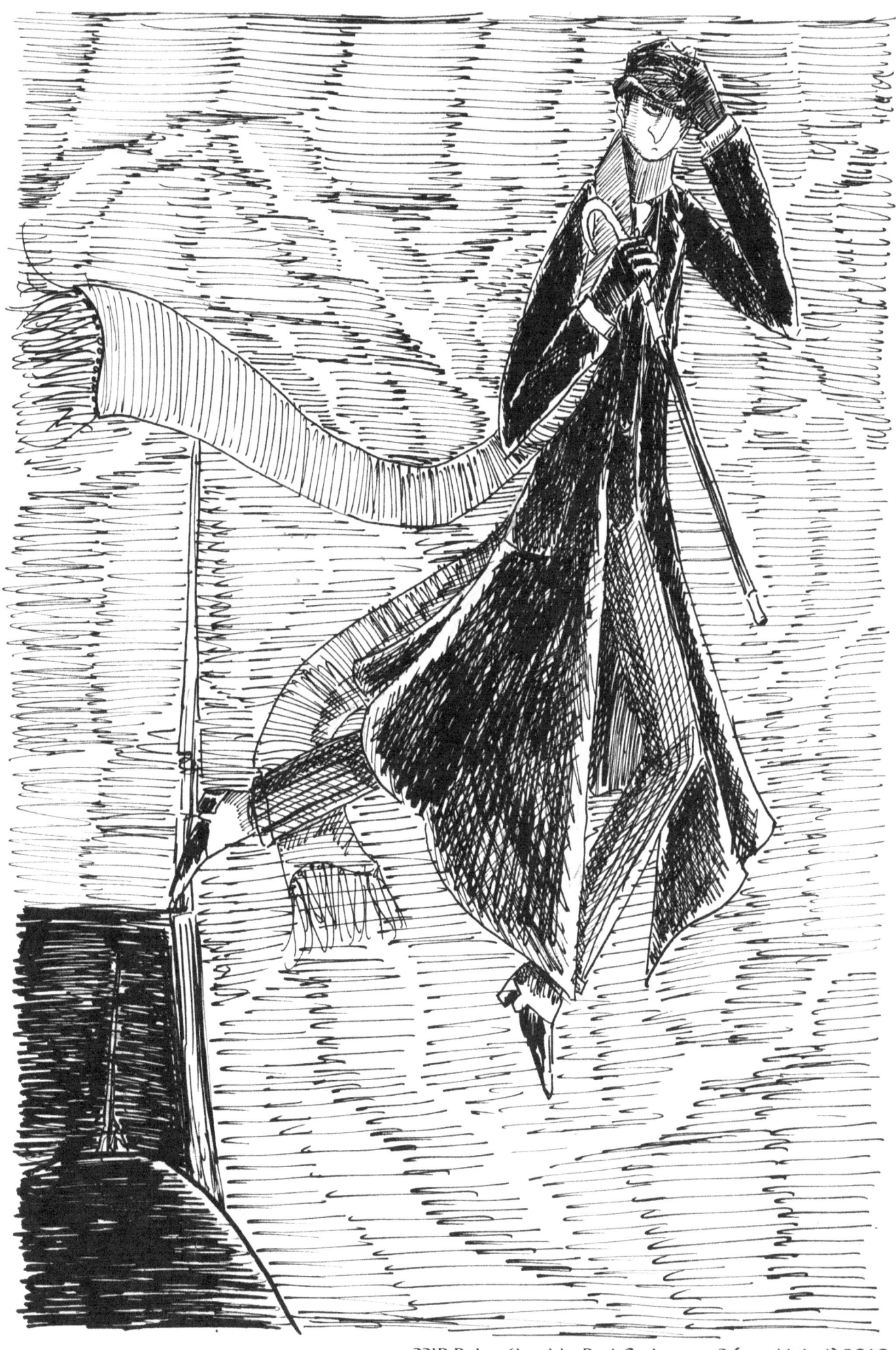

221B Baker Street by Bert Coules page 3 (unpublished) 2010

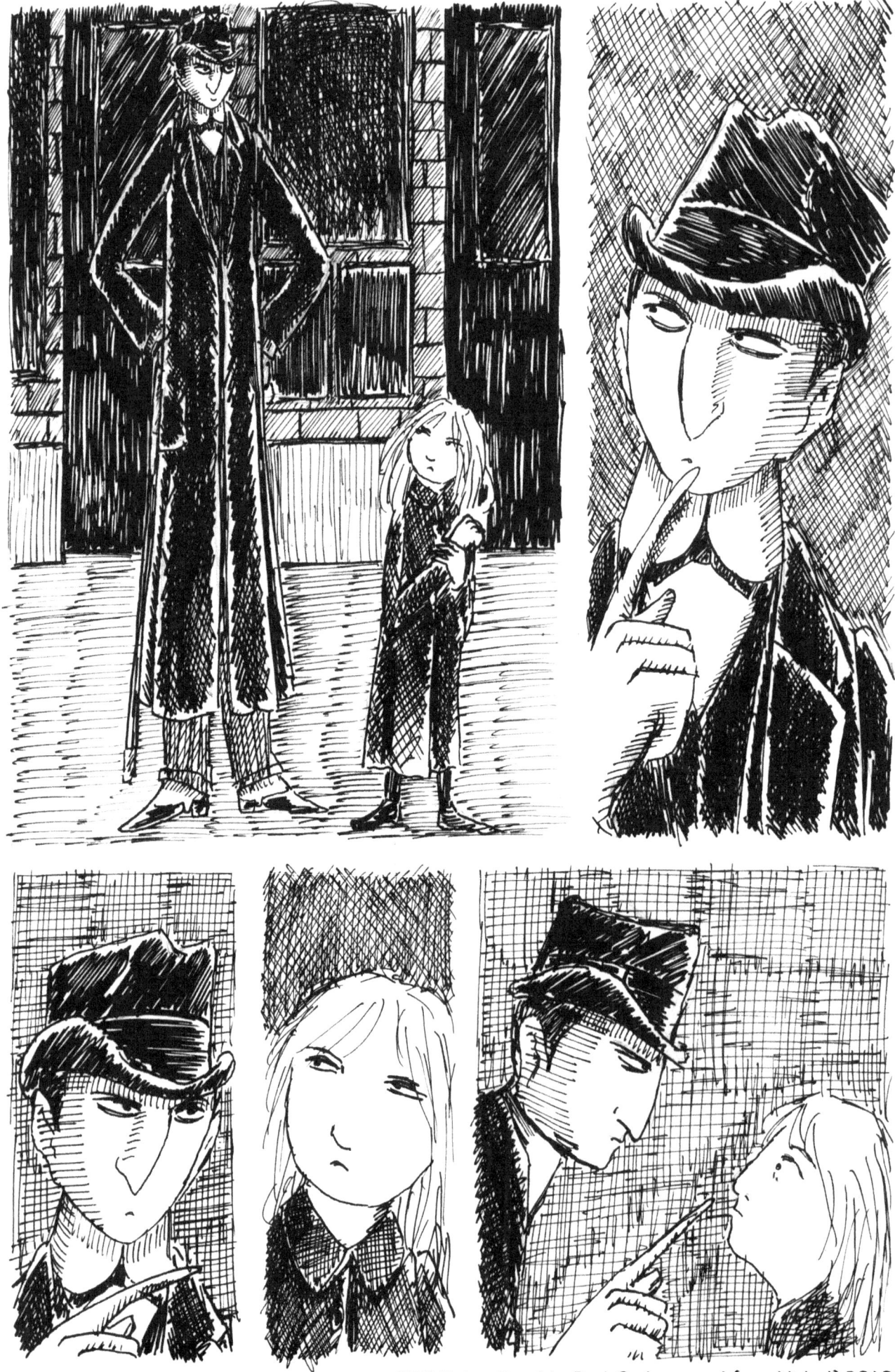

221B Baker Street by Bert Coules page 4 (unpublished) 2010

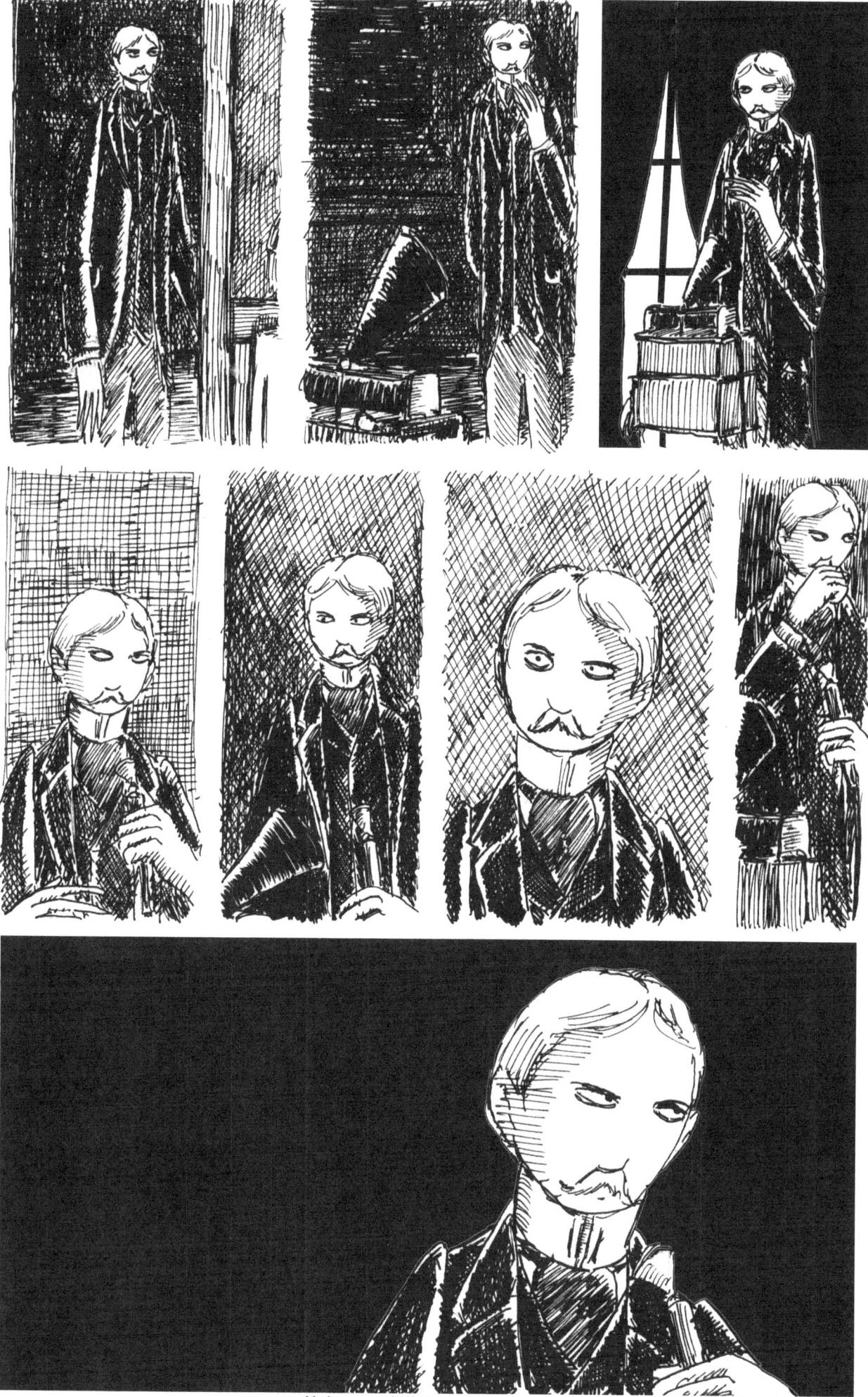

Holmes and Watson by R. Lee Shackleford page 1 (unpublished) 2010
Based on Lee's play (which he starred in as well). The story is set after the events of Reichenbach Falls.

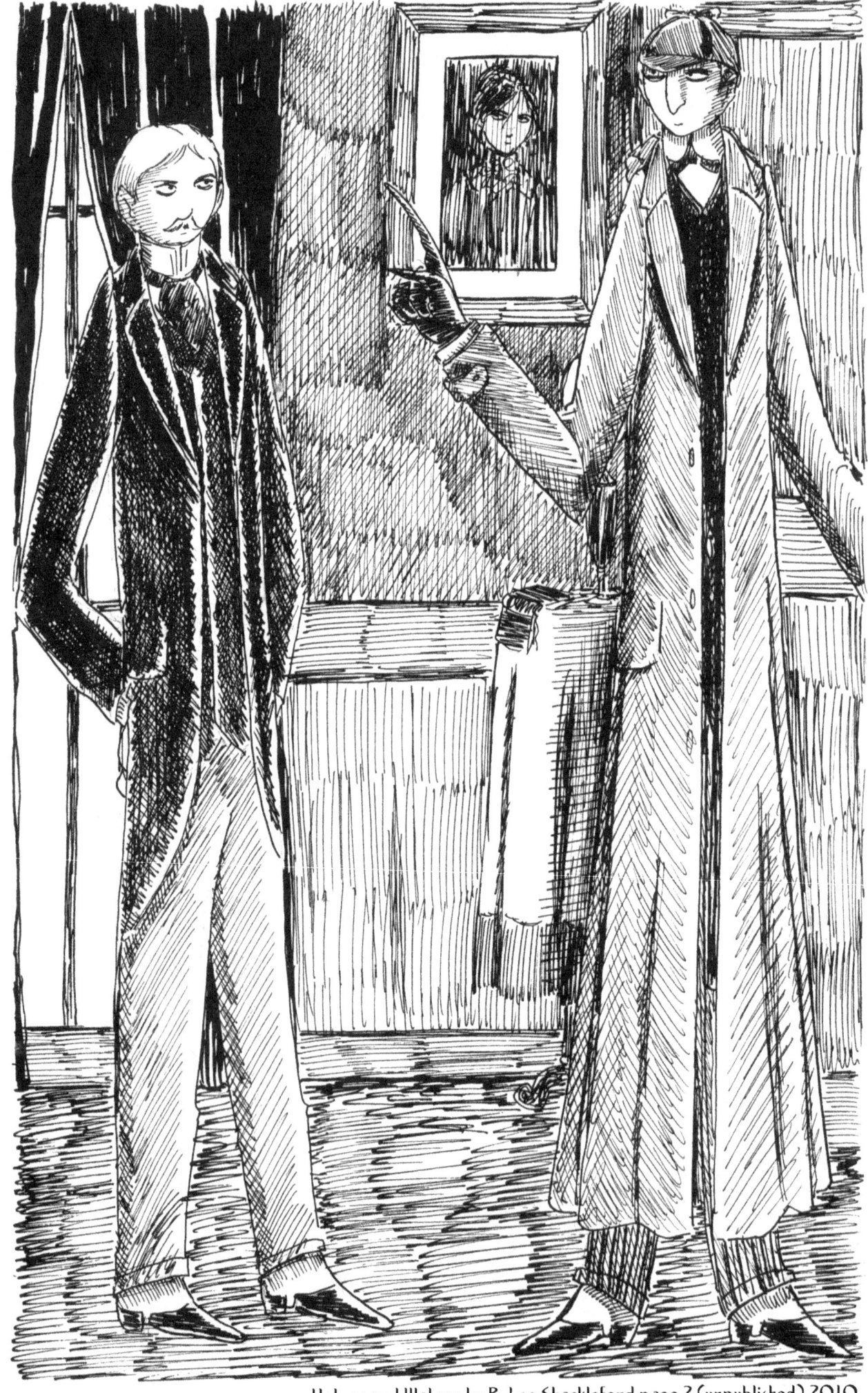

Holmes and Watson by R. Lee Shackleford page 2 (unpublished) 2010

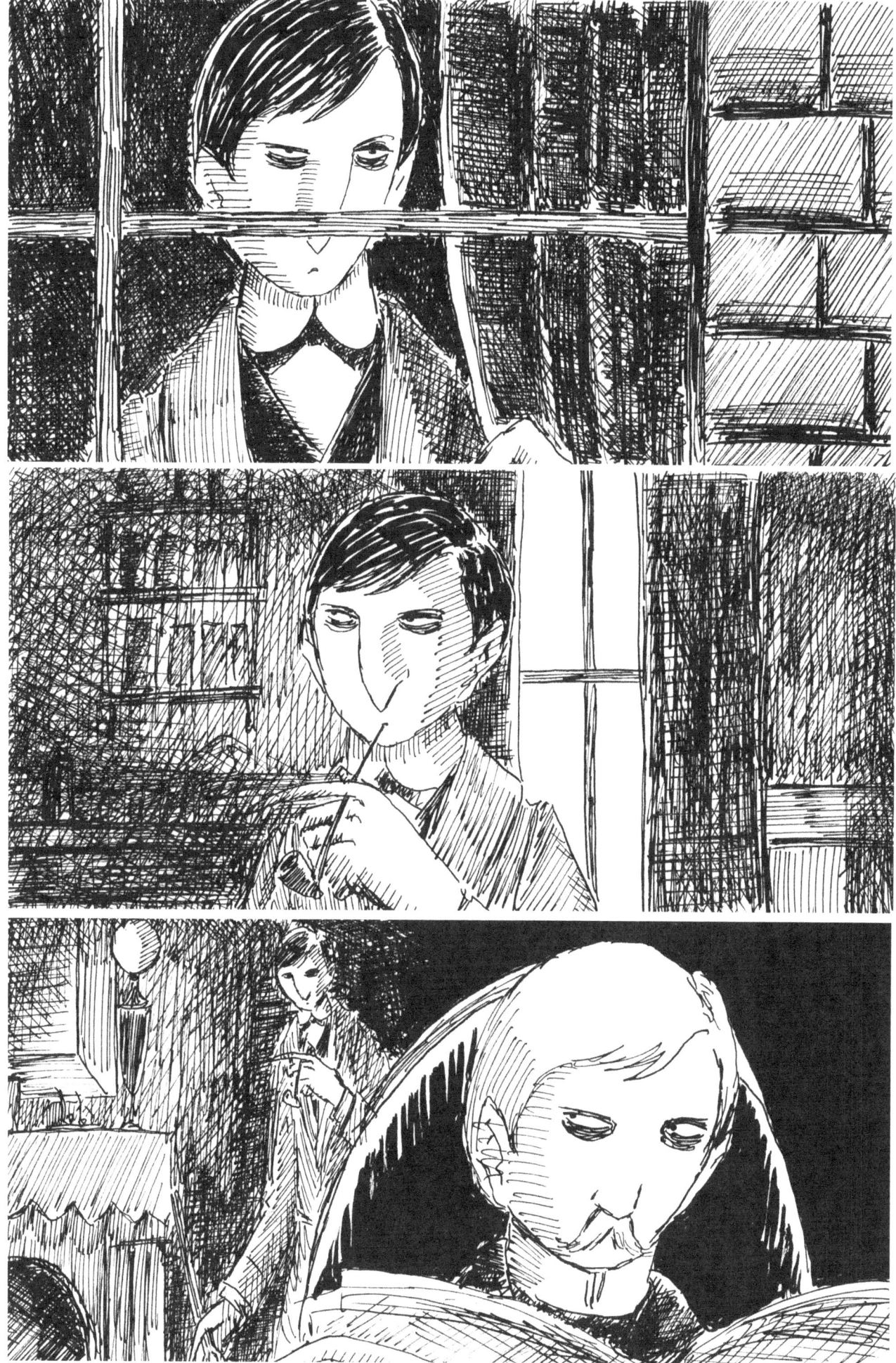

Dust and Shadow by Lyndsay Faye (unpublished) 2012

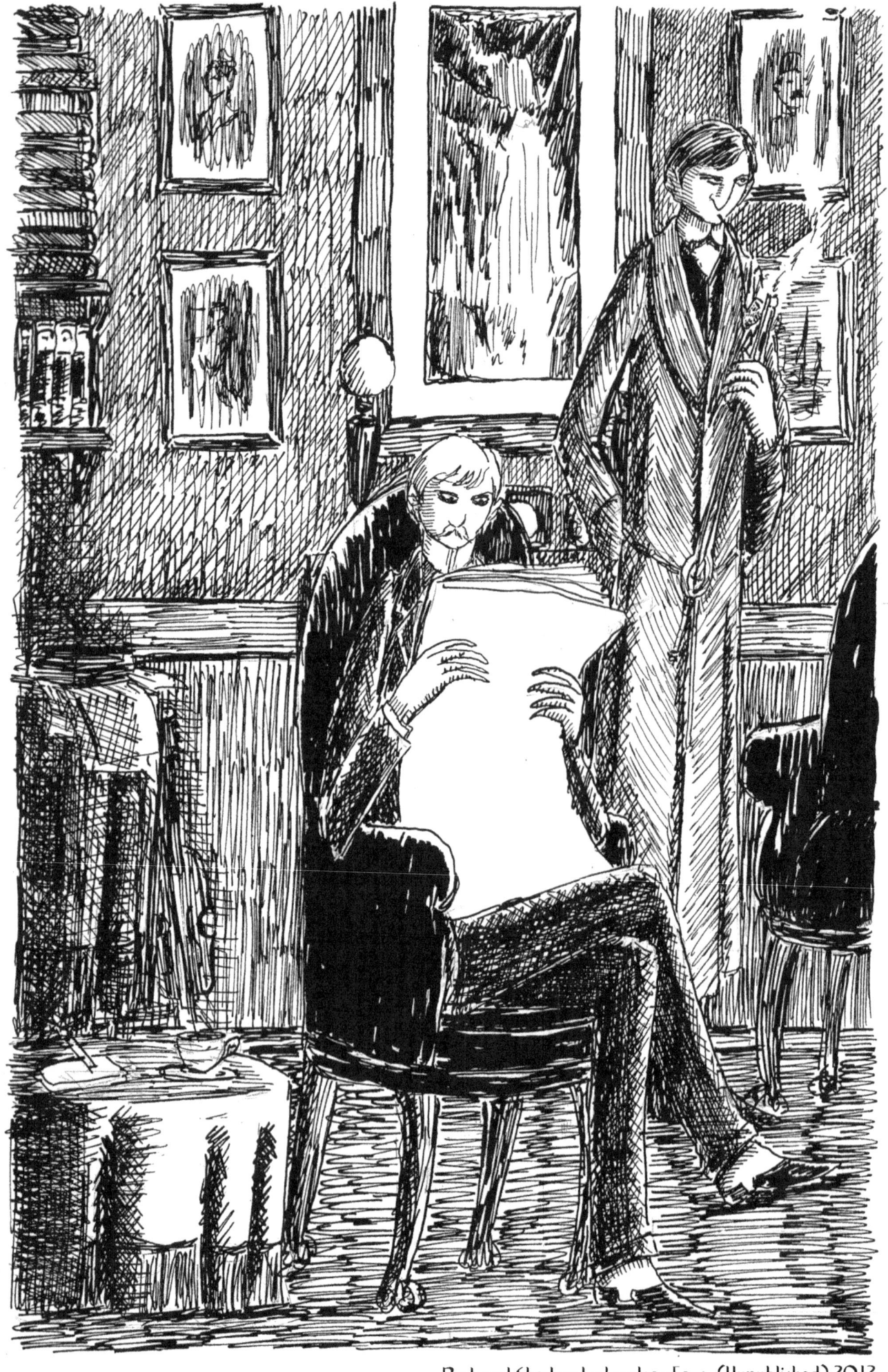

Dust and Shadow by Lyndsay Faye (Unpublished) 2012

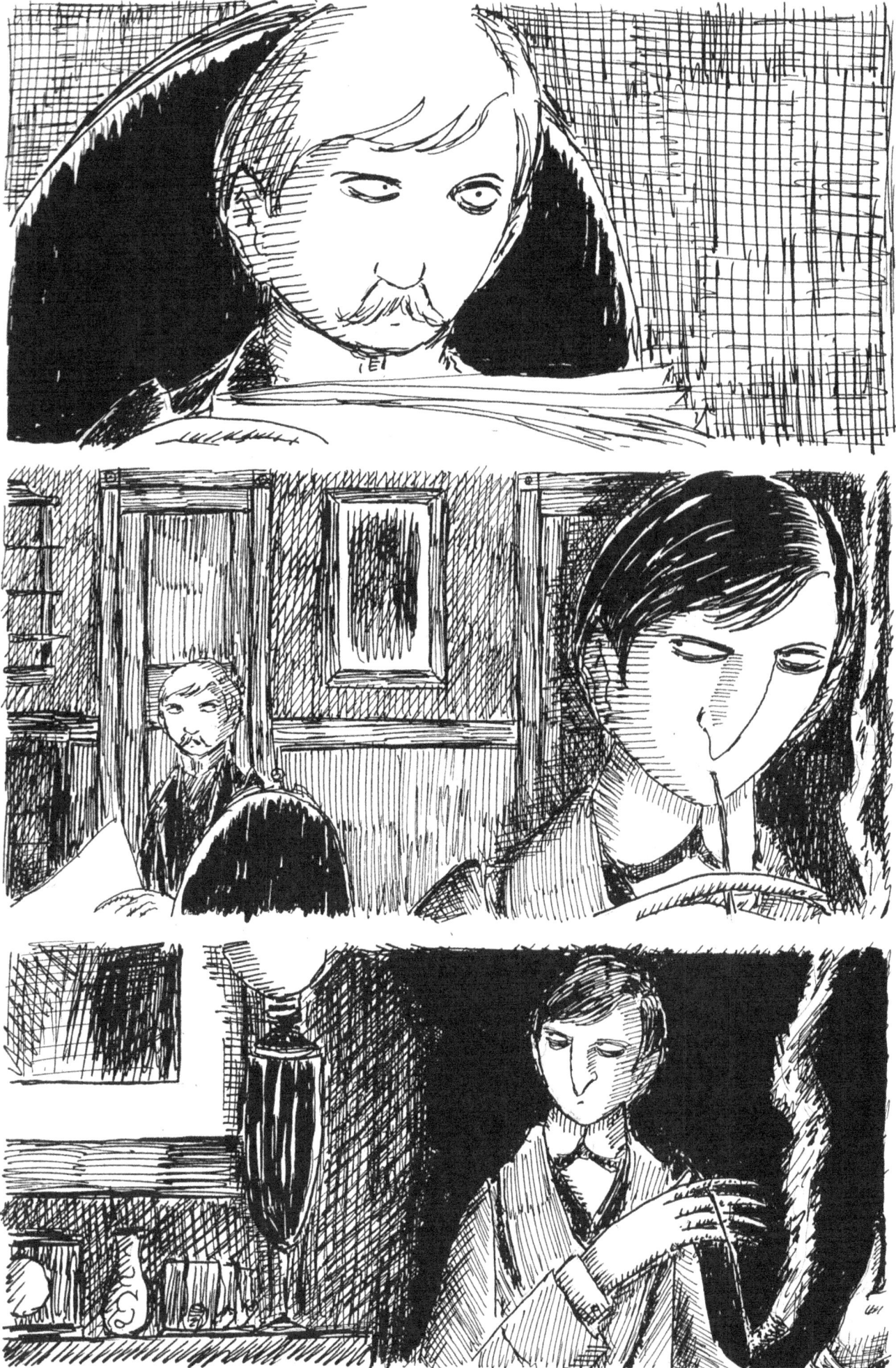

Dust and Shadow by Lyndsay Faye (unpublished) 2012

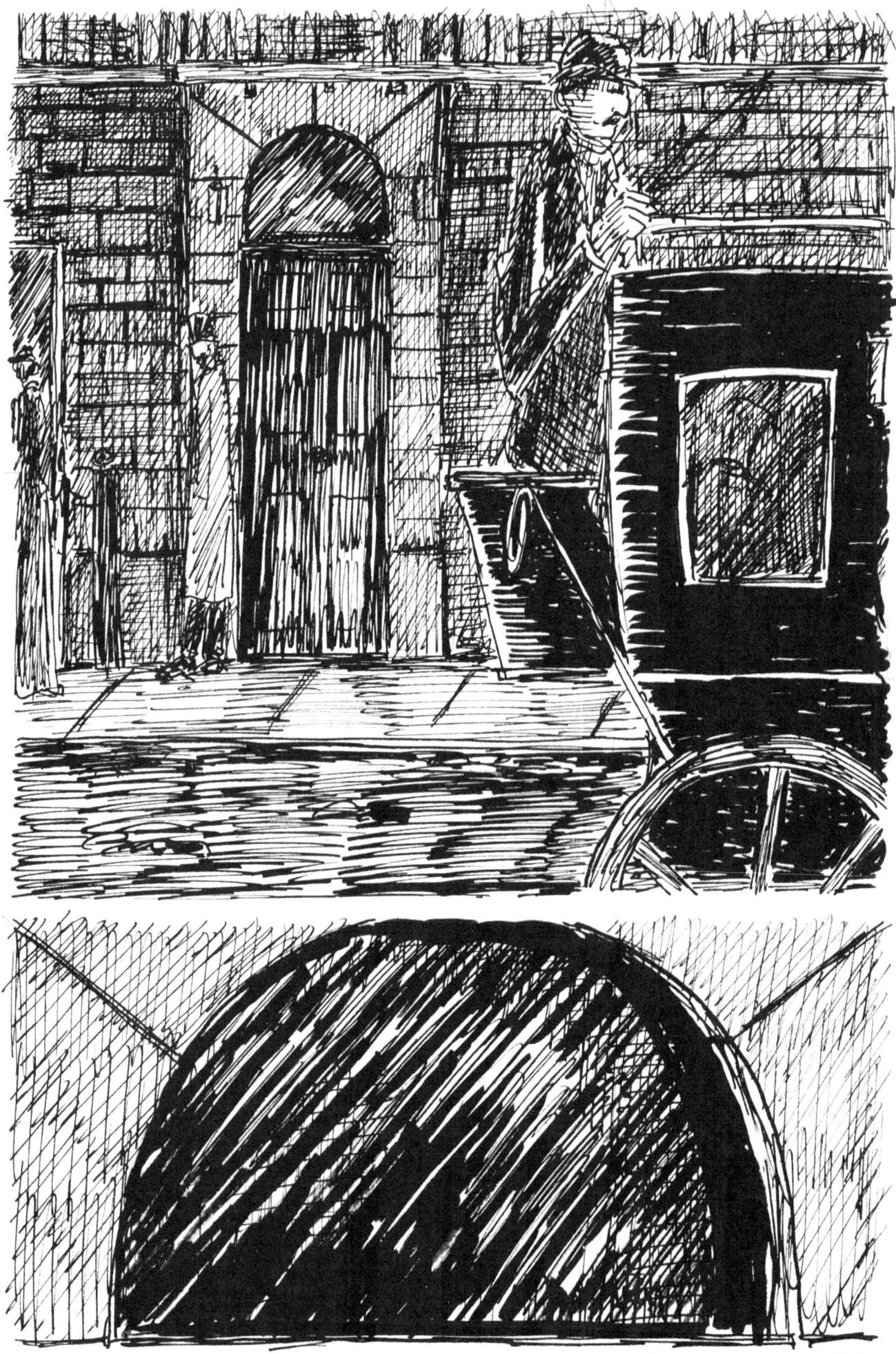

Untitled page 1 (unpublished) 2012

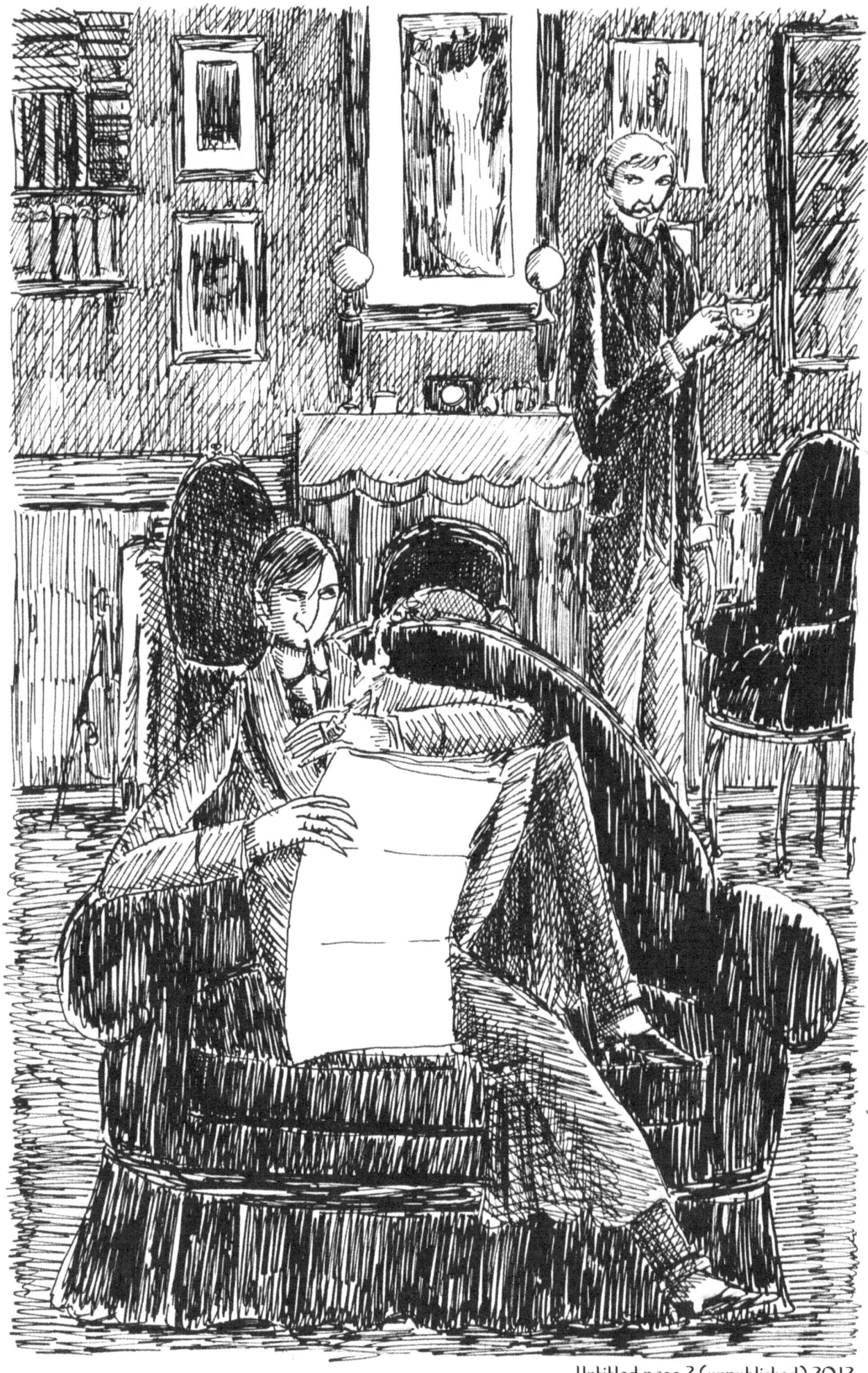

Untitled page 2 (unpublished) 2012

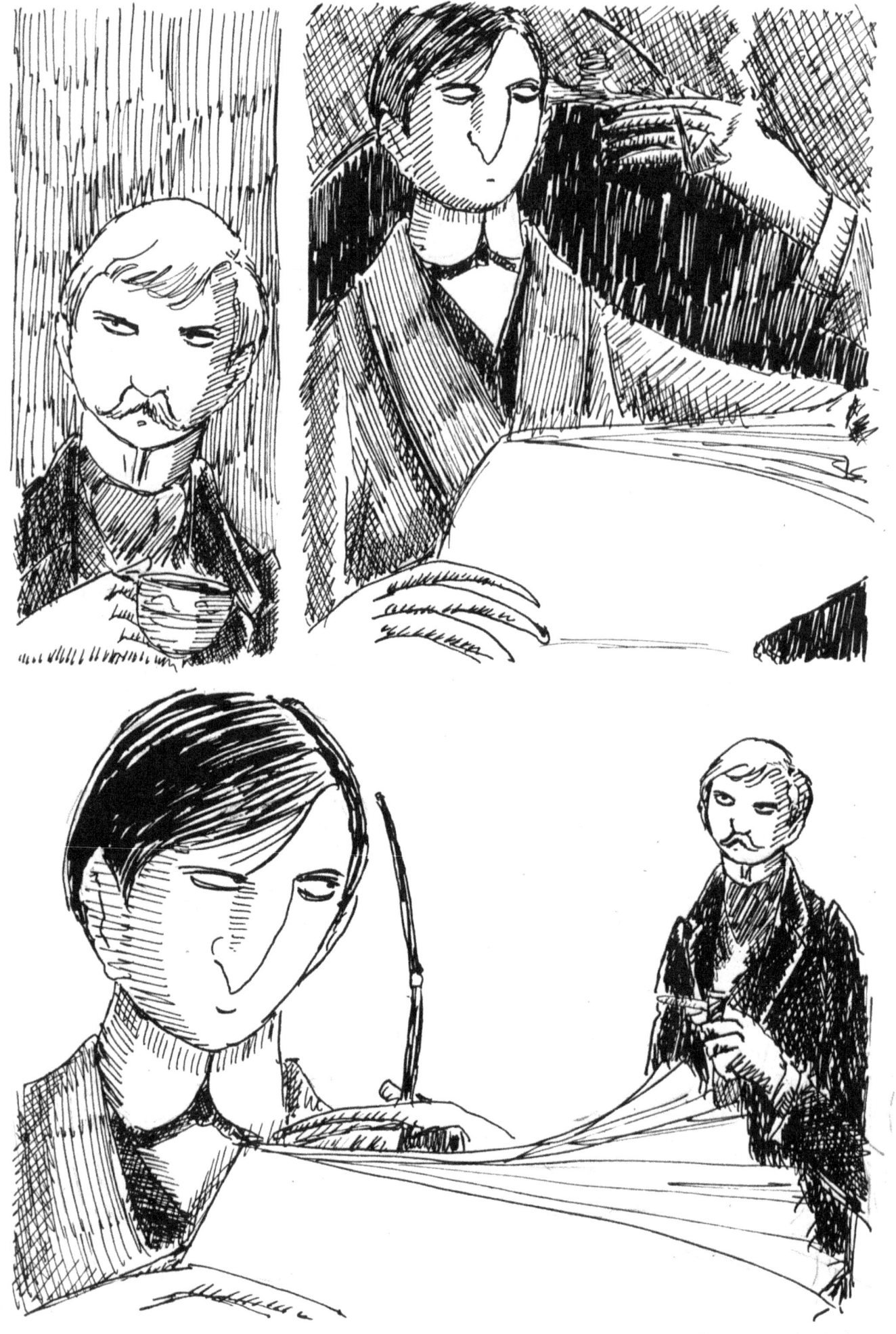

Untitled page 3 (unpublished) 2012

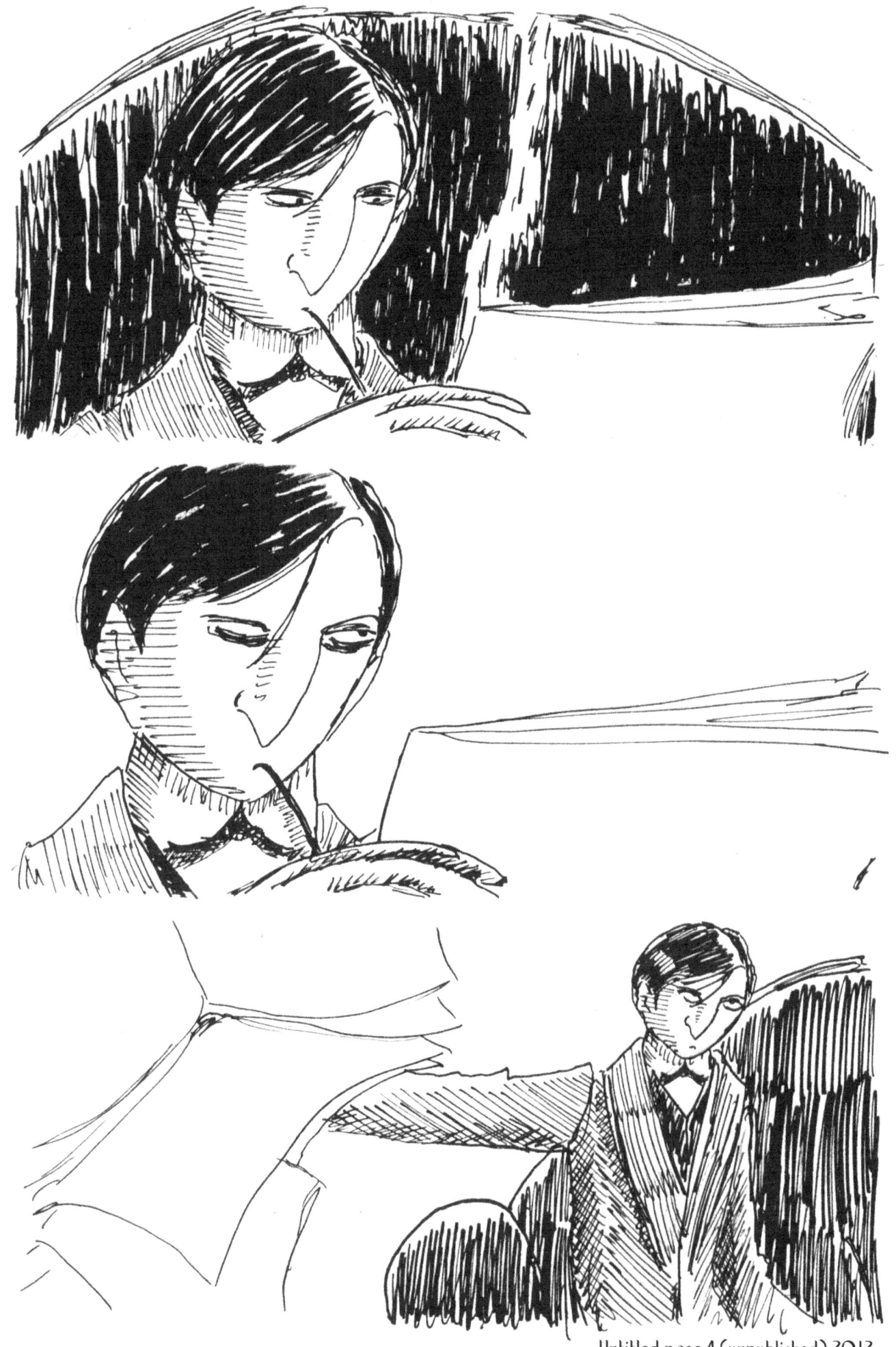

Untitled page 4 (unpublished) 2012

SET DESIGN

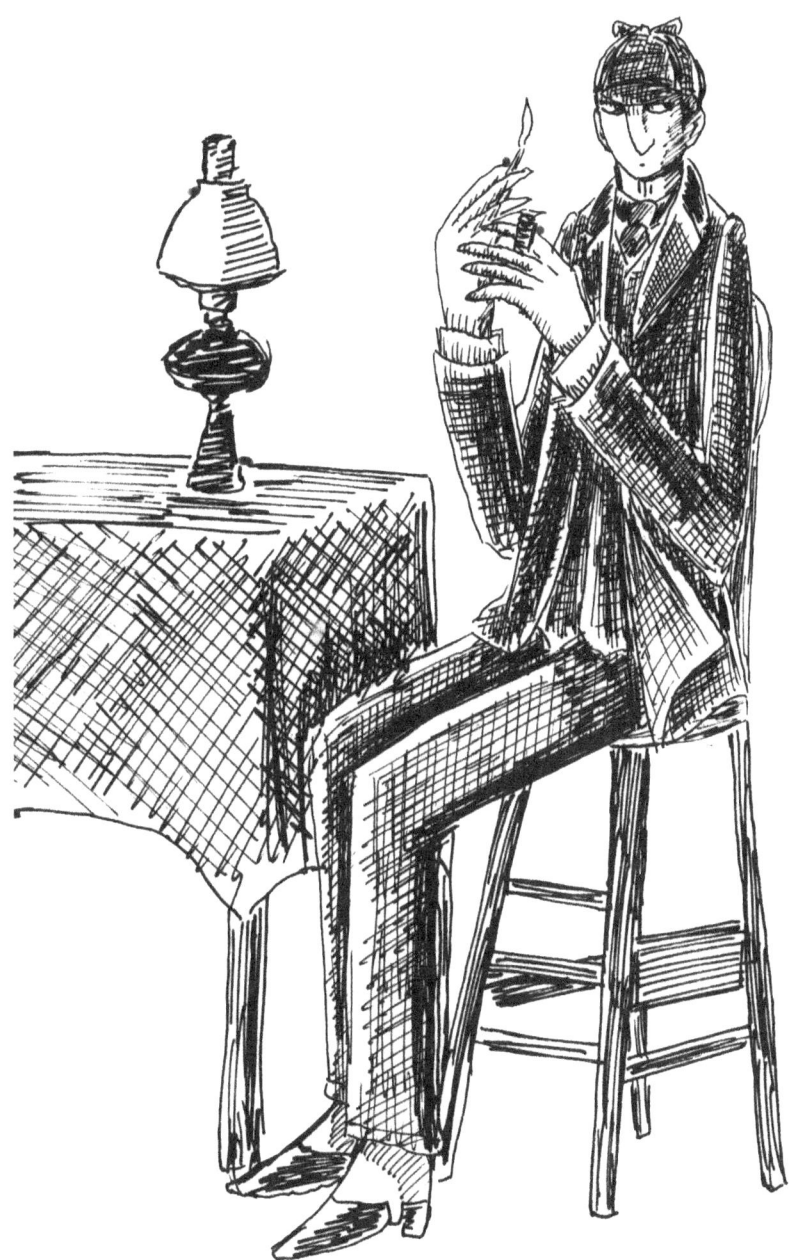

Set design I did for the Kentucky Repertory Theatre in 2012
for their production of William Gillette's 1899 play SHERLOCK HOLMES
based on my graphic novel. And set design I did for my own production of
THE CROWN DIAMOND: AN EVENING WITH SHERLOCK HOLMES
written by Sir Arthur Conan Doyle in 1910. Which took place at Nick's
Bar and Restaurant in 2013

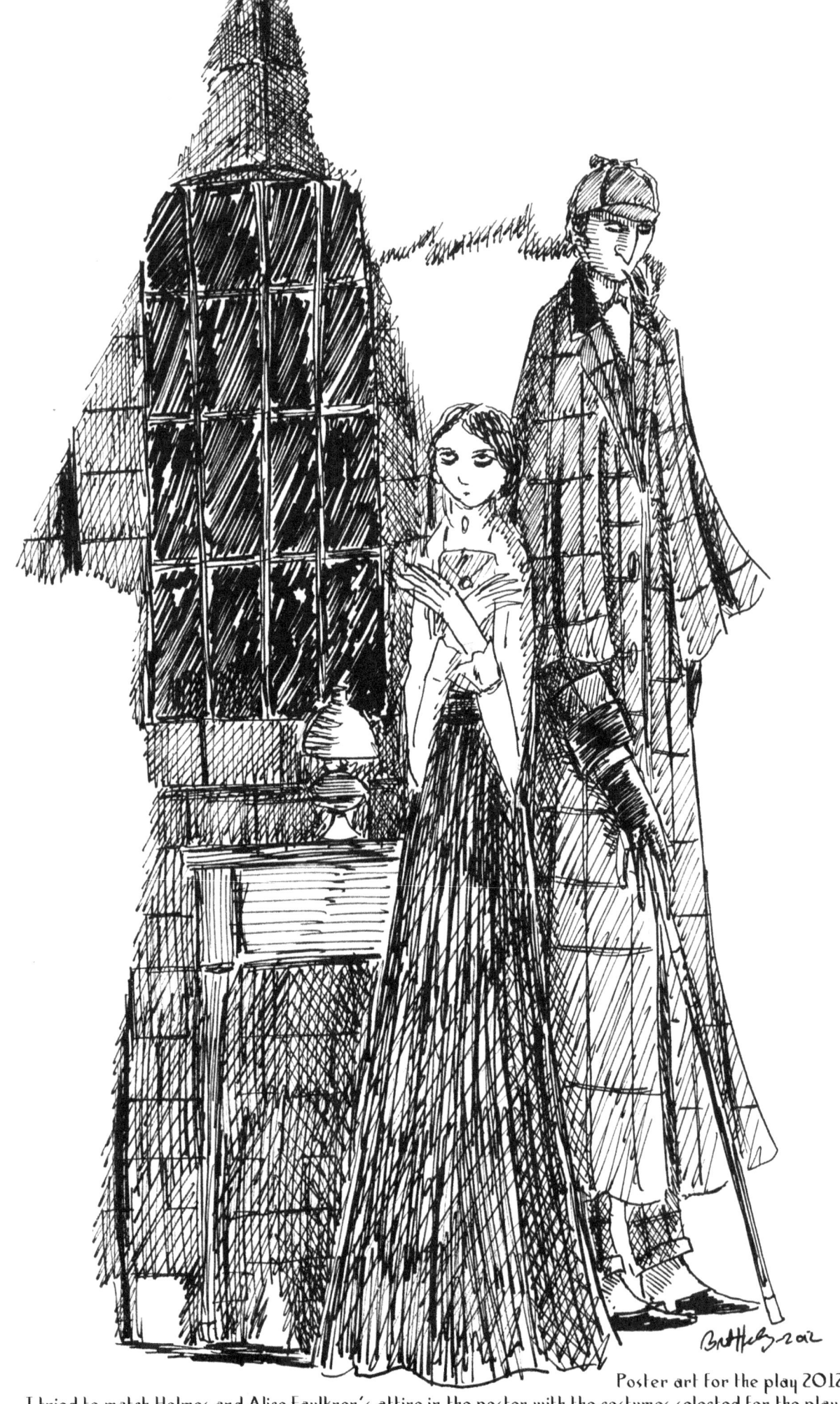

Poster art for the play 2012

I tried to match Holmes and Alice Faulkner's attire in the poster with the costumes selected for the play.

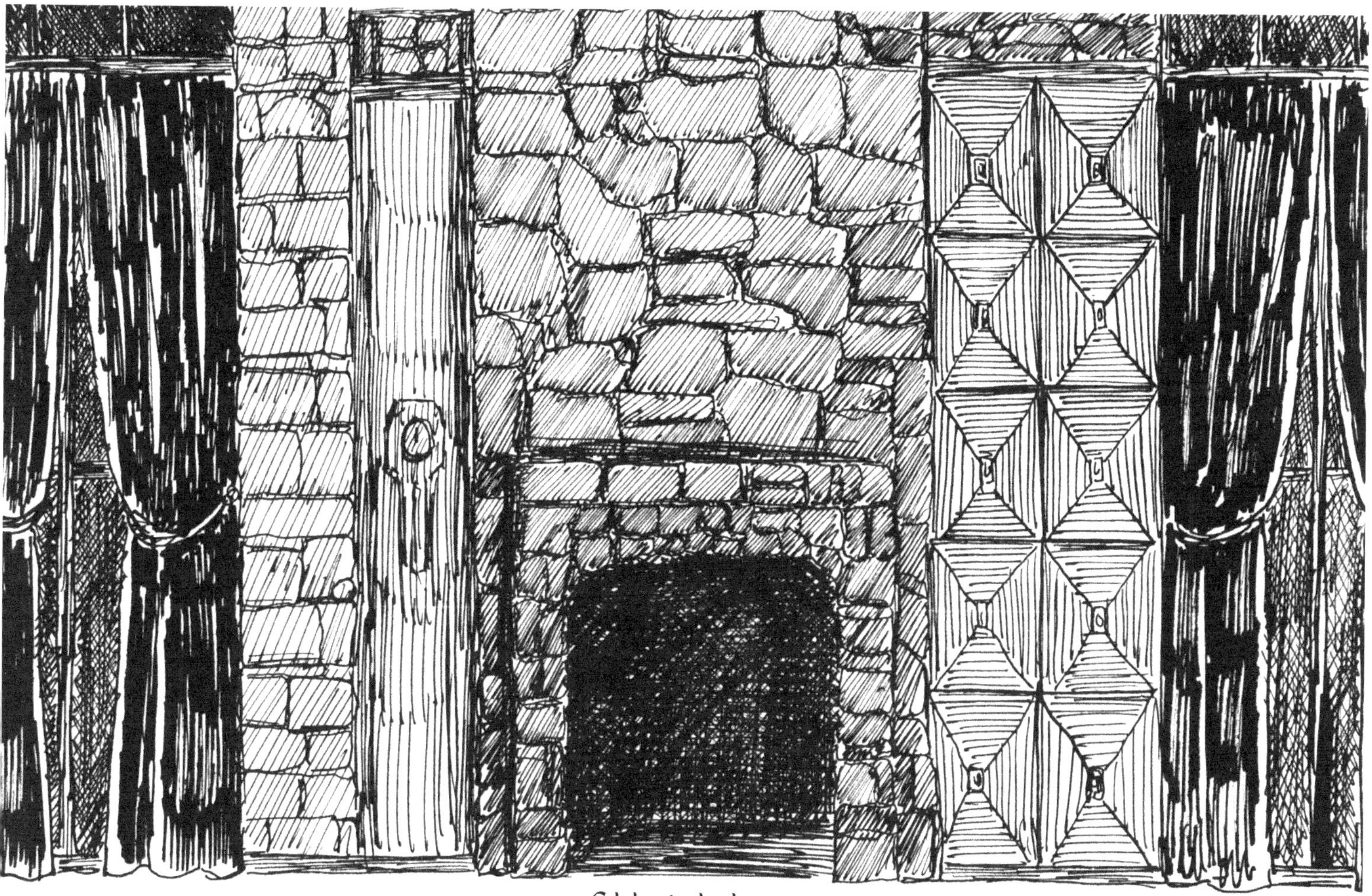

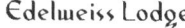

Edelweiss Lodge

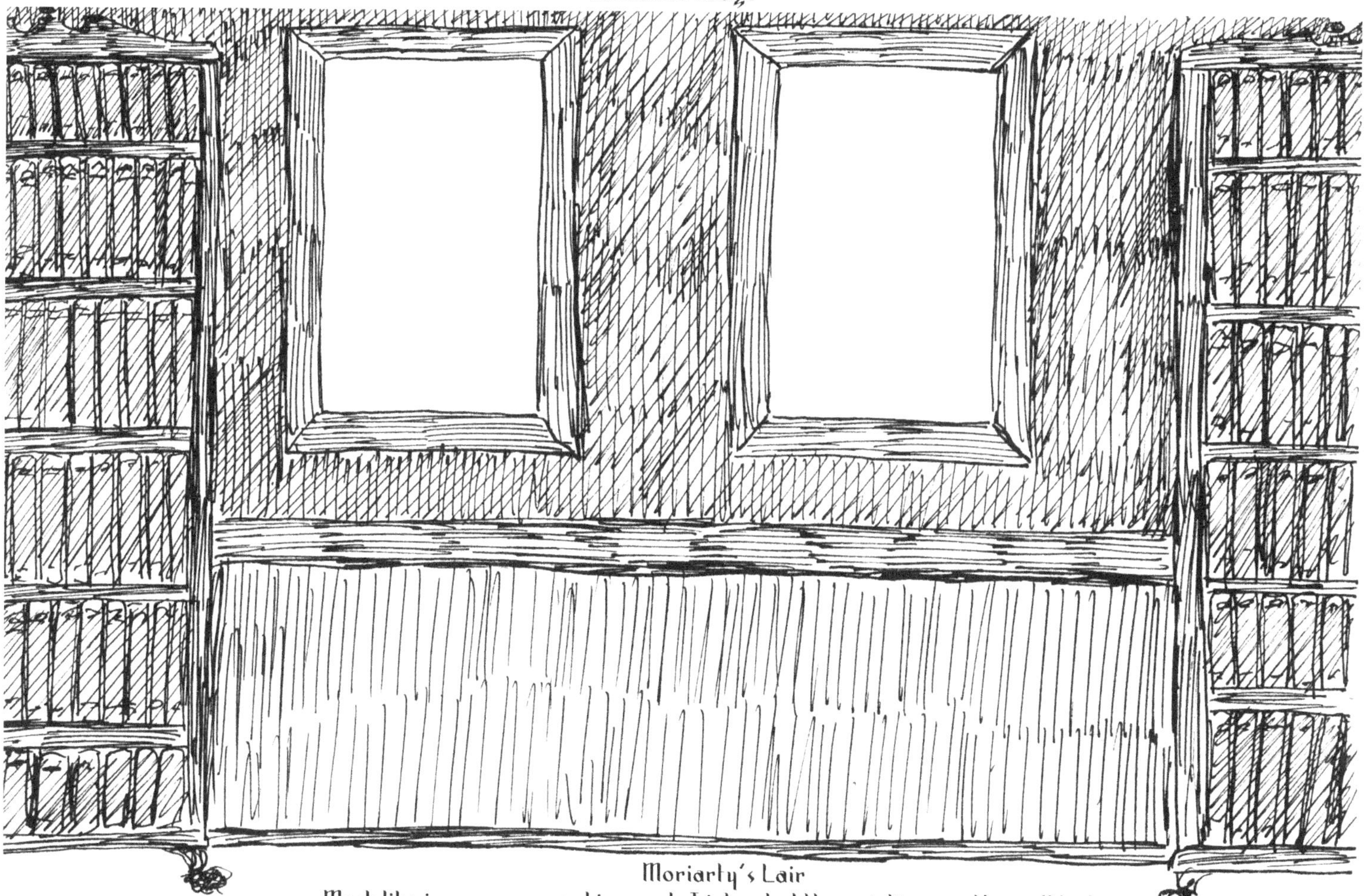

Moriarty's Lair
Much like in my own graphic novel, I intended the paintings on the wall to be
reproductions of Heironymus Bosch's nightmarish artwork. I thought Bosch
would be the ideal artist to hang in Moriarty's lair. The paintings would be added in later.

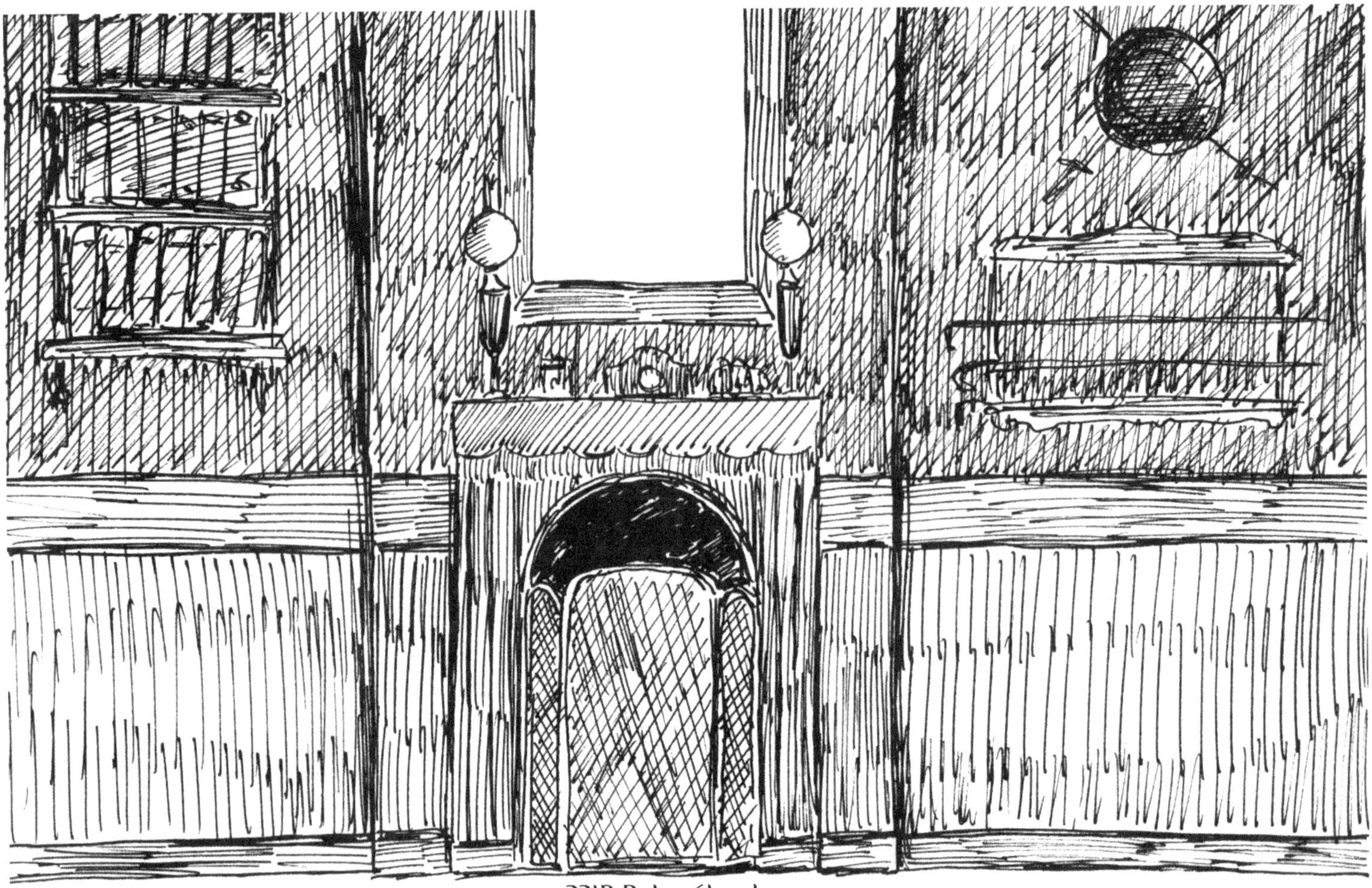

221B Baker Street
A reproduction of the Reichenbach Falls would be the added later for the painting above the fireplace.

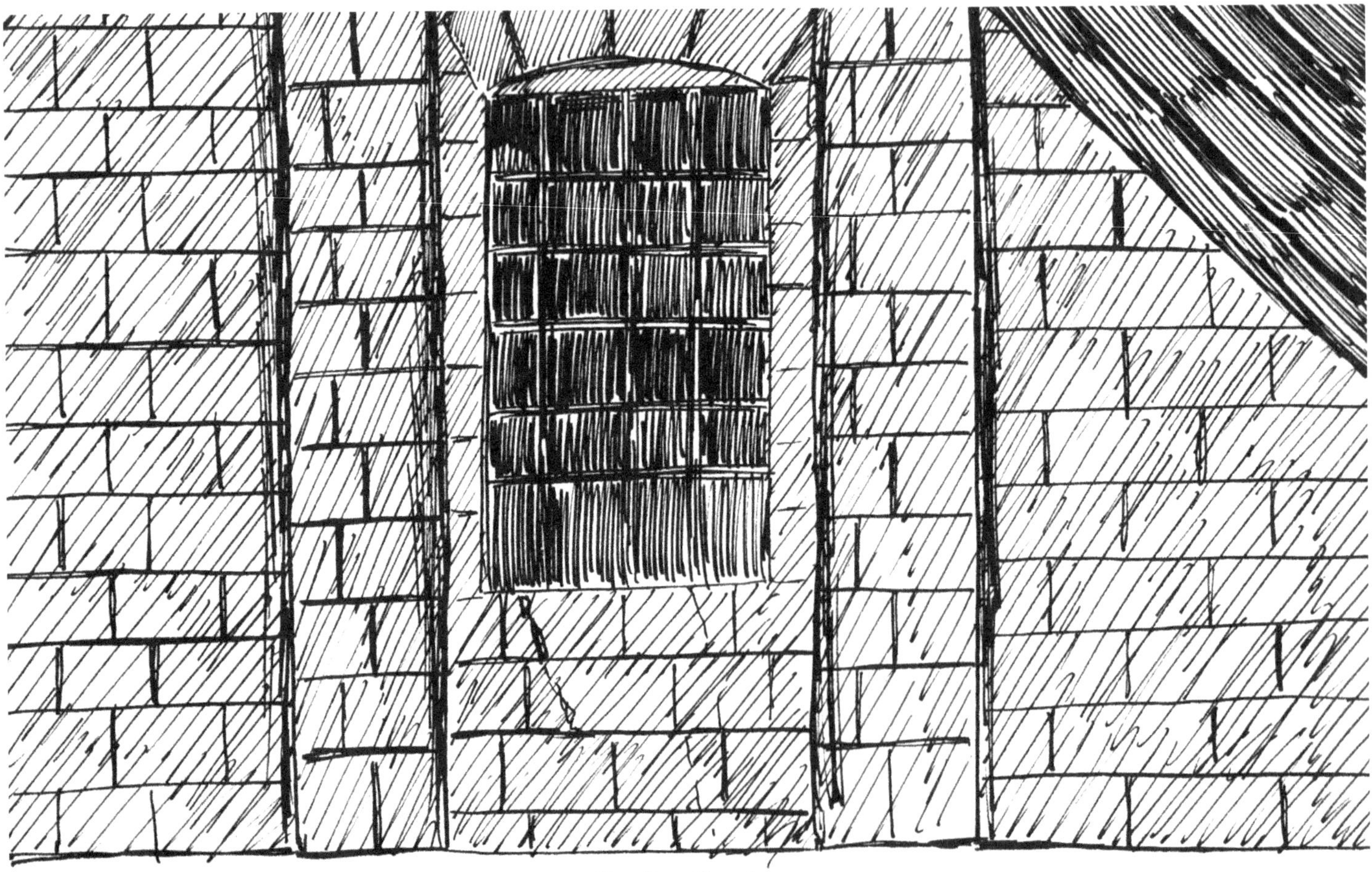

The Gas Chambers
Unlike the other set designs, this one was inspired directly from stills of Gillette's original production

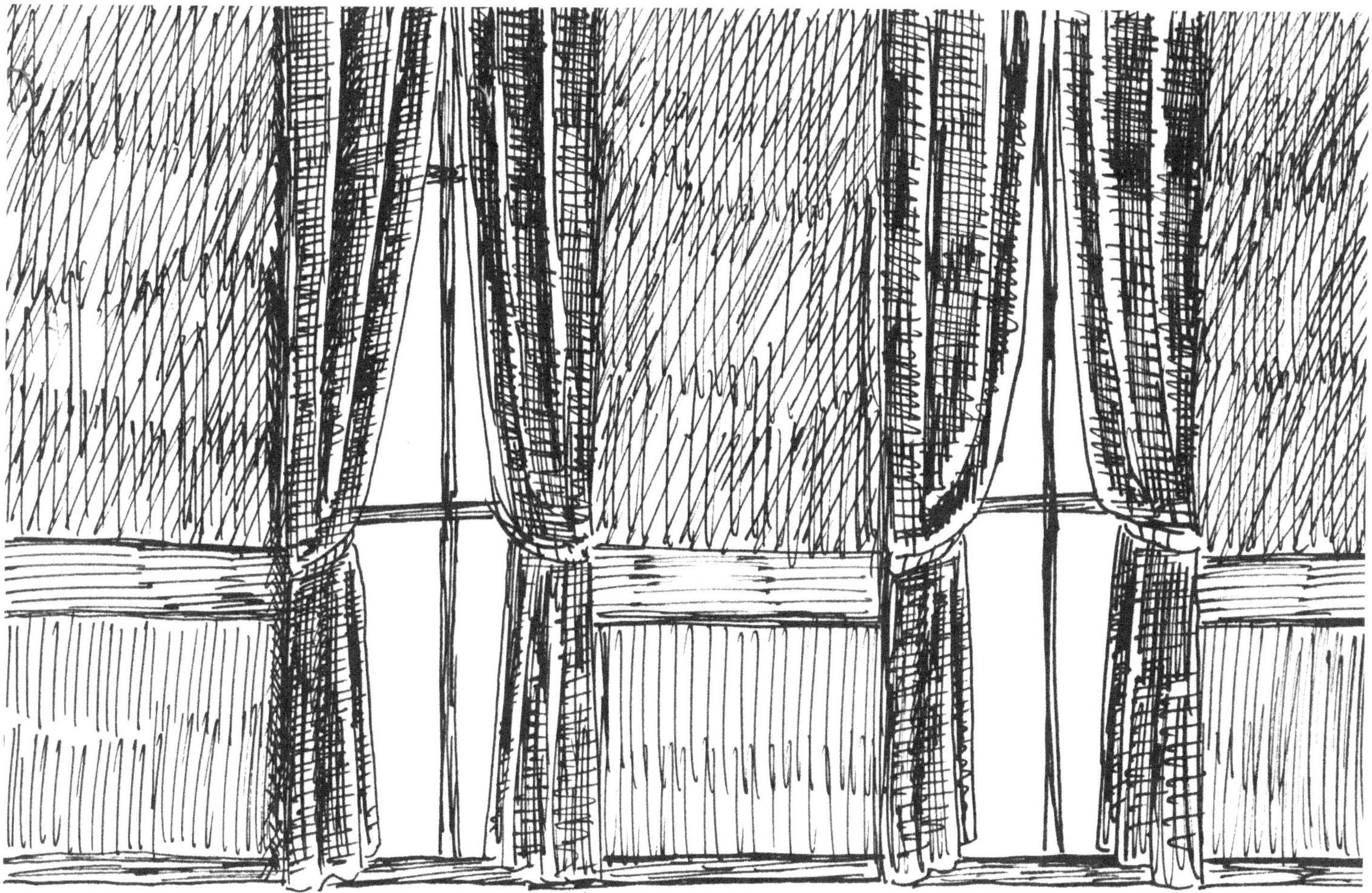

Doctor Watson's Consulting Room, Kensington
When I did my graphic novel of Gillette's play. I changed the ending in Watson's consulting room to Baker Street. Originally in the play we discover that Baker Street has burnt to the ground. I decided to leave all that out in my version.

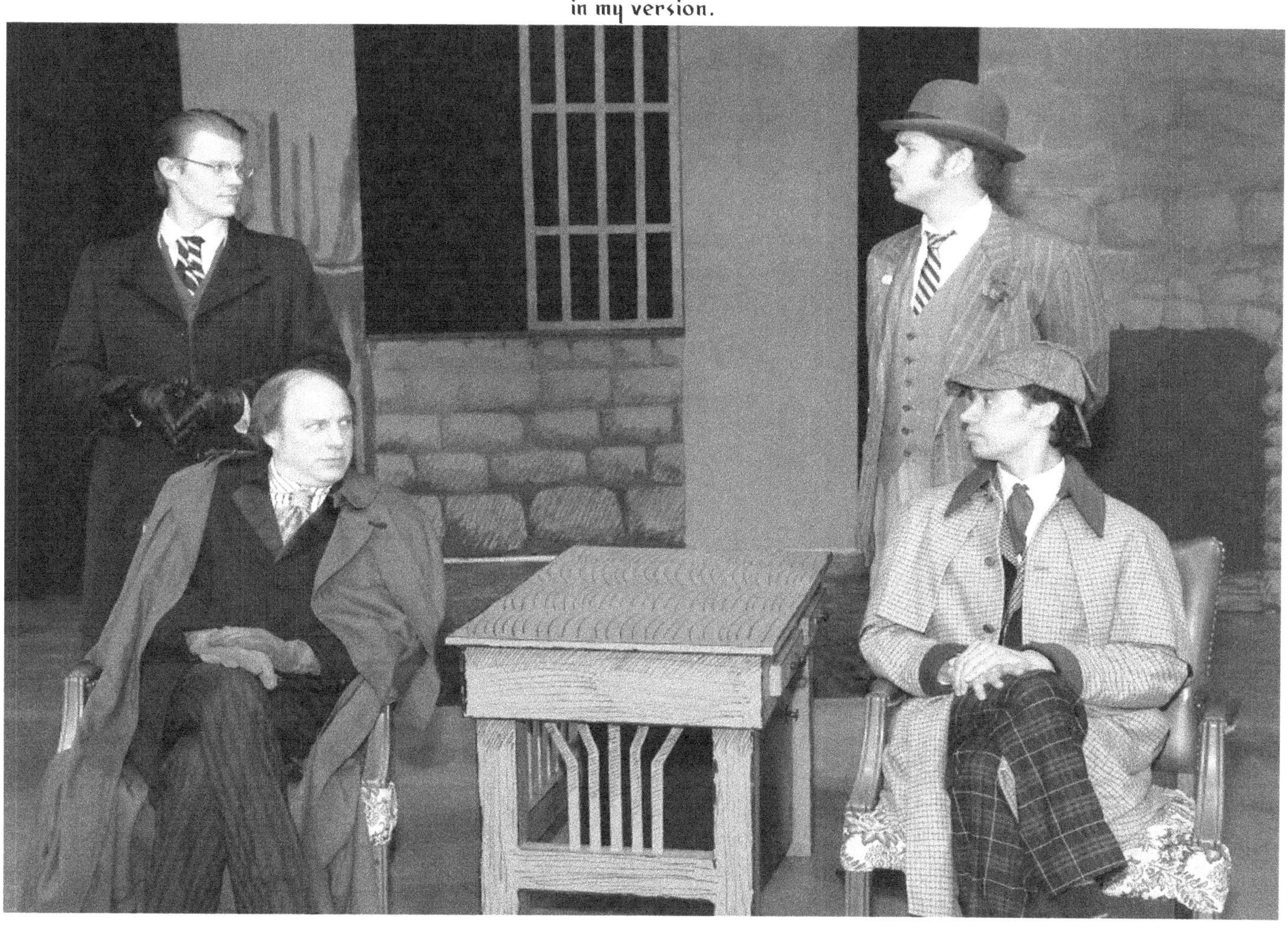

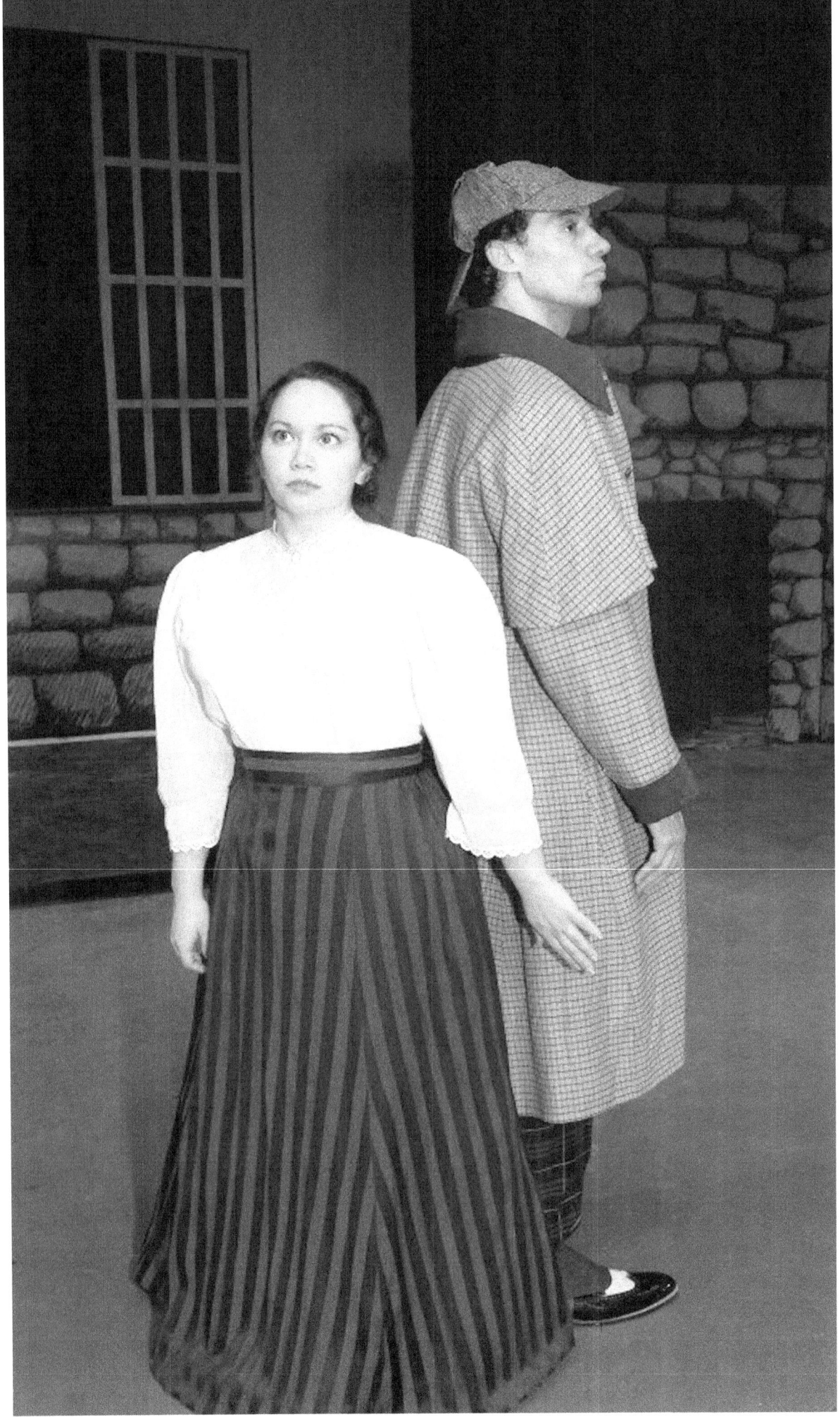

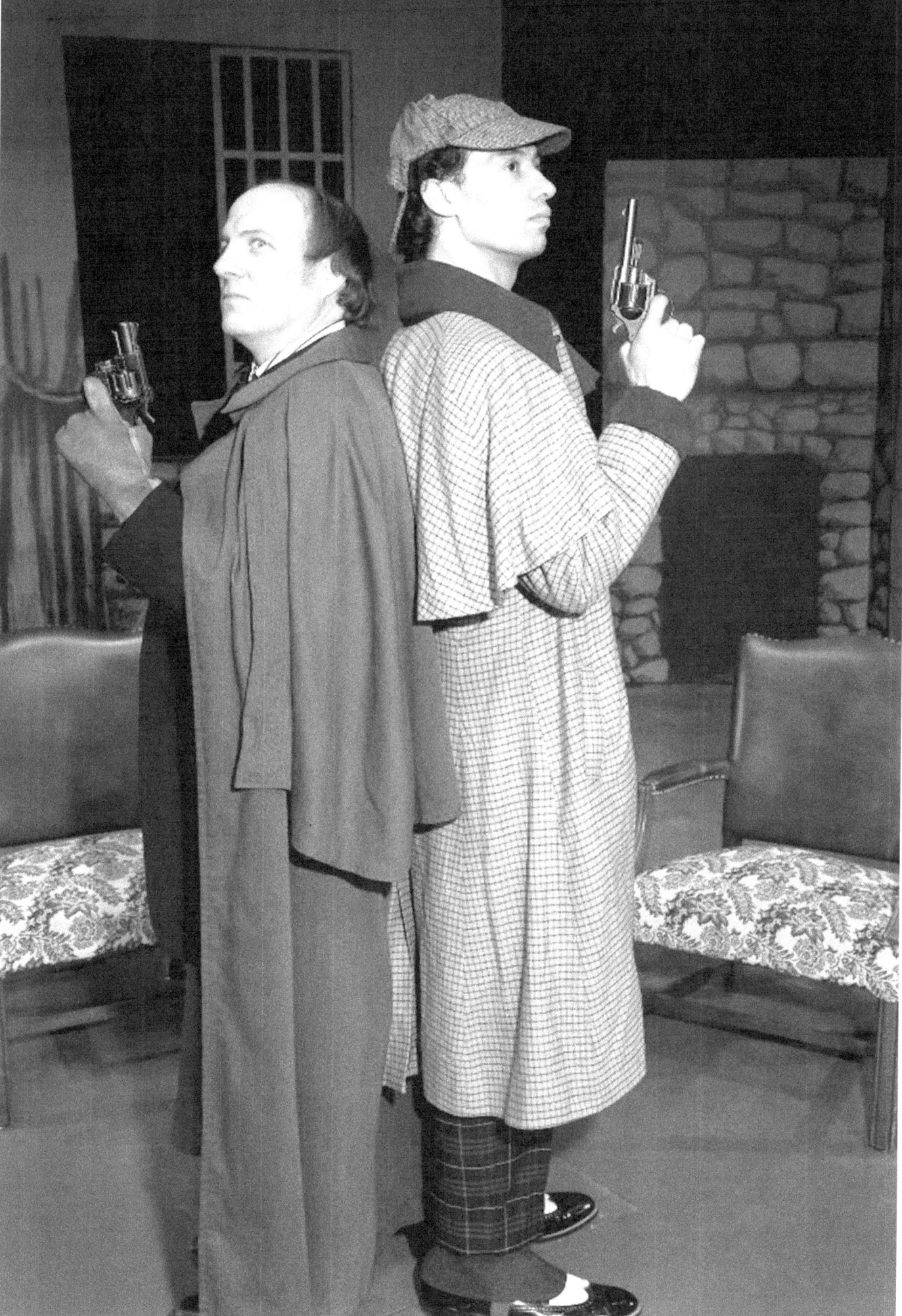

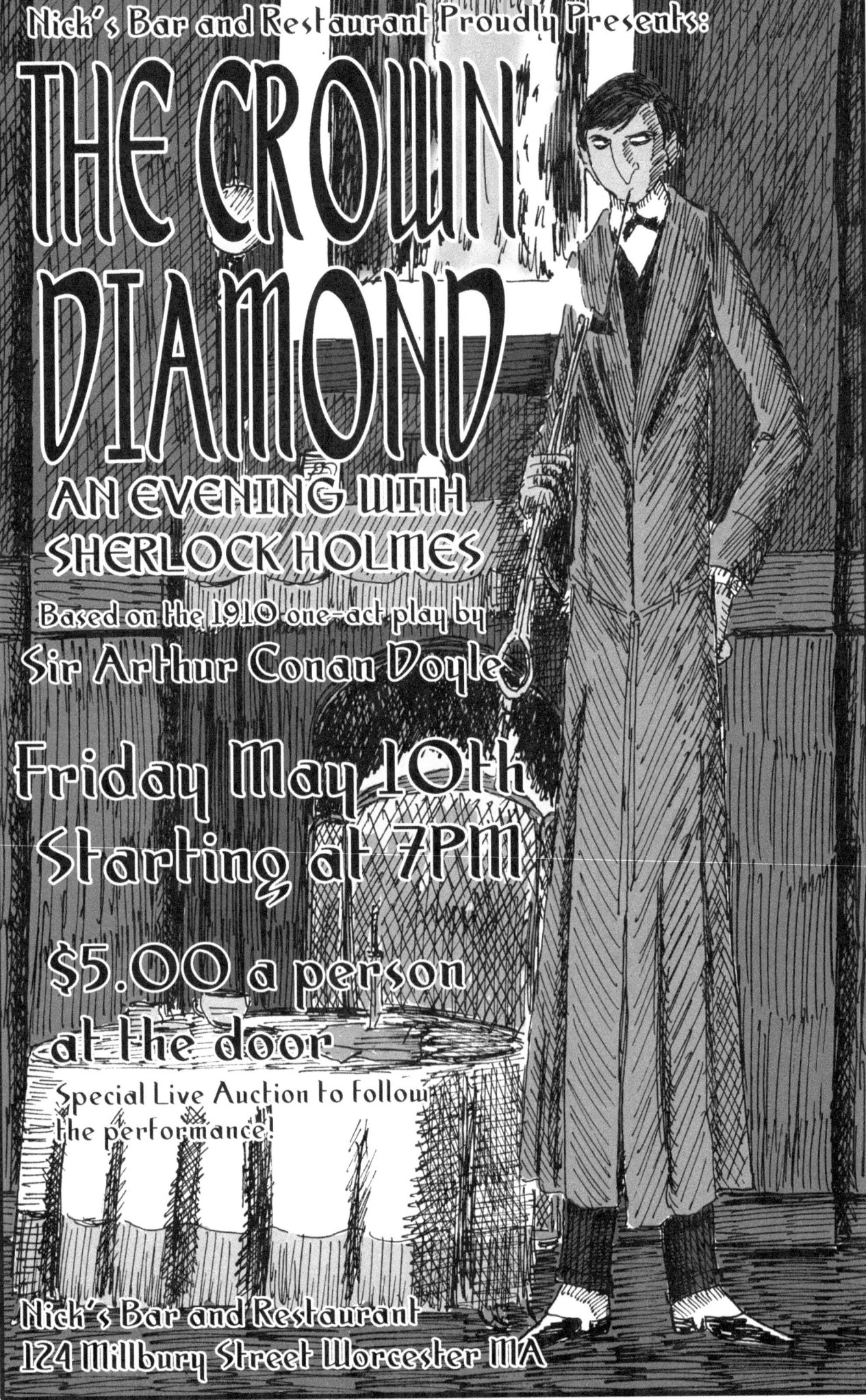

Nick's Bar and Restaurant Proudly Presents:

THE CROWN DIAMOND

AN EVENING WITH SHERLOCK HOLMES

Based on the 1910 one-act play by
Sir Arthur Conan Doyle

Friday May 10th
Starting at 7PM

$5.00 a person
at the door

Special Live Auction to follow
the performance!

Nick's Bar and Restaurant
124 Millbury Street Worcester MA

The original set and some of the costume design I devised for
THE CROWN DIAMOND. Several changes were made in production.
Billy the Page was switched to Mrs.. Hudson and I condensed
the Baker Street set to accommodate Nick's cozy stage.

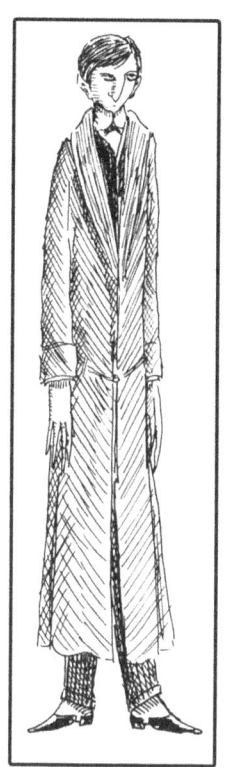

Sherlock Holmes

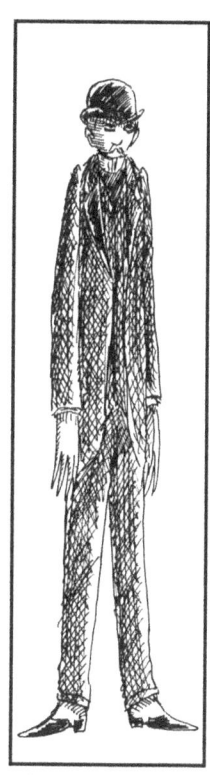

Doctor Watson

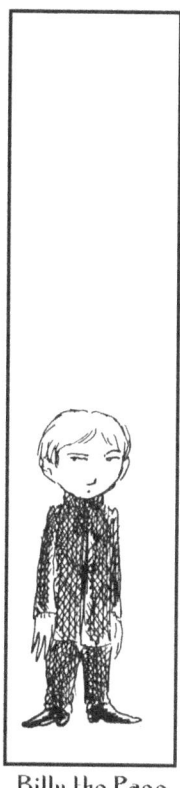

Billy the Page

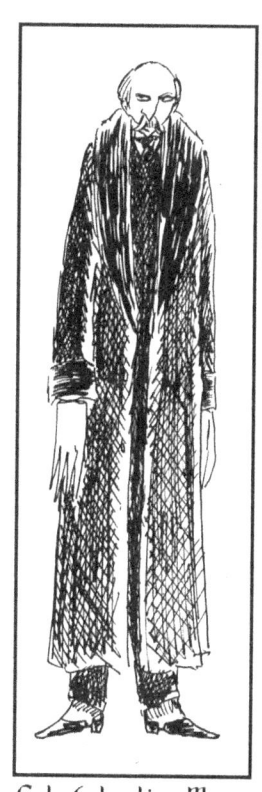

Col.. Sebastian Moran

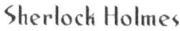

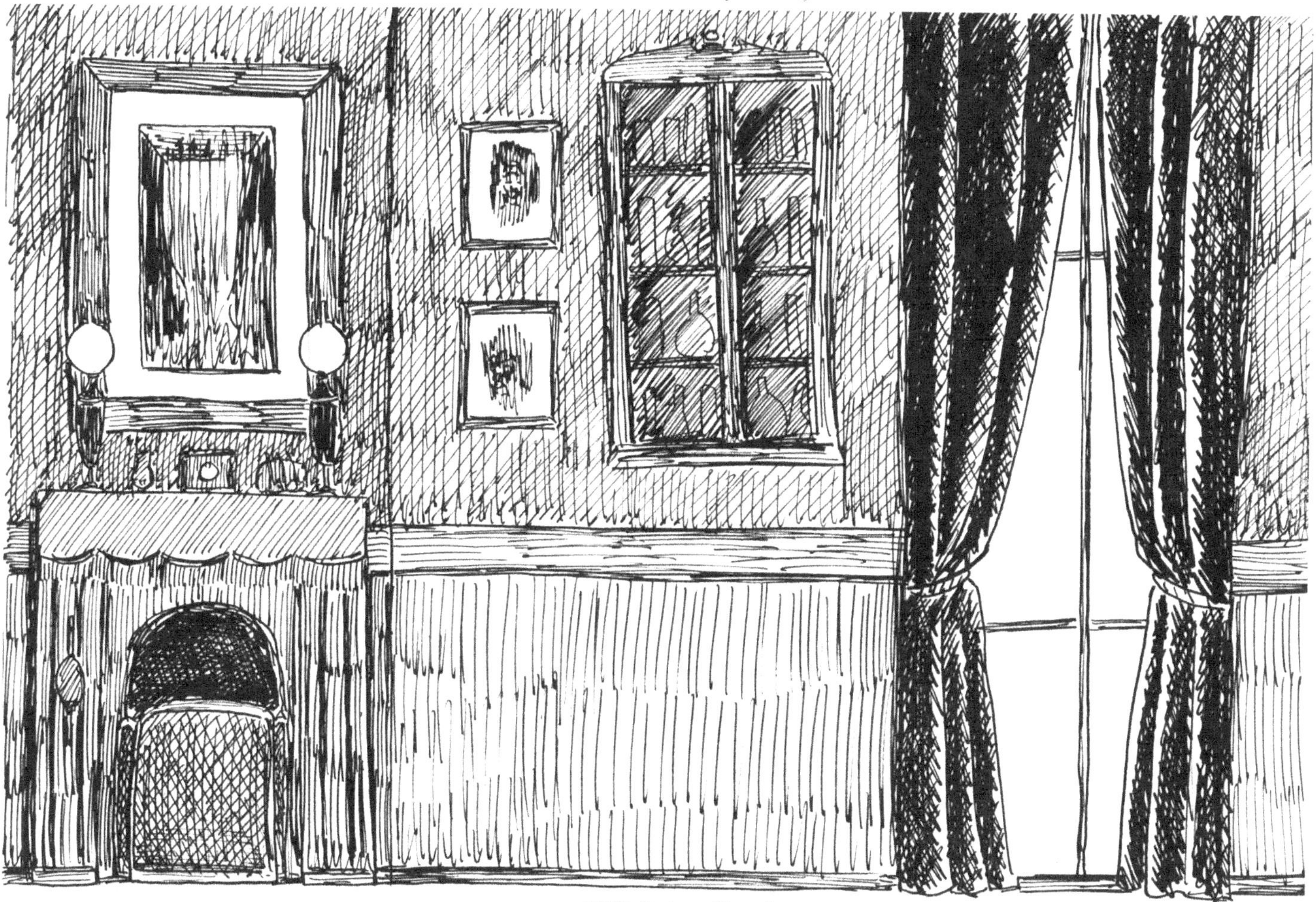

221B Baker Street

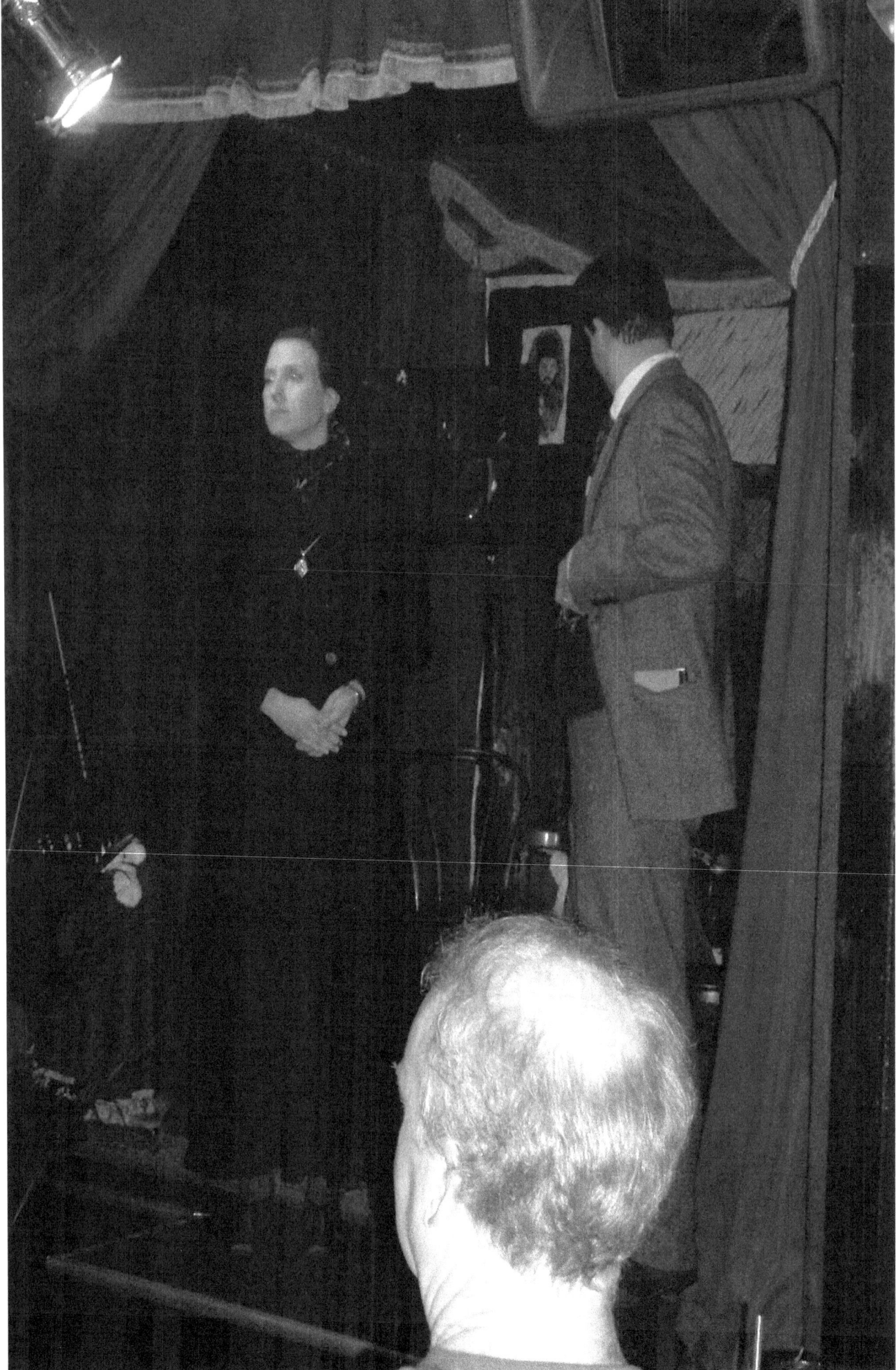

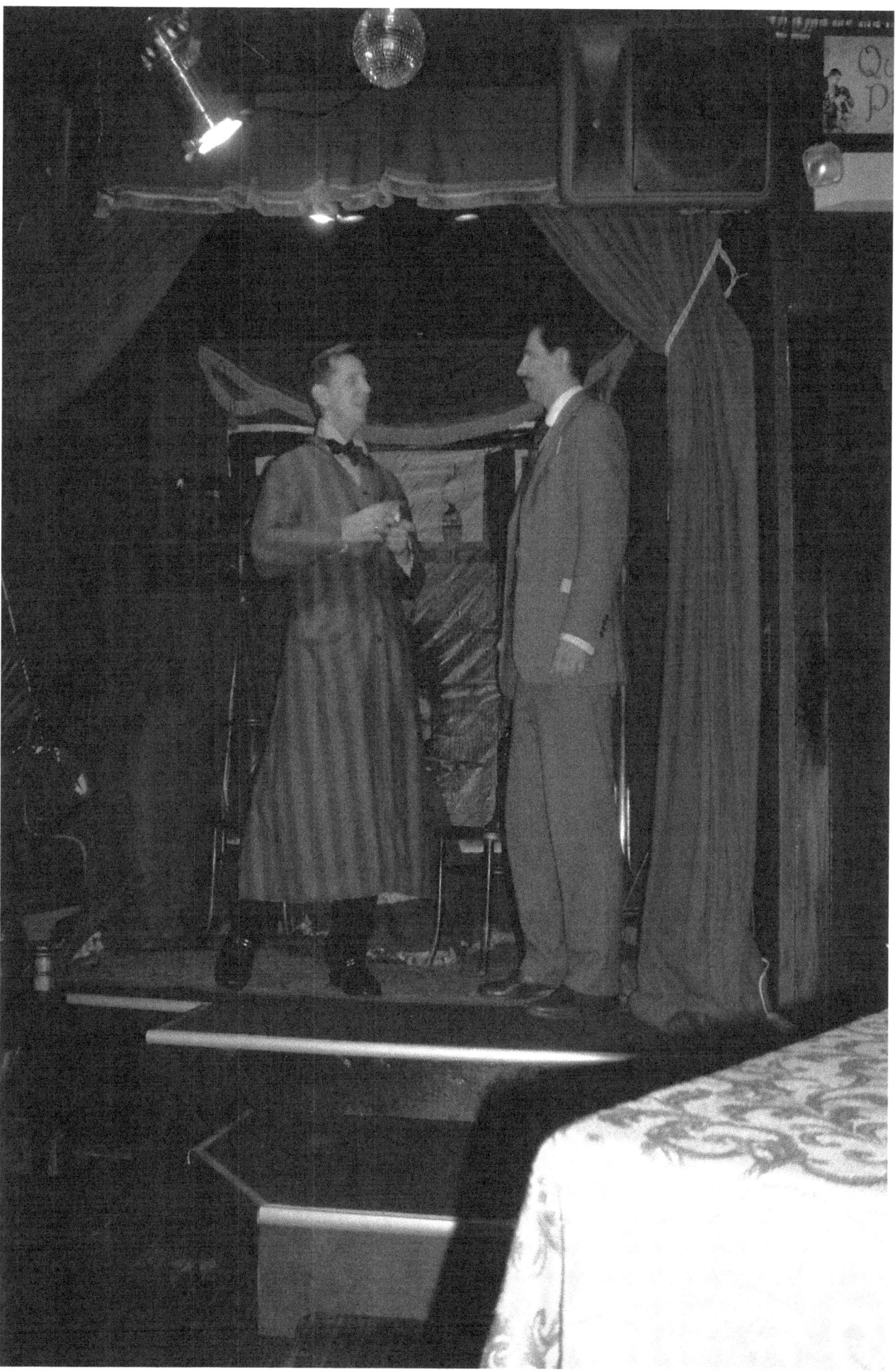

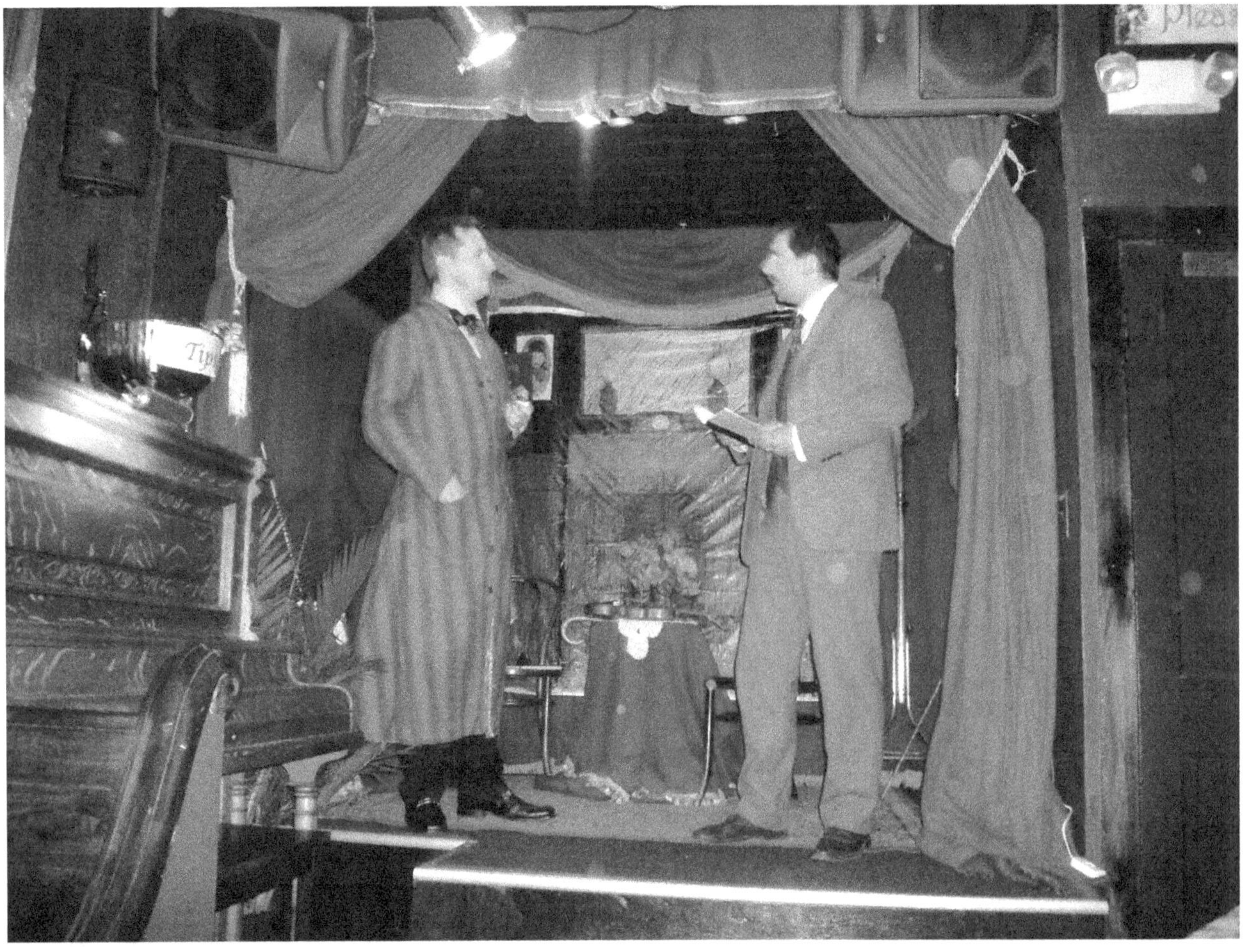

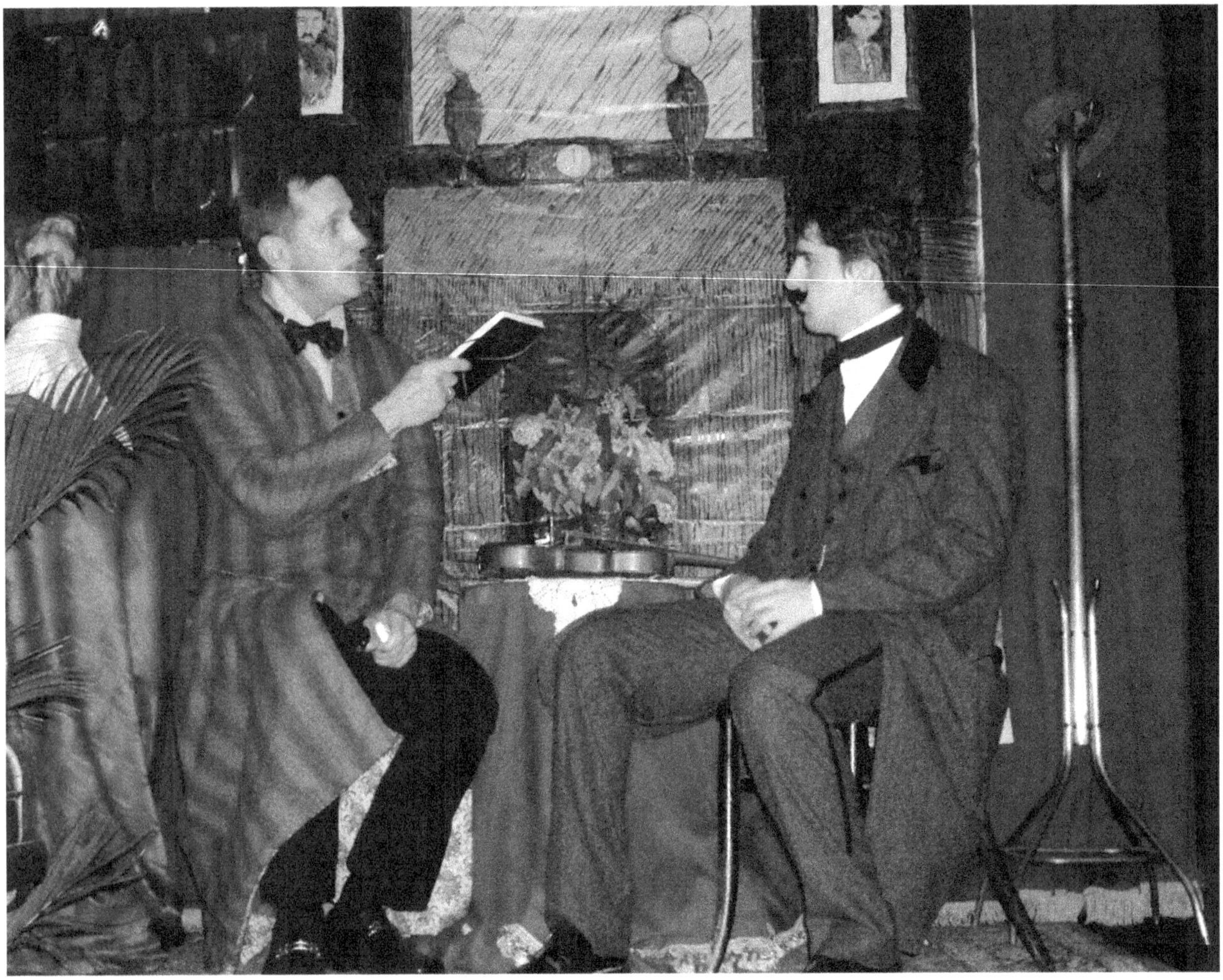

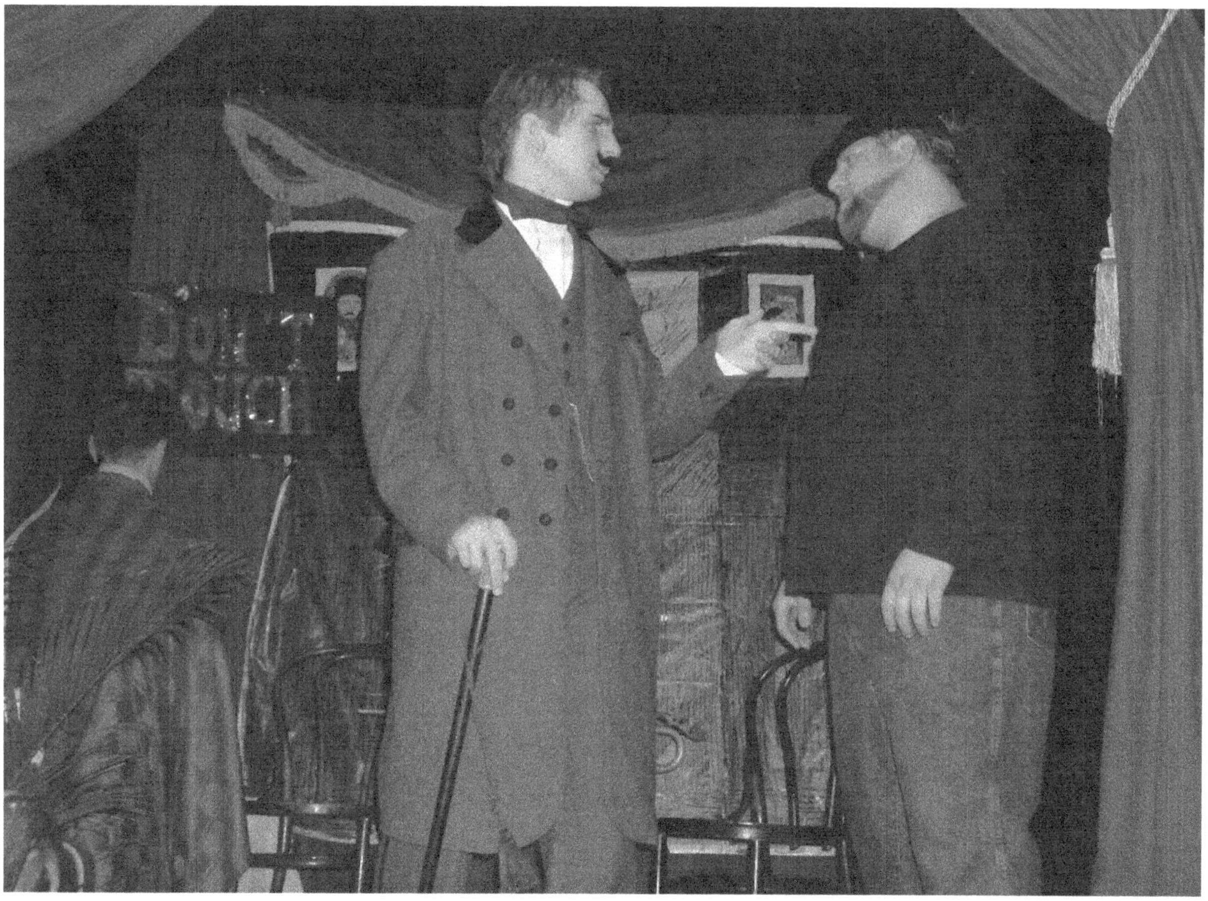

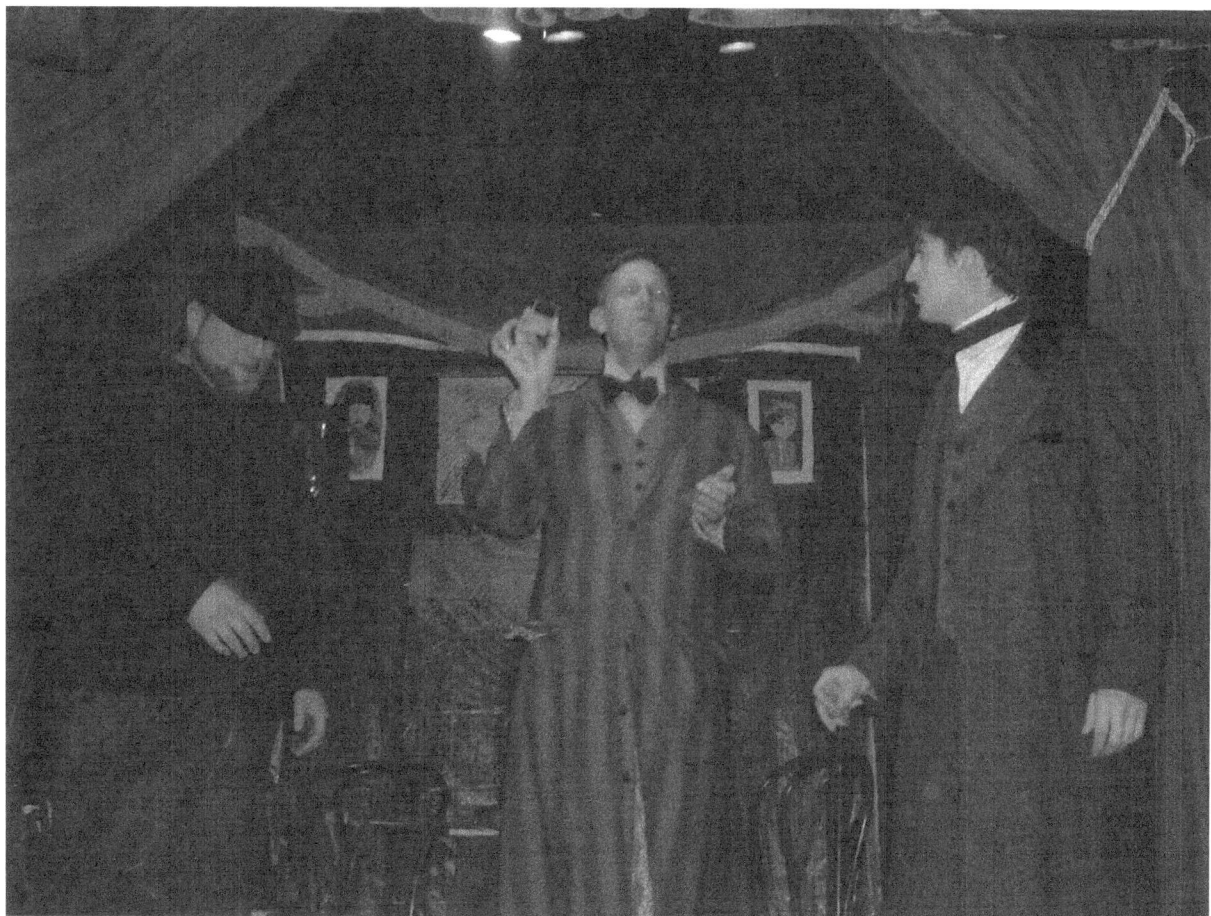

Also by Bret M. Herholz

Diary of the Black Widow

Confessions of a Peculiar Boy...And Other Stories

The Spaghetti Strand Murder

The Adventures of Polly and Handgraves: A Sinister Aura

Sherlock Holmes: The Painful Predicament of Alice Faulkner

Vintage Gray by Joshua Michael Stewart

Gloomy Presentiments of Things to Come by Susurrus Din

The Ninnies by Paul Magrs

12 Weeks of Summer by Joseph J. Andrade

The Casque of Amontillado

Loogie the Booger Genie by N.E. Castle

Memento Mori with Sydney Herholz

Coming Soon!!

Film Noir by Joshua Michael Stewart

Frankenstein A.D.1931 by Andy Fish

Romance with a Croquet Mallet (or a plausibly stirring afternoon at Slougshire Manor)

Available for purchase through Amazon.com, alternacomics.com, Obversebook.co.uk

and wherever fine books are sold!

www.ingramcontent.com/pod-product-compliance
Lightning Source LLC
Chambersburg PA
CBHW081509170526
45166CB00008B/2597